FOCUS ON AGGRESSION RESEARCH

FOCUS ON AGGRESSION RESEARCH

JAMES P. MORGAN
EDITOR

Nova Science Publishers, Inc.
New York

Production Coordinator: Tatiana Shohov
Coordinating Editor: Tatiana Shohov
Senior Production Editors: Susan Boriotti and Donna Dennis
Production Editors: Marius Andronie and Rusudan Razmadze
Office Manager: Annette Hellinger
Graphics: Levani Chlaidze and Magdalena Nuñez
Editorial Production: Alexandra Columbus, Maya Columbus, Robert Brower,
Vladimir Klestov and Lorna Loperfido
Circulation: Luis Aviles, Raymond Davis, Cathy DeGregory, Melissa Diaz, Ave Maria
Gonzalez, Jarred Haynes, Marlene Nuñez, Jeannie Pappas and Vera Popovic
Communications and Acquisitions: Serge P. Shohov

Library of Congress Cataloging-in-Publication Data
Available Upon Request

ISBN: 1-59454-132-9.

Copyright © 2004 by Nova Science Publishers, Inc.
400 Oser Ave, Suite 1600
Hauppauge, New York 11788-3619
Tele.: 631-231-7269 Fax: 631-231-8175
e-mail: Novascience@earthlink.net
Web Site: http://www.novapublishers.com

Printed in the United States of America

CONTENTS

PREFACE

Aggression may be defined as: 1: The act of initiating hostilities or invasion.; 2. The practice or habit of launching attacks; 3. The practice or habit of launching attacks. Aggression is one of the most important and most controversial kinds of motivation. Its use as a category in the psychology of motivation has often been criticized, because it is clear that it encompasses a vast range of phenomena, from modern war and terrorism to squabbles between individuals. There is an important familial component to aggression, antisocial behavior, crime, and violence. Essentially all people are in some way affected by aggression, whether they are targets of it, engage in it themselves, or are charged with observing and controlling it in others. Thus aggression is of concern to victims, perpetrators, and those professionals charged with its treatment because of personal safety, well-being, or obligation. This new book examines the foundations and manifestations of aggression including intimate partner violence, parental aggression, verbal aggression in stepfamilies, childhood teasing, forgiveness in cases of aggression, self and aggression, neurobehavioral aspects of aggression, road aggression, and music and its effects on reducing aggression.

In: *Focus on Aggression Research*
Editor: James P. Morgan, pp. 1-13

ISBN 1-59454-132-9
© 2004 Nova Science Publishers, Inc.

Chapter 1

MEASURING INTIMATE PARTNER VIOLENCE: A COMPARISON OF THE CONFLICT TACTICS SCALE AND THE TIMELINE FOLLOWBACK SPOUSAL VIOLENCE INTERVIEW

Cynthia A. Stappenbeck and William Fals-Stewart

Research Institute on Addictions, University at Buffalo,
The State University of New York

INTRODUCTION

Although once considered a private family matter, intimate partner violence (IPV) is now considered a serious and all-too-prevalent social problem in the United States. IPV prevalence estimates vary widely, due in large part to different definitions of violence and what constitutes an intimate relationship (National Research Council, 1996). although estimates of its prevalence vary significantly due in large measure. However, recent nationally representative surveys indicate that more than two million women are severely beaten by their partners each year, and that one out of six couples experience an incident involving physical assault between partners each year (Straus & Gelles, 1986, 1990). It has been suggested that during the course of half of all marriages, there will be at least one act of IPV (Peachy, 1988). Though these figures are clearly high, it has also been suggested that IPV is vastly underreported and that the reported prevalence rates may be a lower-bound estimate, particular if estimates are drawn from criminal justice system data sets. As an example, in their large national survey of family violence, Straus and Gelles (1990) reported that less than 7 percent of victims of IPV reported the violence to the police.

The number of treatment programs for partner violent men have grown dramatically since the mid-1970s (Pirog-Good & Stets-Kealey, 1985). Most states in the US now mandate intervention programs for convicted perpetrators of IPV, though it has been argued that these interventions are based on practice guidelines developed from "ideologies regarding the causes and course of domestic violence, rather than by empirical research" (Babcock & La Taillade, 2000, p. 37). Debates about the most effective and the most appropriate methods to treat IPV are often contentious. Many models of intervention posit that IPV is the result of long-standing social values that condone and perpetuate the control, and even abuse, of women by men. This type of physical aggression used to dominate and control the female partner has been called "patriarchal terrorism" (Johnson, 1995). One view is that all, or nearly all episodes of IPV are forms of patriarchal terrorism used by men to have power and control over their partners. Others note that not all episodes of IPV are severe; this is often referred to as "common couple violence." The debate evolves over whether all episodes of IPV are viewed as being on a continuum of patriarchal terrorism or if there are different subtypes of IPV that are distinctly different and do not fall under the patriarchal terrorism rubric. These conceptual differences of the nature of IPV are debated by treatment and research professionals, as well as policy makers, and highlight the need for further research in to understand the causes and consequences of IPV.

MEASURING IPV: THE CONFLICT TACTICS SCALE

With a growing concern about the prevalence and treatment of IPV, and the need for well-designed and rigorous research in this area, concerns about how best to assess partner violence have emerged. Methods and measures used to assess IPV have received great scrutiny and, in turn, have been a source of considerable disagreement and debate (Schafer, 1996). The most widely used instrument for the evaluation of couple violence is the Conflict Tactics Scale (CTS; Straus, 1979, 1990), which has been updated and expanded (CTS-2; Straus, Hamby, Boney-McCoy, & Sugarman, 1996). The CTS is a self-administered questionnaire used to measure conflict resolution techniques, including physical and psychological attacks, as well as the use of reasoning and negotiation between partners in a dating, cohabiting, or marital relationship. Although the CTS has been primarily used in research settings, especially in large-scale surveys of family violence, it has also been increasingly adopted as part of general relationship and family assessment batteries.

The CTS-2 differs from the original CTS in several important ways. The wording has been revised to improve clarity and specificity and the format has been simplified to make it a more efficient self-report questionnaire. Additional items were included in the CTS-2; however, despite the extra items (39 compared to the CTS's 19 items), the CTS-2 is still relatively quick to administer, requiring only 10-15 minutes. The CTS consists of three scales designed to assess different facets of conflict: verbal reasoning, verbal aggression, and violence. The CTS-2, however, has an additional two scales, replacing the verbal reasoning scale with a measure of emotional and cognitive facets of conflict negotiation, and renaming the violence scale to avoid confusion with the broader definition of the term violence. Therefore, the final make-up of the CTS-2 consists of the following 5 scales: physical assault, psychological aggression, negotiation, physical injury and sexual coercion. The physical assault scale is then further subdivided into "minor" and "severe" violence.

However, it is important to highlight that the psychometric construction for the CTS and the CTS-2 are, for all intents and purposes, the same. Both versions measure tangible acts and events, including physical violence instead of attitudes about conflict or violence. Second, a defining characteristic of both measures is that it uses 'symmetry in measurement'; the behavior of both the respondent and the respondent's partner is measured. Thus, for every question asked about the respondent's behavior, the same question is asked about the behavior of the respondent's partner (e.g., "I explained my side of a disagreement to my partner," "My partner explained his or her side of a disagreement to me").

The CTS and CTS-2 measure behaviors used by respondents in conflict situations during a specific target interval, which is typically the 12 months prior to administration. The amount of husband-to-wife aggression and wife-to-husband aggression is determined by instructing participants to indicate on an 8-point scale (ie., ranging from 0 = never to 6 = more than 20 times in the past year, and 7 = not in the past 12 months, but it did happen before) the frequency with which (1) they have engaged in these strategies over the past year, and (2) their partners have engaged in these strategies over the past year.

Criticisms of the CTS

Although much of our accumulated knowledge about partner violence is based largely on data from studies that have used the CTS, the measure has nonetheless been the subject of much controversy. The following few sections will highlight some of the issues as well as strategies to overcome them. Because the criticisms discussed here are applicable to both the CTS and the CTS-2, these measures will be referred to collectively as the CTS.

Aggregate Responses

One criticism of the CTS is that it requires respondents to aggregate the episodes and instances of physical aggression that have occurred over the referent time period. For example, a male interviewee who kicked his partner, beat his partner, and used a knife against her in one single episode, would have to report each action separately on the CTS. This type of reporting is problematic because it may seem that these are three distinct, separate episodes (i.e., the male kicked his partner one day, beat his partner another, and used a knife against her on a third day), and the CTS provides no option for disentangling or otherwise understanding if these behaviors happened in one circumscribed episode or were separate, distinct episodes of IPV.

A second problem with the aggregated responses of the CTS is that the interviewee may only report the most severe action taken during any single episode. That is, if the male partner kicked, beat, and threatened his partner with a knife during the same argument, he may only report that he threatened his partner with a knife. Many actions occur during the escalation of an argument that can be forgotten, or thought to be insignificant, therefore, the respondent may pick the one that caused the most serious harm or injury, and report only that one. Reporting only the most severe action is a problem because the smaller, less severe acts of partner violence may not be reported, thereby providing an incomplete account of the episode. In addition, this type of response set will make the overall occurrence of partner violence appear less frequent than it may actually be. Alternatively, it is possible that a respondent could report the least violent incident per episode on the CTS to appear more favorable. In this case, the severity of partner violence could be underestimated, having a significant impact on the intervention provided (e.g., recommending couple counseling for what appears to be common couple violence, when a more intensive treatment may be warranted).

Measuring Violent Acts out of Context

The fact that the CTS measures partner violent acts in isolation of any contextual information is a commonly held criticism. Understanding the context and circumstances in which partner violence occurs may be important to understanding the nature of the violent behaviors, as well as the causes and consequences of the violent acts. Although the CTS elicits information on the frequency of various types of violent behaviors occurred between partners during the target interval, it does not solicit information about *when* the incidents occurred. Such temporal sequencing information could provide valuable insight into factors that might be related to the occurrence of interpartner violence. Determining when physically aggressive acts between partners occur might reveal temporal correlates of domestic violence and factors that predispose partners to the use of these tactics. As an example, for certain dyads, violence may occur around or during major holidays, when financial and social pressures tend to be high. IPV may occur for some couples only, or at least most often, when one or both partners are drinking or using drugs (e.g., Fals-Stewart, 2003; Fals-Stewart, Golden, & Schmacher, 2003).

In addition to lacking temporal information about episodes of violence, the CTS fails to account for the amount of partners' face-to-face contact during the target interval. Relationships in which IPV occurs can be very tumultuous. Depending on the severity of the incidents of IPV, the perpetrator may have been arrested and possibly even spent time in jail. There may even be a series of separations in which the partners do not have contact with each other for a period of time (either court ordered restraining orders or voluntary lack of contact). Quite obviously, when partners do not have contact with each other for whatever reason, the opportunity for physical partner violence is eliminated. Therefore, when attempting to assess the occurrence of partner violence, it is essential to account for periods of time in which the partners had no face-to-face contact, which would allow for an evaluation of 'violence per opportunity'.

Predetermined Set of Violent Acts

The CTS provides a limited set of violent acts for respondents to fit their experiences to. Although the acts on the CTS have been shown to be broadly applicable (Straus, 1990), they do not cover the entire spectrum of acts that could occur during a fight or an argument between partners. Although it would be nearly impossible to ask questions about every possible act of violence that could occur between partners, limiting the violent acts may prevent episodes of violence from being reported, as they do not fit in to the exact descriptions given.

ADDRESSING THE CRITICISMS OF THE CTS:
THE TIMELINE FOLLOWBACK SPOUSAL VIOLENCE INTERVIEW

Given the problems with the CTS outlined above, other investigations have proposed alternative IPV assessment approaches. There are several other measures used to assess partner abuse including the Physical Abuse of Partner Scale (PAPS; Hudson, 1992), the Psychological Maltreatment of Women Inventory (Tolman, 1989), the Index of Spouse Abuse (Hudson & McIntosh, 1981), the Measure of Wife Abuse (Rodenberg & Fantuzzo, 1993), and the Abuse Risk Inventory for Women (Yegidis, 1989). Despite the large number of measures available to assess the occurrence of partner physical abuse, these measures do not account for the majority of problems experienced with use of the CTS. For example, a thorough review of investigations that have used these and other measures to assess domestic violence and published critiques of various spousal violence assessment tools, found no reports that have examined the effect of the amount of face-to-face contact between partners on levels of reported violence.

The limitations of the CTS (and other similar inventories) used to assess partner violence could potentially be addressed by supplementing the data obtained from the CTS with another measure that requires respondents to note on what days spousal violence happens and the types of violent acts that occur on these days. Semistructured calendar interviews have been used in other research areas to ascertain the specific days within a given target interval when certain behaviors occur. Among the most widely used calendar interview is the Timeline Followback (TLFB; Sobell & Sobell, 1996) designed to measure alcohol use, and in particular, frequency and quantity of drinking. An interviewer administers the TLFB using a calendar and other memory aids to gather retrospective estimates of an individual's daily alcohol use over a specified time period.

A calendar-based interview was recently developed and validated for the purposes of assessing IPV. The Timeline Followback Spousal Violence interview (TLFB-SV; Fals-Stewart, Birchler & Kelley, 2003) is based on the TLFB and is used to assess spousal violence in the same way the TLFB assesses alcohol use; frequency and daily patterns of spousal violence (both male-to-female and female-to-male violence) are assessed. The TLFB-SV was shown to have excellent temporal stability and concurrent and discriminant validity (Fals-Stewart, Birchler, & Kelley, 2003).

Individuals interviewed with the TLFB-SV are presented with a daily calendar dating back the number of days in the target interval with standard U.S. holidays noted; they are also asked to mark other days of personal significance (e.g., anniversaries and birthdays). Days during which episodes of male-to-female physical aggression occurred and days during which episodes of female-to-male episodes of physical aggression occurred are entered on the calendar, starting with the previous day. Days during which partners had no face-to-face contact (due to circumstances such as marital separations, separate vacations, court-ordered restraining orders) are also marked.

Interviewees are given a list of possible types of interpartner physical aggression, taken from the eight violence items on the CTS: (a) threw something at partner; (b) pushed, grabbed, or shoved; (c) slapped; (d) kicked, bit or hit; (e) hit, or tried to hit with something; (f) beat up; (g) threatened with a knife or gun; (h) used a knife or gun; or (i) other types of physical aggression not otherwise specified. For violence reported on any given day, the type of violence is categorized using this list and recorded on the calendar. It is possible that more than one type of violent behavior would occur as part of any circumscribed episode; all types of violence are recorded on the calendar. When episodes of violence are reported, interviewers have the option of asking further questions to obtain information about (a) the espisode(s), (b) factors that may have co-occurred with the violent behavior (e.g., intoxication), and (c) the nature of violent interaction.

Addressing the Criticisms of the CTS with the Timeline Followback Spousal Violence Interview

Addressing the Problem of Aggregated Responses

The TLFB-SV interview attempts to address the problem of aggregated responses by interviewing the respondent about the escalation of fights during each episode. With this approach, multiple acts of violence that occur during a single episode can be coded as such, leaving little doubt that these acts occurred during one incident. In a hypothetical scenario where the male partner kicked, beat and threatened his partner with a knife, the interviewer would mark each of those incidents as occurring on that single day, giving more meaning to the responses. Instead of viewing these as three distinct episodes, it can be deduced that, during the course of a single argument or conflict, many different violent behaviors occurred.

Interviewing about violent acts occurring during individual episodes with the TLFB-SV also discourages the respondent from reporting only the most severe (or least severe) action taken during a specified episode, as can occur with the CTS. For example, it is rare that an individual would use a knife against his partner exclusively. Therefore, if a respondent indicated that he had used a knife against his partner, interviewers administering the TLFB-SV would ask follow-up questions to determine if that was the only violent act that occurred that day or within the given violent episode.

The TLFB-SV also provides flexibility to record multiple episodes that may occur in one day. For example, if an argument occurred in the morning that led to physical violence toward one or both of the partners, that would be noted as one episode. If the respondent then reports another conflict later in the day that also led to physical violence, a second episode would be recorded with the codes for the acts that occurred during that argument.

Addressing Violent Acts Measured out of Context

As previously mentioned, one problem with the CTS is that it ignores the context in which partner violent acts occur. Semi-structured calendar interviews like the TLFB-SV, on the other hand, have been used to ascertain the specific days within a given target interval when certain behaviors occur making it more likely to see patterns and trends in the occurrence of IPV. This information could be critical when working with the victim on strategies to avoid potentially dangerous situations, and can help guide the perpetrator's treatment when triggers for violence can easily be identified. In addition, the TLFB-SV allows interviewers to gather specific information about the time of day that partner violent acts occurred, whether it preceded episodes of, say, drinking, drug use, or a verbal argument, and what the order of events was during the escalation of the conflict.

Lets take as an example a husband who comes home from a bar intoxicated and begins to argue with his wife. After the argument, the wife pushes him and begins to punch his chest. The husband then retaliates by slapping her across the face and pushing her down the stairs. Because of the semistructured design of the TLFB-SV interview, much more information is gathered about the dynamics of this conflict and the order of events. Knowing this information may be more useful in research or clinical practice.

In contrast to the CTS, the TLFB-SV accounts for days of contact between partners. A recent study conducted by Fals-Stewart, Lucente and Birchler (2002) highlighted the importance of the amount of face-to-face contact and partners' frequency of domestic violence. The authors found that the number of days of face-to-face contact was significantly associated with the frequency of male-to-female and female-to-male verbal aggression and overall physical violence, both at the baseline and 12-month follow-up assessments. These findings suggest that increased face-to-face contact between partners creates more opportunity for physical violence, as well as the need to consider the amount of face-to-face contact when interpreting frequency of interpartner violence and its likelihood in the future.

The importance of face-to-face contact is highlighted in the following example. A male respondent indicates on the CTS he has punched his partner 6-10 times in the past year; on the TLFB-SV, the male partner indicates that this behavior occurred across 9 days. However, the piece of information captured on the TLFB-SV interview (and not on the CTS) is that the partners only had face-to-face contact 12 days in the past year. Therefore, the fact that violence occurred more than 50% of the time that the partners had contact would be considered by many to be a much more serious situation than the one in which the male punched his partner 6-10 times in the past year, but had contact with her every day.

Addressing the Predetermined Set of Violent Acts

Although the questionnaire format of the CTS limits the partner violent acts that can be queried, the TLFB-SV interview allows for more comprehensive interviewing about the nature of the violence episodes. On the TLFB-SV, the respondent is provided with a list of possible acts of partner physical aggression that are broadly taken from the CTS (e.g., pushed, grabbed, or shoved); they also have the opportunity to report an aggressive act that is not subsumed under any category (i.e., other types of physical aggression not otherwise specified) and provide further elaboration about all episodes. Thus, the highly structured format of the CTS allows for a more efficient evaluation of IPV, but a consequence of its format is a certain loss of flexibility. Although more complicated to administer, the TLFB-SV's interview format allows interviewers to collect more complete descriptive information about the episodes.

Case Example 1

Carlos, a 27 year-old Latino male, and Sonya, a 29 year-old African-American woman have been married for four years. They have two children; their daughter, Tisha, is three years old, and their son, Lamar, is 18 months old. For the past nine months of their marriage, Carlos and Sonya have been legally separated. Their family and friends report that Carlos is easily angered and has been accused of hitting Sonya in the past. After their separation, Sonya denied him access to their children, which angered Carlos. After Carlos threatened to hurt her if she didn't let him see his kids, Sonya filed for a restraining order. She did not have contact with Carlos between November 17th and January 21st. After a phone conversation on January 21st, Sonya believed that Carlos had settled down and deserved a chance to see his kids, so she invited him over. The kids were taking a nap when Carlos arrived at their house. Not long after his arrival, an argument ensued. During the course of the argument Carlos (a) insulted and yelled at Sonya, (b) grabbed Sonya and pushed her against a wall, (c) slapped her, (d) threw a chair at her, (e) pulled her hair, (f) kicked her, and (g) beat her up. When Tisha came downstairs from her nap to witness what was happening, Carlos stopped and ran out of the house. Sonya did not see him for the rest of the month. Carlos was later evaluated for treatment and was administered both the CTS-2 and the TLFB-SV, the results of which are displayed in figures 1 and 2, respectively.[1]

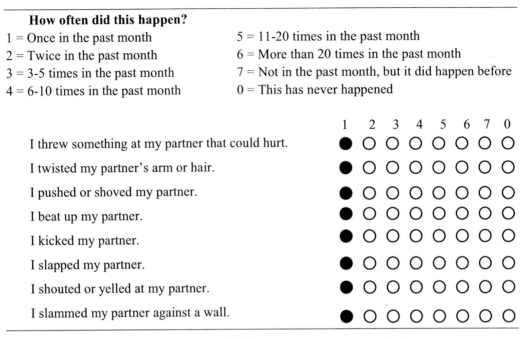

How often did this happen?

1 = Once in the past month
2 = Twice in the past month
3 = 3-5 times in the past month
4 = 6-10 times in the past month

5 = 11-20 times in the past month
6 = More than 20 times in the past month
7 = Not in the past month, but it did happen before
0 = This has never happened

Figure 1. Items from the CTS-2 and Carlos' response to the items.
This figure corresponds to Case Example 1.

			January			
Monday	**Tuesday**	**Wednesday**	**Thursday**	**Friday**	**Saturday**	**Sunday**
			1 New Year's Day Kwanzaa Ends NC	2 NC	3 NC	4 NC
5 NC	6 NC	7 NC	8 NC	9 NC	10 NC	11 NC
12 NC	13 NC	14 NC	15 NC	16 NC	17 NC	18 NC
19 Martin Luther King Jr. Day NC	20 NC	21 RP – 1, 2, 3, 4, 6	22 NC	23 NC	24 NC	25 NC
26 NC	27 NC	28 NC	29 NC	30 NC	31 NC	

Figure 2. A month excerpt of Carlos' TLFB-SV calendar.
This figure corresponds to Case Example 1. NC = days of no face-to-face contact;
RP = respondent-to-partner violence; 1 = pushed, grabbed, or shoved; 2 = slapped; 3 = threw something; 4 = kicked, bit, or hit with a fist; 6 = beat up.

---

[1] This figure is used to illustrate how the client from each case example would respond to some of the items on the CTS. For the purposes of the figure we choose not to show items indicating violent acts the respondent's partner has done toward him or her and we changed the referent time period to 30 days, rather than the 12 month period that is usually employed to make a direct comparison to one month of the TLFB-SV interview.

There are several critical differences that become apparent immediately upon reviewing the CTS-2 and the TLFB-SV calendar. First, there are a significant number of items endorsed on the CTS-2, even though all of the types of behaviors occurred in the context of one episode. In addition, it is not possible from the information provided on the CTS-2 to ascertain the lack of contact between the partners and how that may have influenced the frequency of behaviors.

In contrast, more information is provided on the TLFB-SV calendar. The TLBB-SV reveals that Carlos engaged in one episode of violence toward his partner during the 30-day period in question. The other important piece of information the TLFB-SV calendar provides is that Carlos and Sonya had no face-to-face contact any other day during the 30-day period. This information may be important to evaluators and treatment providers, who may wish to interpret frequency of violence in terms of opportunity.

Case Example 2

Sam is a 47 year-old Caucasian man, and Heather is a 45 year-old Caucasian woman. Sam and Heather have been married for 15 years and do not have any children. Sam has struggled with his temper and has sought treatment for domestic violence in the past. He recognizes that when he drinks, he gets in to more arguments with Heather, which is when he has the tendency to be physically aggressive toward her. Sam is currently seeking treatment for his physical aggression toward his wife and reports having several episodes in which he physically attacked her over the past month. Upon entering treatment, Sam was administered the CTS-2 and the TLFB-SV. The results can be seen in Figures 3 and 4, respectively.[1]

How often did this happen?

1 = Once in the past month
2 = Twice in the past month
3 = 3-5 times in the past month
4 = 6-10 times in the past month
5 = 11-20 times in the past month
6 = More than 20 times in the past month
7 = Not in the past month, but it did happen before
0 = This has never happened

	1	2	3	4	5	6	7	0
I punched or hit my partner with something that could hurt.	○	●	○	○	○	○	○	○
I beat up my partner.	●	○	○	○	○	○	○	○

Figure 3. Items from the CTS-2 and Sam's response to the items. This figure corresponds to Case Example 2.

January						
Monday	**Tuesday**	**Wednesday**	**Thursday**	**Friday**	**Saturday**	**Sunday**
			1 New Year's Day, Kwanzaa Ends	2	3	4 RP – 1, 2, 5
5 NC	6 NC	7 NC	8	9	10	11
12	13	14	15	16	17 RP – 1, 2, 3, 6	18
19 Martin Luther King Jr. Day	20	21	22	23	24	25 RP - 3, 5
26	27	28	29	30	31	

Figure 4. A month excerpt of Sam's TLFB-SV calendar.
This figure corresponds to Case Example 2. NC = days of no face-to-face contact;
RP = respondent-to-partner violence; 1 = pushed, grabbed, or shoved; 2 = slapped;
3 = threw something; 5 = hit, or tried to hit, with something; 6 = beat up.

According to Sam's responses on the CTS-2, he kicked, bit, or hit Heather with a fist once during the past month and hit, or tried to hit Heather with something twice in the past month. A review of the TLFB-SV calendar reveals much more information about Sam's behavior toward his wife in the past month, revealing three distinct episodes of IPV, with multiple violent behaviors occurring within each episode. The most severe acts in each episode were (a) kicked, bit or hit, and (b) hit or tried to hit with something. There were also three consecutive days where Sam and Heather had no face-to-face contact with each other. Given the information provided on the TLFB-SV calendar, it is apparent that when Sam was filling out the CTS-2, he chose to indicate only the most severe violent act during each episode. This creates a certain degree of distortion in the description of the IPV episodes, which evolves from the aggregated responses solicited by the CTS.

CONCLUSION

Although the above case examples illustrate certain advantages the TLFB-SV interview may have over the CTS, there are several other situations in which using the TLFB-SV interview may also be beneficial. In particular, the TLFB-SV was designed to assess temporal relationships among events. Thus, for those interested in understanding the temporal sequencing of behaviors that may influence IPV, the TLFB-SV responses can reveal important patterns. As an example, a large and growing body of research suggests a substantial proportion of incidents of interpartner physical violence occur during alcohol or drug intoxication (for a review, see Quigley & Leonard, 2000). In addition, the prevalence of IPV is substantially higher among couples in which one or both partners abuse alcohol or other drugs when compared to nonsubstance abusing couples (e.g., Murphy & O'Farrell, 1994). Given these findings, the functional role of substance use in the occurrence of partner physical aggression was recently investigated (Fals-Stewart, 2003). Fals-Stewart (2003) concluded that men entering a domestic violence treatment program and domestically violent men entering an alcoholism treatment program were roughly 8 times more likely to report any incidence of male-to-female physical aggression on days of drinking than on days of no drinking. Additionally, the odds of severe male-to-female physical aggression were more than 11 times higher on days of men's drinking than on days of no drinking. Conducting this study, and understanding the day-to-day relationship between alcohol use and partner violence, was made possible, in part, by the availability of psychometrically-sound calendar interviews for both IPV and drinking.

It is also important to highlight the advantages of using the CTS compared to the TLFB-SV. First, the CTS is brief and requires less training. The TLFB-SV, on the other hand, is more labor intensive, and requires the respondents to discuss, in detail, single episodes of partner violence occurring within the past 12 months, and needs to be administered by a well-trained interviewer. Also, depending on the depth of the information that is desired, the CTS can give a quick overview of the nature of partner violence that may be occurring between partners. The CTS can be used in contexts where subject burden is of concern. For example, it would be impractical to use the TLFB-SV when conducting national surveys of IPV prevalence and frequency, whereas the CTS is ideal for such data collection. Despite the criticisms of the CTS, this measure remains one of the most widely used and cited measure of partner abuse. The authors of the CTS do acknowledge its limitations and note that the CTS is intended to be used in addition to other measures that gather other information relevant to the investigator (e.g., background, and outcome variables relevant for the study or the clinical situation; Straus et al., 1996).

The TLFB-SV, while being a viable alternative to the CTS, is not, however, the only one. New technologies in the area of interactive voice response (IVR) have been developed to collect daily data over an extended time frame by using touch-tone telephone pads to report daily behaviors (Mundt, Perrine, Searles, & Walter, 1995; Searles, Perrine, Mundt, & Helzer, 1995). One recent study also investigated the use of cellular telephones in IVR to provide a flexible way to collect data and found that the use of cellular phones may be a viable alternative to traditional paper-and-pencil self report measures (Collins, Kashdan & Gollnisch, 2003). Because the TLFB-SV interview attempts to collect information about daily behaviors, it would be possible to collect information about incidents of partner violence using similar IVR techniques.

In addition to IVR, computerized ecological momentary assessment (EMA; Shiffman & Stone, 1998) is an alternative in which participants use handheld computers to enter information about a target behavior such as drinking (e.g., Collins et al., 1998). EMA has several advantages to traditional paper-and-pencil questionnaires including the collection of data in real time, and monitoring of participation and compliance. Again, with technology like EMA already existing for the assessment of alcohol consumption, it is feasible that this technique can be used to record and assess the occurrence of IPV.

In conclusion, the CTS is a widely used and accepted measure of partner violence, but has been shown to have certain limitations with accurate measurement of the information related to the occurrence of partner abuse. The TLFB-SV interview attempts to address many of these issues by providing a more comprehensive overview of the occurrence of partner physical abuse. The TLFB-SV interview allows investigators to determine temporal relationships, accounts for days of no face-to-face contact between partners, and provides a clear picture of when each violent act occurs, and whether multiple acts occur within each episode. Although the TLFB-SV interview does address many of the criticisms of the CTS, recent technology is providing interactive means of collecting data that may be even more useful in the future.

REFERENCES

Babcock, J.C., & La Taillade, J.J. (2000). Evaluating interventions for men who batter. In J. Vincent & E. Jouriles (Eds.), *Domestic Violence: Guidelines for Research-Informed Practice.* (pp. 37-77). Philadelphia, PA: Jessica Kingsley.

Collins, R.L., Kashdan, T.B., & Gollnisch, G. (2003). The feasibility of using cellular phones to collect ecological momentary assessment data: Application to alcohol consumption. *Experimental and Clinical Psychopharmacology, 11,* 73-78.

Collins, R.L., Morsheimer, E.T., Shiffman, S., Paty, J.A., Gnys, M., & Papandonatos, G.D. (1998). Ecological momentary assessment in a behavioral drinking moderation training program. *Experimental and Clinical Psychopharmacology, 6,* 306-315.

Fals-Stewart, W. (2003). The occurrence of partner physical aggression on days of alcohol consumption: A longitudinal diary study. *Journal of Consulting and Clinical Psychology, 71,* 41-52.

Fals-Stewart, W., Birchler, G.R., & Kelley, M.L. (2003). The timeline followback spousal violence interview to assess physical aggression between intimate partners: Reliability and validity. *Journal of Family Violence, 18,* 131-142.

Fals-Stewart, W., Golden, J., Schumacher, J.A. (2003). Intimate partner violence and substance use: A longitudinal day-to-day examination. *Addictive Behaviors, 28,* 1555-1574.

Fals-Stewart, W., Lucente, S.W., & Birchler, G.R. (2002). The relationship between the amount of face-to-face contact and partners' reports of domestic violence frequency. *Assessment, 9,* 123-130.

Hudson, W.W. (1992). *The WALMYR Assessment Scales Scoring Manual,* WALMYR Publishing, Tempe, AZ.

Hudson, W., & McIntosh, S. (1981). The assessment of spouse abuse: Two quantifiable dimensions. *Journal of Marriage and the Family, 43,* 873-888.

Johnson, M.P. (1995). Patriarchal terrorism and common couple violence: Two forms of violence against women. *Journal of Marriage and the Family, 57,* 283-294.

Murphy, C.M., & O'Farrell, T.J. (1994). Factors associated with marital aggression in male alcoholics. *Journal of Family Psychology, 8,* 321-335.

Mundt, J.C., Perrine, M.W., Searles, J.S., & Walter, D. (1995). An application of interactive voice response (IVR) technology to longitudinal studies of daily behavior. *Behavior Research, Methods, Instruments, & Computers, 27,* 351-357.

National Research Council. (1996). *Understanding violence against women.* Washington, DC: National Academy Press.

Peachy, R. (1988). *Consulting in research and psychiatry: Statistics.* Philadelphia, PA: National Clearinghouse for the Defense of Battered Women.

Pirog-Good, M., & Stets-Kealey, J. (1985). Male batterers and battering prevention programs: A national survey. *Response to the Victimization of Women and Children, 2,* 223-233.

Quigley, B.M., & Leonard, K.E. (2000). Alcohol, drugs, and violence. In V.B. Van Hasselt & M. Hersen (Eds.), *Aggression and violence: An introductory text* (pp. 259-283). Boston: Allyn & Bacon.

Rodenberg, F., & Fantuzzo, J. (1993). The measure of wife abuse: Steps toward the development of a comprehensive assessment technique. *Journal of Family Violence, 8,* 203-217.

Schafer, J. (1996). Measuring spousal violence with the Conflict Tactics Scale: Notes on reliability and validity issues. *Journal of Interpersonal Violence, 11*, 572-585.

Searles, J.S., Perrine, M.W., Mundt, J.C., & Helzer, J.E. (1995). Self-report of drinking using touch-tone telephone: Extending the limits of reliable daily contact. *Journal of Studies on Alcohol, 56*, 375-382.

Shiffman, S., & Stone, A.A. (1998). Introduction to the special section: Ecological momentary assessment in health psychology. *Health Psychology, 17*, 3-5.

Sobell, L.C., & Sobell, M.B. (1996). *Timeline followback user's guide: A calendar method for assessing alcohol and drug use.* Toronto, Canada: Addiction Research Foundation.

Straus, M.A. (1979). Measuring intrafamily conflict and violence: The Conflict Tactics (CT) Scales. *Journal of Marriage and the Family, 41*, 75-78.

_____ . (1990). The Conflict Tactics Scale and its critics: An evaluation and new data on validity and reliability. In M.A. Straus & R. J. Gelles (Eds.), *Physical violence in American Families: Risk factors and adaptations to violence in 8,145 families.* (pp. 49-73). New Brunswick, NJ: Transaction Books.

Straus, M.A. & Gelles, R.J. (1986). Societal change and change in family violence from 1975 to 1985 as revealed by two national surveys. *Journal of Marriage and the Family, 48*, 465-479.

_____ . (1990). How violent are American families? Estimates from the National Family Violence Resurvey and other studies. In M.A. Strauss and R.J. Gelles (Eds.), *Physical violence in American families: Risk factors and adaptations to violence in 8,145 families* (pp. 341-367). New Brunswick, NJ: Transaction Publishers.

Straus, M.A., Hamby, S. L., Boney-McCoy, S., & Sugarman, D.B. (1996). The revised conflict tactics scale (CTS2). Development and preliminary psychometric data. *Journal of Family Issues, 17*, 283-316.

Tolman, R. (1989). The development of a measure of psychological maltreatment of women by their male partners. *Violence and Victims, 4*, 159-177.

Yegidis, B.L. (1989). *Abuse Risk Inventory for Women.* Palo Alto, CA: Mind Garden.

In: *Focus on Aggression Research*
Editor: James P. Morgan, pp. 15-39

ISBN 1-59454-132-9
© 2004 Nova Science Publishers, Inc.

Chapter 2

"HOW COULD THEY DO THAT?" PARENTAL AGGRESSION: ITS IMPACT ON CHILDREN'S ADULT MENTAL HEALTH, ITS LINK TO UNDERSTANDING SOCIAL VIOLENCE

*Henry Massie and Nathan Szajnberg**

ABSTRACT

The Brody longitudinal study which followed the emotional development of 76 individuals from birth to age 30 – volunteer families from all socioeconomic groups – provides a kind of naturalistic laboratory for examining how violence in childhood affects adult mental health. The study illuminates: 1) psychological conditions that lead parents to maltreat their children, 2) the appearance and evolution of emotional problems in the children, 3) resilient coping, and 4) the inevitable scars which trauma always leaves on personality development.

Specifically, of the 76 study participants 10 (13%) experienced severe physical abuse and/or severe emotional rejection from one or both parents, an incidence similar to that found in large-scale surveys. All 76 were followed from birth with parent interviews, filmed mother-infant and mother-child interactions, psychodiagnostic projective testing, and school observations to age 7. They were followed up with extensive interviews and psychodiagnostic testing at ages 18 and 30. Those who escaped trauma in childhood provide a comparison group to the less fortunate whose adult mental health was globally compromised.

Favorable mothering in infancy provided only limited psychological protection against traumas later in childhood and adolescence. However, only 1/3 of the parents of the 76 children were effectively empathic, responsive, and organized with their children in the first years of life, raising the question of what societal and internal psychological forces degrade

* Henry Massie, M.D. is Clinical Associate Professor of Psychiatry, University of California School of Medicine, San Francisco, CA, and in private practice of child, adolescent, and adult psychiatry in Berkeley, CA. Address communications to Dr. Massie at 3036 Regent St., Berkeley, CA 94705. Nathan Szajnberg, M.D. is Clinical Professor of Psychiatry, University of California School of Medicine, San Francisco, and in private practice of psychoanalysis and child and adult psychiatry.
The research on which this essay is based has been supported by grants from the California Wellness Foundation and International Psychoanalytic Association Research Advisory Board.

the nurturing of young children, which ideally occurs in a relatively smooth, instinctual, and normative manner. Further, aggression within families provides a model for understanding some aspects of violence in the larger society.

"All cruelty springs from weakness,"

Seneca (4 BC - 65 AD)

INTRODUCTION

The Fifth Commandment, "Thou shall not kill," undoubtedly exists because of humankind's entrenched violence and the enduring need to prevent it. The Golden Rule offers alternatives to violence: "Do onto others as you would have them do onto you," and "Love thy neighbor as thyself. However, as George Bernard Shaw (1903) observed with mordant humor, "The Golden Rule is that there is no Golden Rule."

To explore the dilemma of aggression and its often tragic consequences we take a close look at data related to violence in our longitudinal study of 76 families and their children's emotional development from birth to age 30 (Massie and Szajnberg, 2002). The cases we examine show disturbances of aggression, as opposed to the normative expression of forcefulness which allows people to exploit their potential for the sake of mastering the challenges of raising families and existing in their environment as harmoniously as possible. We also examine what the data show about the pernicious effects of violence on the psychological life of children, and how some children rise above its effects to raise their own children with sensitivity and aggression healthily channeled or sublimated to the tasks of parenthood.

To present the study this paper first describes the background of the longitudinal project, then focuses on the 10 families out of the 76 followed to age 30 in which physical abuse and/or extreme emotional abuse occurred. In narrowing the lens to these 10 families, the paper presents, first, the pervasive way in which violence harms the children's development well into adulthood; then describes the fathers' physical aggression, the mothers' emotional hostility, and their psychological sources. Three detailed individual case histories follow. The concluding discussion considers the very high incidence of impaired parenting not only in our study but also in other research studies. Finally we return to the dilemma of whether human violence is inevitable, instinctual, or rooted in the specific psychopathology of a relatively few people.

Background – the Longitudinal Study

Sylvia Brody, a psychologist and psychoanalyst, and Sidney Axelrad, a sociologist, at the City University of New York, began the project in 1963 and 1964 with 132 families expecting the birth of a child. The parents – largely middle-class but from all socioeconomic groups and many ethnicities – had responded to a call for volunteers in obstetrical clinics in New York City for a study of children's psychological development. Not a study of aggression or of child abuse per se, its core hypothesis was that children whose mothers were most favorable would fare better as time went on. Brody (1956), a pioneer in the study of mother-infant interactions, had analyzed the many elements of nursing and feeding, which the longitudinal study condensed for statistical purposes into four maternal categories – responsiveness, empathy, organization, and loving behavior (showing affection, offering endearments). Dr. Brody had also shown how the feeding relationship was a paradigm of the overall quality of the mother-child relationship. This was the first study to combine psychoanalytic developmental theory, modern research design, filmed mother-child interaction for analysis, and to be carried to the adulthood of the participants. Figure 1 outlines the research procedures through age 18.

Figure 1

Procedures from the Third Trimester Through Age 18

Child's Time-line		Procedures
3rd trimester		Interviews with mother
Birth (1964)	– Neonatal assessment	(pregnancy–age 7: attitudes to child,
6 Weeks	– Filmed feedings	hopes, anxieties, routines, child's
6 Months	– Developmental assessments	training, education, events in life,
1 Year	– Maternal classifications	sibling & spousal relationships,
	Child observations	parent's childhood)
3 Years	– Filmed mother-child play	
4	– Psychodiagnostics (WISC, CAT,	Interviews with father
5	human figure drawings)	(age 4–7: same semi-structured
6	– School observations	format as mothers)
7	– Teacher reports	
18 Years (1982)	Interviews with youths (family, health, education, goals, leisure, friendships, attitudes to self, others and society, anxiety, conflicts, symptoms, early memories)	
	Psychodiagnostics (WAIS, TAT, Rorschach, Bender, human figure drawings)	

Figure 1. Research Procedures Birth to Age 18.

At the 1, 12, and 18 years of age follow-ups (Brody and Axelrad, 1970; Brody and Axelrad, 1978; Brody and Siegel, 1992), the original hypothesis bore out: Children of the more effective mothers were more emotionally robust in terms of having more maturity, more mature psychological defenses, fewer psychiatric symptoms such as anxiety and depression, better peer relationships, and having school performance more consistent with their I.Q.s than the children who had had less effective mothers in infancy. But at each of the junctures the relationship between mothering and outcome grew statistically weaker. The 30 year followup illuminated why this was happening.

The 30-Year Followup

In 1994, the research participants reached age 30 and a new team, directed by Dr. Massie, took on the project. Seventy-eight of the 92 whom Dr. Brody had interviewed at age 18 (from the original group of 132) were located, and of these 76 elected to participate in the followup study. The new team audio- and video-recorded semi-structured interviews that covered pre-set topics but also allowed subject and interviewer to digress and explore areas that seemed especially interesting, conflictual, affect laden, or unclear. The first 1 1/2 hours of the followup was the Adult Attachment Interview (AAI) (George, Kaplan and Main, 1985) which provides a picture of the interviewees' mental representation of attachment to their parents based on their recall of events related to security in childhood, parental discipline, losses of attachment figures, and the manner in which the interviewees talk about these experiences. The second 1 1/2 hours of the followup focused on life after 18 – friendships, education, continuing relationship with family, work, partnerships, health, psychiatric symptoms if any, fears and ambitions for the future, recurring night-time dreams, earliest childhood memories, and the subjects' own children if they were already parents. In the case of participants who were parents, we filmed them feeding and/or playing with their children just as the project's original researchers had filmed their mothers with them a generation earlier. Figure 2 summarizes the 30-year followup procedures.

An additional aspect of the 30-year followup was a reexamination of the original researchers' classification of mothers into Favorable and Less Favorable groups. Contemporary measures of the quality of the mother-child interaction were applied blind to original classification and subsequent history with a subset of the original childhood films, the results of which validated the original groupings (Bahadur, 1998). The overall Brody project data from birth to age 30 includes approximately 300 pages of records and many hours of films for each participant, the analysis of which is reported in detail elsewhere (Massie and Szajnberg, 2002). All coding and assessments of the 30-year olds were made blind to the subject's mother's original classification, and blind to any information from the research record through age 18. Subsequently, we constructed psychodynamic biographies of each participant from the information from all years of the study.

For the first time in the course of the longitudinal study, the participants' outcomes betrayed the original hypothesis. In brief, the children who received the most effective mothering in infancy were *not* doing better as adults than those who had received less favorable mothering: They were no more likely to be Secure in their representations of childhood attachment; they did not have higher Global Assessment of Functioning (American Psychiatric Association, 1994) ratings of psychological, social and occupational functioning; and their Eriksonian psychosocial levels (Hawley, 1980) were no higher than adult children of the less effective mothers. Further, the children of the more effective mothers were *no* freer of psychiatric diagnoses as adults than children of less effective mothers.

Figure 2

Flow Chart of 30-year Followup Procedures

3-Hour Semi-Structured Interview

Adult Attachment Interview (AAI)

Focuses on security, loss, trauma
in first 18 years of life

Ages 18–30 Interview

Family relationships, education, health,
career, relationships, leisure, sexuality,
children, psychiatric history, early memories, recurrent & striking dreams, future
wishes

House-Tree-Person Drawings

Analysis & Scoring of Interviews (Measures used)

Defensive Functioning Scale	**Global Assessment of Functioning**	**Psycho-social Functioning**	**AAI**	**Diagnosis**
Maturity of psychological defence mecha- nisms	Competence, contentment, adjustment, impact of symp- toms, if any	Attainment of Erikson psycho- social stages	Mental repre- sentation of security in family in childhood	DSM-IV Axis I or II diagnosis, if any

Psychodynamic Synthesis of Outcome & Archival Record of Childhood History

Figure 2. 30-Year Followup Procedures.

Only one area supported the infancy predictions: Adult children of the more effective mothers had more mature psychological defense mechanisms as rated by the Defense Scale (Vaillant, 1994). For example, they were significantly more likely to have highly adaptive defenses; while children of less effective mothers were prone to defenses at the level of mental inhibitions and minor image distortions. We theorized that this occurred because the mother's own defense mechanisms mediate how she cares for her child, and as time passes the child internalizes and identifies with the mother's ministrations and her manner of responding in habitual and stressful situations. The mother's mediation of early childhood emotional regulation becomes the child's own mode of managing unpleasant thoughts, feelings and stress, and maintaining equilibrium – in essence the mother's defense mechanisms become the child's in the process of core psychological structuralization which is relatively complete by approximately six years of age.

The Role of Psychological Trauma

Encounters with trauma in childhood and adolescence explained why children of the more effective mothers failed to live up to their original promise (aside from maturity of defenses). Table 1 lists the kinds of damaging experiences the children met, their incidence, and their impact on lowering GAF scores. As can be seen, physical and emotional abuse were the most common traumas in the study.

Table 1. Incidence of Childhood Traumas and Adult Outcome of Children
with Two or More Traumas Compared to Children with None or One

76 Families: Divorce (9), Alcoholic Parent (9), Severe Psychiatric Illness in Parent (4), Abusive Parent (10), Sexual Molestation (2 - outside family), Severe Physical Illness or Injury to parent or Sibling (3), Severe Physical Illness, Handicap or Injury to Child (2), Witnessing Death or Severe Injury (2).

Families with 0 or 1 Trauma/Adversity (n = 68)	Mean Global Assessment of Functioning = 82.21 std dev 12.05
Families with 2 or more Trauma/Adversities (n = 8)	Mean Global Assessment of Functioning = 72.38 std dev 11.30 t- 2.195 p - 0.031*

* Significant difference

The findings are not surprising; Bowlby (1969) predicted them in positing that threats to the emotional security of a developing child will lead to insecurity which, like a pebble's ripple effect in water, expands toward anxiety, depression, and compensatory psychological maneuvers that are often pathological to maintain emotional equilibrium. For example, a parent's illness threatens family security; divorce typically removes a large measure of security; an abused child experiences loss of love; a child's personal illness or injury (or being beaten) threatens the child's sense of physical mastery; and witnessing a parent's or sibling's illness, injury or beating (even witnessing a non-family member's severe injury or death) profoundly violates the child's sense of bodily and emotional integrity.

The theory of cumulative traumatic strain (Kahn, 1963; van der Kolk, 1996) also explains the findings: Traumatized children and adults have some emotional resilience, but the strain of repeated emotional assaults overwhelms the human organism's plasticity, distorting personality and possibly altering neuroendocrine function permanently.

CHILD ABUSE

Ten of the 76 children experienced child abuse – the most frequent trauma in the study – and 5 of 76 (6.6%) were physically beaten, a rate slightly higher than the 5% reported in community surveys (McKay, Fanning, Paleg, and Landis, 1995). Child maltreatment was linked with parental alcoholism and/or divorce in several of the families. The divorces all occurred after the children were seven years old. Parents kept the extent of family violence and hostility hidden from the original researchers so that it only came out during the participants' 30-year interviews, pointing up the difficulty of identifying and therefore preventing child abuse. During the interviews at age 18, the youths – even many of those beaten by parents – tended to idealize their families, gloss over unhappiness, or adopt counter-phobic attitudes that they could manage in spite of having parents who did not understand them, did not meet their needs, or worse. For teenagers, denial generally won out over remembrance; but as adults – physical and psychological individuation and separation from their childhood families generally accomplished – they recalled specific details about abusive childhood experiences, a capacity for reflection that characterizes the transition from adolescence to adulthood which we have described more fully elsewhere (Szajnberg and Massie, 2003).

The adult memories of the participants painted vivid pictures of physical attacks five suffered at the hands of fathers; five others recalled severe emotional abuse in the form of continued denigration or rejection by one or both parents. When physical abuse occurred in our families it was always at the hands of the father; in the cases of emotional abuse without physical violence mothers were the perpetrators in four of five instances. In only one family in which abuse occurred had the mother been originally classified as Favorable as a caretaker during her child's first year of life (see Nita's case below). Although the original research team was unaware of the full extent of hostility and violence in the families, they did observe how the mothers' care of their babies was already perturbed in the other 9 families. They offered the parents educational feedback and referrals for counseling, but none made use of these offers.

Table 2, Adult Outcome of Abused Children Compared to Non-Abused Children, shows that the maltreated children as adults fare badly in all measures – Global Assessment of Functioning, presence of psychiatric diagnoses, security of attachment, psychosocial level, and maturity of psychological defenses. As other studies of abused children have found (Green, 1978; Steele, 1980; McCloskey, Figueredo, and Koss, 1995), they have handicaps in many areas of their lives. There is no statistically significant difference in outcome between the children who were physically abused and those who were emotionally maltreated in our study, but sample sizes are small.

Table 2. Adult Outcome of Abused Children Compared to Non-Abused Children

GLOBAL FUNCTION (GAF)	DEFENSE LEVEL	ERIKSON PSYCHO-SOCIAL LEVEL	PSYCHIATRIC DIAGNOSIS	ATTACHMENT STATUS (AAI)
ABUSED (N = 10)				
Mean = 69.1 (SD = 9.3)	Mean = 4.83 (SD = 1.3)	Mean = 27.8 (SD = 6.2)	8 (80%)	2 (20%) Secure
Mild symptoms; Some difficulty functioning.	Minor distortions of images of the self and others; Disavowal of the unacceptable	Moderate attainment		
NON-ABUSED (N = 66)				
Mean = 82.6 (SD = 12)	Mean = 5.96 (SD = 1.06)	Mean = 32.6 (SD = 6)	18 (27.3%)	39 (59%) Secure
No or minimal symptoms; Good functioning in all areas	Mental inhibitions & compromise formations	Generally high attainment		
t = 3.39 p = .001*	t = 3.06 p = .003*	t = 2.38 p = .02*	Chi2 = 10.73 p = .002*	Chi2 = 5.34 p = .02*

* Significant

The Parents' Aggression

The project had a deeper understanding of the mothers because their contact with the researchers began in the third trimester of pregnancy. Fathers formally joined the study with yearly interviews from age 4 to 7, although some fathers had informal contact with the researchers earlier. The fathers' relatively late entry into the study was an artifact of the era in which the project began, a time when it was still believed that a father's role in children's development was peripheral in the first years. Today, although mothers still provide most infant care in all cultures, we know that the father's influence begins in infancy, facilitating or hindering a baby's psychological individuation, providing a model for identification, and facilitating the mother's capacity to nurture through his supportive presence.

The parent interviews, the mother-child observations and films, occasional father-child observations, and the children's own interviews reveal a range of causes for the parents' aggression toward their children. Capsule presentations – with names and some details changed to protect confidentiality – summarize these sources of parental hostility.

Physically abusive fathers: *Victor's father* had been abandoned by his own father, which greatly impaired his self-esteem. A professional actor, he was admired on the stage, but in the rough-and-tumble of family life where conflict often over-rode adulation, he couldn't control his temper. He left the family for weeks and months at a time to look for affirmation elsewhere; then returned home consumed with guilt. Diagnostically (American Psychiatric Association, 1994) he appeared to suffer from a Borderline Personality Disorder – he was erratic, needy, guilty, loving and hostile; as well as prominent features of a Narcissistic Personality Disorder. *Ted's father*, a sufferer of chronic Post-Traumatic Stress Disorder, lost his parents in World War II and was raised in displaced person camps. He brought to parenthood little experience with intimacy, and tried to emulate the autocratic models of discipline he learned in the camps after the war. When dispirited or frustrated in the family, he used alcohol as a form of self-medication even though it fueled rage that he took out on his children. When Ted's mother finally put herself definitively between the father and Ted, the father fled the family. *Ulla's father* was a driven, competitive, economically successful executive. Described as a self-involved "cocky man with a cold, hard stare" by an early interviewer, he had no patience for family life. A Narcissistic Personality, he believed his wife and children should draw admiring attention so that people in turn admired him. However he did not view himself as having a role in their accomplishments, for his image of a husband was simply a man who made money. When Ulla was seven years old, the parents divorced. During Ulla's teenage visits with her father, he invited her to use drugs with him to try to create an illusion of camaraderie; their visits, however, usually ended in confrontations, and once he pushed her down a flight of stairs.

Larry's and Nita's fathers were both extremely rigid Obsessive-Compulsive Personalities. Larry's father had also been orphaned young and he was raised with little love by relatives who forced him prematurely to support himself by his mid-teens. Both men worked hard trying to gain footholds in the middle class in order to give their children opportunities they never had. When they felt over-worked, over-whelmed, unappreciated – and sometimes paranoid that misfortune was singling them out – they erupted with anger. After seeing her children endure several years of beatings, some that led to emergency room visits, Larry's mother threatened to turn to a boyfriend and leave with the two children. The father never raised his fists against the family again. By contrast, Nita's mother (the one mother rated Favorable of the 10 abused children) said to her interviewer that she wanted to leave her husband, "But with 5 children and no money, where would I go?" Nita's father continued to hit his daughter until she made a suicide attempt when she was 20 years old and left home.

Emotionally Abusive Mothers

Lisa's parents were both neglectful in the extreme. The research team recognized early on that the mother acted in a very child-like manner. Anxious and insecure from being belittled by her own self-involved parents (diagnostically an Infantile Personality), she had little notion about how to care for a young child. Lisa's father was entirely invested not in his daughter but in entrepreneurial schemes that usually failed. The self-occupied parents entrusted the child to a series of poorly chosen nannies. By the time Lisa was in high school, the parents moved abroad to escape creditors and left their daughter behind in her own apartment. *Vicki's mother* was also very self-centered, an outgrowth of imperious self-certainty rather than anxiety.

Diagnostically, also a Narcissistic Personality and professionally an entertainer, she focused on her appearance and traveled a great deal with her husband, Vicki's father, who was also the mother's manager. During visits to the research project, the mother pushed her daughter about roughly, and showed no warmth, patience, or understanding. Vicki, however, was more fortunate than Lisa: she had a kindly aunt who lived in the family home to turn to for comfort.

Ken's mother was the most behaviorally brutal of the mothers. Shortly after the baby was born, rigidly obsessive-compulsive, the mother enunciated her child-rearing tenets: "I will get rid of a child who doesn't mind me." "Indulging children is a weakness and they will find you out." "Getting a child to sleep, to use the toilet, and to behave is just a matter of conditioned reflexes." Her joyless, domineering behavior with her son followed her words. Fixated on cleanliness, the mother spanked Ken regularly from a very young age when he didn't keep his room clean. The milquetoast father timidly kept his peace and didn't intervene. When Ken was 18 years old, he was meek and bland but had a clearer-eyed view of his childhood than the great majority of the teenagers. He told his interviewer, "It was not as if I felt deprived of love as a kid because I didn't know what it was to have any." He added hard won insight about his mother, "I should have stood up to her more, but the few times I did she became more angry or started crying so I backed down. I guess I thought she would fall apart or something." Ken grasped that his mother's brittleness – her rigid routines and tyranny – warded off uncertainty and self-doubt. Like his father, Ken kept his peace and now lives far away, almost entirely out of contact with his parents.

Janet's mother combined the disturbed qualities of both Lisa's and Ken's mothers. Like Lisa's, she was child-like and emotionally immature, with only rudimentary understanding of how to go about caring for a baby and child. For her own inadequacy she substituted obsessive-compulsive rules of behavior and expectations that were beyond Janet's years and capacity. Constantly critical, controlling, and denigrating, she demanded household chores that were far too advanced for her daughter. Life was a constant round of spankings, room confinements, and punitive deprivations – all in the belief that this was how one raised a child. The father was considerably more tolerant of Janet, but had one grave disappointment in her that he couldn't contain: she wasn't the son he wanted. He unfairly and regularly compared her to the fantasized golden boy he wished he had – in such mundane ways as mocking her for not throwing a ball like a boy, and in critical ways by not supporting her education in the belief that it was not important for girls to be educated.

David's mother didn't know how to connect with people; she was remote and lonely – an only child who saw little of her parents growing up because of the long shifts both worked, one during the day and the other at night. David's father was also little available to his wife or son because of his work in the restaurant business which kept him out late into the evening. Increasingly the mother used alcohol to comfort herself, which drove the father further away and largely out of the boy's life when he was in sixth grade. Even more embittered, the mother drank herself to death by the time David was in his 20s. Sometimes sober and functional during the day, the mother lost all restraint at night under the influence of alcohol; in outbursts of resentment, she cursed her children, swung at them with her fists, and threw objects at them. David escaped by wandering the streets at night, sleeping in backyards, and returning in the morning to dress for school.

As early as David's infancy, the research team recognized that the mother was troubled. She felt her son was a burden but couldn't ask for or accept help. In her childcare, she ascribed feelings to the baby that she herself felt (such as seeing him as restless or difficult to calm). Responding to the mother's sense of estrangement from David, a researcher wrote, "Her denial of the baby's misery was so great that I found it hard to believe and tolerate. The baby cried whenever the mother picked him up. At no time did she speak to him fondly or cuddle him and clearly disliked him. I attempted to model for the mother and when I held David he calmed, smiled and reached toward me. I was struck by how connected his irritability seemed to the interaction with his mother. They were clearly a miserable mother-child pair."

Summary of Psychological Liabilities Underlying the Parents' Aggression toward their Children

Reviews of maltreating parents typically describe behavior (Milner and Chilamkurti, 1991; Bancroft and Silverman, 2002) to the detriment of the parents' underlying psychodynamics and psychiatric diagnoses which we emphasize. In the Brody study *pathological narcissism* (extreme self-involvement) led directly to two fathers' and one mother's rage. Kohut (1972) has delineated how narcissistic rage erupts when people hold too dearly to their own self-image. Clinging to their pride because they feel an underlying lack of personal esteem, their egos are easily bruised. Other narcissists, by contrast, over-value themselves because they were raised with too much adulation, too many indulgences, and too few limits. When narcissists of either stripe feel slighted or undervalued, they are prone to attack with a vengeful rage that has few limits and frequently distorts reality with paranoia. Further, pathological self-involvement prevents parents from experiencing effective empathy with a child, for empathy requires putting one's own feelings aside and caring for the child first.

Rigid, obsessive-compulsive expectations for how things should be done in a family led to three parents' aggression toward their children. Parents with over-developed obsessive-compulsive personalities place rules and routines over feelings. This in itself is not abusive. Organization, order and consistency are valuable qualities for parents to bring to childcare. Mature parents, however, have access to their own and their children's feelings, and this gives them sufficient flexibility to temper their need for order. Pathologically obsessive-compulsive parents are as likely to be alienated from their own feelings as from their children's; they are self-disciplined and disciplining to the point of lovelessness. Such parents who feel the threat of losing control may resort to physical violence against their children to reassert control.

Two parents had *Infantile Personalities*. Out of ignorance of how to otherwise raise a child, this led one to severely neglect her daughter; while the other adopted obsessive-compulsive rote routines and harsh, unrelenting discipline.

Alcohol abuse was central to two parents' violent outbursts. One mother, chronically addicted to alcohol, became incoherent, violent, and paranoid at night. One father's worst explosions occurred when he was intoxicated; his drinking was episodic and in the context of his chronic post-traumatic reaction to war-time violence, loss of his own parents, and chronic loneliness in displaced person's camps and orphanages.

Table 3. The Evolution of Symptoms in 10 Maltreated Children from Infancy to Adulthood

CASE	ABUSE	AGE 1	AGE 7	AGE 18	AGE 30	GAF
VICTOR	Beaten & neglected by father	———	Many fears Excessive sibling rivalry	Anxious Self-doubting Self-critical Perfectionistic Compulsive Controlling	Chronic Depression (Dysthymia) – – – Physical Injuries	73
TED	Beaten & abandoned by father	———	———	Uncertain of abilities Compulsive trends Tense, feels physically vulnerable	Major depression Alcohol abuse – – – Physical injuries	60
ULLA	Beaten & neglected by father	Slow development Anxious Sad	Slow development Anxious Sad Enuretic Insomnia	Needs recognition Anxious Poor self-esteem Uneven concentration Underlying depression Longings for tenderness	Narcissistic personality – – – Substance abuse in past – – – Injuries	84
LARRY	Beaten by father	Angry Excessive auto-erotic behavior	Over-compliant Anxious Depressed Impulsive Head banging, rocking	Tense Self-doubting Wants direction Passive Emotionally restricted Concrete	– – – Insomnia Lethargy Dizzy Spells	65
NITA	Beaten by father	———	Trying to keep up Becoming depressed	Rigid Suspicious Anxious Emotionally hungry Poor self-esteem Impulsive Clinging to dependency	Chronic depression (Dysthymia) Anxiety – – – Major depression in past – – – Overweight	61
DAVID	Emotionally abused by mother Neglected by father	Uneven development	Impulsive Poor frustration tolerance	Anxious, inhibited Depressed Anhedonia Impaired self-esteem Passive-aggressive Self-critical, dutiful Resentful Obsessional	Chronic depression (Dysthymia) – – – Injuries	63
LISA	Neglected by mother & father	Depressed	Depressed	Anxious Counter-phobic Grandiose Oppositional Tangential Unstable identity "As-if" quality	Chronic depression (Dysthymia) – – – Major depression in past Anorexia Alcohol abuse in past	60
VICKI	Emotionally abused by mother Neglected by father	Depressed Anxious	Anxious Depressed	Unsure of self Constricted, inhibited Avoidant, suspicious Sad, longing for maternal care	Anxiety – – – Headaches Stomach distress	80
KEN	Emotionally abused by mother	Hyperactive Poor frustration tolerance Poor attention span	Passive Anxious Sad Impaired self-esteem Loner	Shy, bland, meek Emptiness Poor sense of self Withdrawn Eyes averted Depressed, Schizotypal	Schizoid personality	65
JANET	Emotionally abused by mother	Sad	Sad	Emotionally hungry Lonely, dutiful Constricted Under-developed personality	– – – Major depression in past Overweight	80

Henry Massie, MD

CASE HISTORIES – THE EFFECT OF AGGRESSION OVER TIME

Unbridled parental hostility broadly damages children. Figure 3, The Evolution of Symptoms in 10 Maltreated Children from Infancy to Adulthood, summarizes the developmental course of each of the children of the above described parents. In the figure, the first 5 children were physically abused by their fathers, the second five were emotionally abused by mothers or by both parents. The figure notes the type of parental maltreatment and then the children's gradually emerging problems, culminating in specific psychiatric diagnoses at age 30. The average Global Assessment of Functioning Score of the 10 was 69.1 (mild symptoms; some difficulty functioning) compared to an average score of 82.6 (no or minimal symptoms; good functioning in all areas) for the non-abused group (see Table 1).

In spite of their adult difficulties, all of the formerly maltreated children are now managing without crippling, major psychiatric disorders such as psychoses. As adults they are all self-supporting. Four (Victor, Larry, Lisa, David, and Janet) are in satisfying intimate relationships, which is the same rate as for non-abused participants. Nita, divorced, and Janet, contentedly married, have children – a rate similar rate to that of the comparison group. Thus these children of abuse may be termed resilient to the extent that they meet phenomenological criteria of adapting positively in the face of adversity which students of the subject have posited (Werner and Smith, 1922; Heller, et al, 1999; Luther, Cicchetti, and Becker, 2000).

The concept of resilience may, however, dangerously over-simplify the long lasting results of abuse in children. Seemingly adequate coping can, if accepted as the measure of success, camouflage specific ways in which abuse in childhood distorts personalities. Such thinking can serve the purpose of social policy makers to over-look the consequences of adversity in children's lives. In this section, three condensed but detailed case histories illustrate different developmental, psychological courses that the lives of abused children can take. Case 1 is an outcome with an adult symptom disorder (depression and anxiety), Case 2 an outcome in the form of a personality disturbance (narcissistic personality disorder), Case 3 a mood disorder (anhedonia – lack of pleasure in life).

Case 1. Symptom-Personality Disorder: Depression and Anxiety

"My life is a longing," Nita responded to the question about a sadness in her life. "Lately I'm always on the verge of tears. I don't want to be in this apartment or working. I want to be in a real house with my children. I should be the one on school trips with my children, not my mother. But I have to work. My main frustration is feeling that life has thrown me through a hole. I rationalize that I was a promiscuous, rotten kid and I'm paying my debt to society, and one day I'll have the life I want. I have to feel that maybe there is a Mr. Right out there for me…When there are rumors of layoffs at work, I have anxiety attacks. I can't breathe and the house goes to a mess." Feisty, overweight, and thoughtful, Nita knows that her teenage promiscuity came largely from her anguished relationship with her father. "I spent my childhood trying to make him love me and never felt I succeeded. When I was six or seven I was using a blow-dryer on my Barbie's hair and my father was watching TV, and there was static on the screen. He thought it was the blow-dryer, so I put it away. But there was still snow on the TV and my father beat the crap out of me. I can't tell you how many bloody noses he gave me from smacking me. He hit me maybe twice a week. I don't know why my teachers never did anything because I was always had black eyes or bruises. Anytime I started getting a little confidence he was there to smash it. He would say, 'You shouldn't do things like that and I won't have to hit you.' My mother was kinder and would say that my father loved me but in his own way. You can imagine the relationships I had as a teenager. I was on a path to destruction, drinking with boys when I was 13. Sex was my way of looking for something to show that someone cared, but because it was always physical it left me feeling worse than before."

Nita's father last hit her when she was 20, pushing her head into a wall so hard she went to the hospital, following which she left home. Not long afterward she attempted suicide with an overdose of pills and was hospitalized psychiatrically. During a family session at the hospital, the therapist enlisted an apology from the father which ultimately led to an end to the physical and verbal father-daughter confrontations. In her early 20s, Nita had a failed marriage and two children, whom her mother helps raise today while Nita works in a grocery store. As a parent she says, "My strengths come from my fear of being like my parents. What children need most is affection and someone to depend on."

The early research record shows that Nita's mother was *the only mother* among the mothers of the ten abused children to be classified as effective (Group A). She was supportive of her daughter, informed, and took pride in her child. Nonetheless, the original team noted limitations in the mother's readiness to respond to her daughter's needs (e.g. once an observer had to intervene when the baby began to play with an electrical outlet because the mother was unconcerned). The mother did report her controlling, perfectionistic husband's rages but could not steer him into treatment or imagine raising her children without him. The researchers noted, "This is a home with continuous stress and dissension. It is hard to see from what source the child will find help in learning to govern her feelings."

By school age, Nita was insecure, worried that she would be left out; she used bravado and impetuosity to mask feelings, and didn't perform to her ability. By 18, her psychological testing showed oedipal longings and unmet dependency needs. Guilt over her anger further depleted her self-worth. Projection of anger and repression of affect impacted her functioning so that she was egocentric, clinging, unreflective, and lonely. Dr. Brody wrote, "Over and above her irritability, I was aware of a deep sadness in this girl because she is not quite burned out, and is somehow still tying to fight for life."

At age 30, she has held on to life and matured considerably. She has stopped substance abuse (except for over-eating); her rigid repression of threatening affects has abated; she can now self-reflect; she is capable of humor; and presently sublimates urges for creativity into gratifying care of her children. She would like to obtain more education but lacks the confidence. Her earliest memory—going back to about age four – encapsulates her frustrated longings for affection, and shows the distance she has been able to achieve from her past conflicts: "I used to stand on the front steps of our house every day in the morning to ask my father for a kiss and hug goodbye when he left for work. One day he said really gruffly, 'I'm not leaving yet. Go away!' After that I never waited around for him to leave anymore. I think it was the time that I began to feel rejected. In retrospect he was probably running late or having a bad mood, and didn't want me to have to wait outside for him." (Global Assessment of Functioning: 61 [mild symptoms and difficulty functioning]; Adult Attachment Interview: Earned-secure; Diagnosis: Dysthymia [past history Major Depression])

Case 2. Personality Disturbance: Narcissistic Personality

UIIa was beaten and neglected by her father also, but less frequently and severely than Nita. Ulla's mother, on the other hand, was much less effective and more self-absorbed and self-centered than Nita's. Dr. Brody described Ulla at 18 years of age as "swamped by neglect" because of her affect hunger and depleted self-worth. However with time, Ulla channeled her emotional needs into a narcissistic self-involvement. When we met her at 30 she was smiling, blithely self-absorbed, and attractively fit from regular workouts. Recently divorced, the failure of her brief marriage seemed to have made little impact on her, and she was eager to start graduate school in Communications for a career on television. In essence, she had made herself an object of her own love.

Tracing this developmental process begins with Ulla's birth into a caustically unhappy marriage. The father (the man project staff described as "cocky" and "cold") pushed the family into many business-related moves in his daughter's first years, and exercised fatherhood distantly as a financial provider. The mother was preoccupied with her appearance and routinely annoyed with her child. According to the record, she showed no positive emotional connection or communication with her baby, once commenting, "Wouldn't it be marvelous if all children were healthy and away on their own except when we're out on the street and people are admiring them." Ulla's mother had a big, warm, pretty smile which she often beamed at the little girl when the baby was upset. The smile drew the child out of her bad mood but only temporarily because the mother's manner lacked real intimacy. An observer wrote, "The mother's smile and her liveliness seemed intended to ease the child out of her distress without really taking note of it."

By six months, Ulla was irritable and appeared sad. At 12 months, she showed marked cognitive and motor lags, and was socially inhibited. Her examiner wrote,

"She seems hungry for company. It is as if this child is bottling up real anguish and distress in her chronic state. The baby seems most concerned with her own body, making loud groaning and grunting noises to relieve distress, and brings things to her mouth all the time to soothe herself."

At three years, Ulla appeared "like a frightened, lost soul;" at five, she could barely separate from her mother; at six, she was passive and sad. By the time Ulla was seven, her father had left the family and would visit his daughter only occasionally for the next several years. The child began showing anger and assertiveness for the first time, which had the positive effect of spurring her motor and cognitive development so that the delays disappeared.

As a teenager Ulla reconnected with her father in a destructive way. He invited her to spend time with him during which he'd ask her to join him in using marijuana and alcohol, but when intoxicated he sometimes lashed out at her, once knocking her down a flight of stairs. At 30, she spoke of these experiences, "He'd be saying he was sorry for what he did, pouring drinks and his heart out at the same time, and then he'd turn mean and hit. I don't trust him to this day but I love him. A real father is somebody who gives you orders and you rebel, but my father just tried to be a friend and I wanted him to like me. I wanted to be neat like his girlfriends, and in good shape like he was, but at the same time I knew he was fucked up."

Her 18 year psychological testing showed anxiety, a poor self-image, self-absorption, and fantasies of achieving power and fame to compensate and to ward off depression, dependency, and loneliness. Her interviewer noted, "At this time in her life her main felt emotion appears to be anger and excitement that comes out in action. When sadness surfaced in her interview, she shied away from it and reassured herself that she would pull through."

Not surprisingly, Ulla's twenties were fitful. Although she was expelled from college for vandalism while inebriated, she became a fashion model; eventually returned to school and graduated; and afterward had several jobs in fashion and sales.

At 30 Ulla appears candid and honest about what she has been through. Knowing she can rely on her mother for financial assistance contributes to her continued, muted optimism. Nonetheless, her emotional neediness, noted by the researchers in childhood and adolescence, crept in when, at the end of their time together, she asked her interviewer slightly plaintively if he thought she would present well on television. Further, her psychologically traumatic background leaves her with underlying sadness and the sense of a foreshortened future:

> "When I have children I'll give them all the love I can because life is too short for fighting, because the next thing you know it's lights out." (Global Assessment of Functioning: 84 [absent or minimal symptoms]; Adult Attachment Interview: Earned-secure; Diagnosis: Narcissistic Personality)

Case 3: Mood disorder: Anhedonia (Admixed with Schizoid Personality)

"How could they do that?" Ken, at 30, asked his interviewer about his mother's unremitting hostility to him and his father's refusal to stand up for him as a child. The research record confirmed Ken's appraisal, describing how the mother was cruelly harsh and rejecting throughout his childhood. She was joyless and domineering with her son, spanking him regularly from a young age when he didn't meet her draconian demands for cleanliness. In her view, "Indulging children is a weakness…training is just a matter of conditioned reflexes…I would get rid of a child who wouldn't mind me." The only person who supported Ken and offered him kindness for many years was his childhood babysitter.

By his first birthday, Ken's development was slowing. On developmental testing he quickly gave up on challenging test items. In his preschool years, he sometimes resisted his mothers demands with tantrums but as months passed he lapsed into compulsive, perseverative, lifeless play such as incessantly taking things apart and putting them back together. His speech was impoverished and his moods narrowed to crossness and bland smiles. By five years, he was inattentive, depressed, vacant, awkward and too cautious to join children in play. He began stealing from school mates, secreting candy and cutting off the hair from toy figures. A teacher commented, "He is wishy-washy. He can follow rules but seems to do it out of fear." At six and seven years, he transiently asserted himself with what can be termed a hypomanic escape from his mother by identifying with her aggressiveness: racing through testing, talking non-stop, boasting that he was smart, belittling questions as stupid, telling his mother to stop giving him orders, and clowning grandiosely and bossily at school. However he couldn't maintain this assertiveness and by eight years again lapsed into apathy. When his interviewer asked him the most unpleasant thing he could think of, the schoolboy replied, "Me, 'cause I'm mean to myself." In his insightful though debased self-image, we see his loss of will to fight back, and his internalization of his mother's life-long criticism of him. Timidity, over-compliance, perfectionistic and compulsive trends – identifications with aspects of his parents' personalities *as well as* mechanisms for achieving approval at school and avoiding fights with his mother – had crystallized in his personality.

At 18, Ken's once bright IQ had fallen to average. He appeared sad, colorless, lonely, and without ambition. And he could not conceive of having felt deprived of love as a child since, as he said, "I didn't know what it was to have any." His clinical interviewer concluded, "He has a loving, gentle quality but his will has been squashed. He is emotionally starved with some awareness of this but doesn't know how to get rid of it, his feelings are so tied up in rage and sadness." His psychodiagnostic testing showed defenses of avoidance, identification with the aggressor, restriction, and turning of aggression against himself. His most optimistic defense was reaction formation in which he took the role of helper of others to ward off feelings of being deprived and sad.

As an adult, Ken rarely contacts his parents and has no close friends or social life. A brief, passionless marriage ended when his wife left him without explanation. Bland and ingratiating, he has found competence and gratification as a personnel benefits administrator for a small company. This is an effective sublimation and choice of work, foretold by his defense mechanism of reaction formation years earlier, and also reflective of an identification with his caring childhood babysitter whose favorite rocking chair he keeps in his apartment to this day. He speaks of his company as a family in which he is the supportive, benign, disciplining parent of the workers who come to him for assistance with their benefits. Cloyingly nice to avoid conflict, his efforts seem to drain him and his life is joyless. He suppresses his sense of himself as bad through multiple defenses. And although Ken functions adequately in work and has no discrete psychiatric symptoms, his intellectual detachment, withdrawal from desire for relationships, and fear that he can never have a trusting relationship render him a schizoid personality. (Global Assessment of Functioning: 65 [generally functioning pretty well]; Adult Attachment Interview: Insecure; Diagnosis: anhedonia, Schizoid Personality)

Three Axes of Adult Emotional Sequelae of Child Abuse

The above case histories emphasize the psychodynamics of abused children. To summarize their intrapsychic adaptation to maltreatment, Figure 4 (10 Cases of Child Abuse and the 3 Axes of its Emotional Sequelae in Adulthood) is a schematic conceptualization of the psychological functioning of the adults victimized as children on three axes: 1) Personality Disorders-Symptom Disorders, 2) Joy/Pleasure-Anhedonia (mood disorder axis), and 3) Defenses (mature to primitive) .

Each of the ten cases shows a primary adaptation as an adult along one of these three axes. For example, ongoing clinical symptoms of depression and/or anxiety mark six of the ten, placing them on the symptom disorder arm of the personality-symptom disorder axis (e.g. Nita, Case 1). An anhedonic lack of pleasure in life (blunting of will, affect and desire, e.g. Ken, Case 3), which is distinguishable from clinical, symptomatic depression, indelibly stamps four of the ten, placing them at the anhedonic pole of the mood axis. However emotional functioning is not simply on a single axis or at its pole, for a subject with evident anhedonia (affect axis) may also show less obvious sequelae on another axis (in a personality disturbance such as schizoid personality, e.g. Ken, Case 3); or an individual with primarily symptoms such as anxiety and depression may have personality problems such poor self-esteem (e.g. Nita, Case 1). Likewise, an individual with a personality disturbance may show sequelae on the defense mechanism axis (a schizoid person may have an effective sublimation that wards off clinical depression, e.g. Ken, Case 3; an individual with a narcissistic personality may use acting out as a major defense, e.g. Ulla, Case 2).

Figure 3
10 CASES OF CHILD ABUSE AND THE 3 AXES OF ITS EMOTIONAL SEQUELAE IN ADULTHOOD

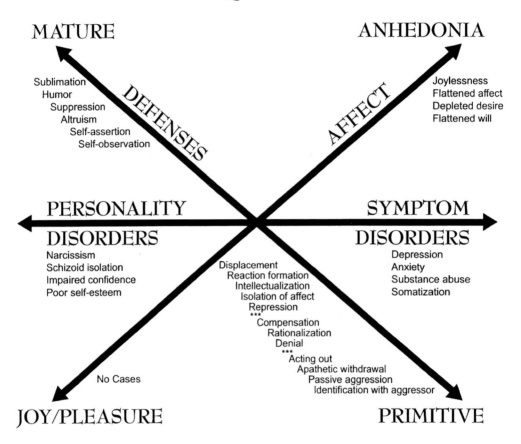

The axes schematize the effects of abuse in childhood on development. <u>Axis A, Affect:</u> The prevailing emotional tone in adulthood is joylessness. <u>Axis B, Symptom vs. Personality Disorders:</u> Psychiatric syndromes in adulthood are likely to be personality disorders characterized by impaired self-esteem and self-protective, disturbed personality adaptations to avoid feeling impaired self-esteem; or symptom disorders with anxiety, depression, & substance abuse. Personality disorders appear to "protect" against symptom disorders. <u>Axis C, Defenses:</u> Adulthood defense mechanisms range from healthy & mature to primitive to manage conflicts and anxiety arising from childhood abuse. However, their defenses cluster at a less mature level than those of non-traumatized adults.

Figure 3. 10 Cases of Child Abuse and the 3 Axes of its Emotional Sequelae in Adulthood

While everyone – healthy or not – has a range of psychological defense mechanisms, the defenses of those mistreated as children cluster at immature levels of the defense axis. Capsule vignettes illustrate this by pointing to specific defenses children in the longitudinal study typically evolved to cope with the shame, pain, rage, confusion, sadness and loneliness inherent in the experience of abuse. Beginning at the higher level of more mature psychological mechanisms, one participant, Ted, used *rationalization* and *intellectualization* to give positive value to his experience when he said at 30, "I wouldn't wish my parents on anybody, but I learned to be who I am from them, and I'm proud that I survived, can support myself, and can care for others." His mother was the severe, violent alcoholic described above and his father had left the family when he was young. Ted also used the valuable psychological maneuver of *humor* to deal with pain. He laughed sardonically at the memory of his mother's drink and fury-infused cooking: "For a time she was into purees and would whip the spinach until nothing was left but black liquid." Another participant chuckled at the recollection of her compulsively neat father's anger at the indelible blood stains on the carpet from her bloody nose after he slapped her. Her laughter serves to exert retribution on her father and to rebel in memory while maintaining control of the level of aggression.

Several of the highest functioning formerly abused participants had mature capacities for *self-observation* and *sublimation*. The aforementioned man whose mother died of alcoholism is a writer: "Going into my mind and creating stories kept me sane. It kept me from being a teenage suicide." His mother supported his writing, and his absentee father sent him "books bound in gold" *in lieu* of companionship. His stories resemble those of Edgar Allen Poe (who was also neglected and witness to his mother's slow death), melding anger, bleakness, blackness, ambivalence, and hope. "My writing often scares me, and sometimes I see how it relates to my life and the working through of my demons." Child rearing is an effective sublimation for two women, and the creative, sublimatory expression of distress through painting works well for another other participants.

Compensation appears frequently as a less mature defense of the formerly traumatized. For example, the writer hopes literary fame will pay him back for the pain and self-discipline he has endured. Compromise formations such as *displacement* are frequent less mature mechanisms – defenses at the level Vaillant (1994) terms mental inhibitions. They mediate and ameliorate the conflicts between urges and restraining ego forces, reducing tension while also giving some satisfaction to the impulse, although they generally also bring a degree of unconscious inhibition. Thus, one subject is writing a graduate dissertation using aspects of his formerly abusive father's professional work. He hopes this will bring him closer to his father, but unfortunately he has a writer's block that impedes his progress. The participant whose mother was an alcoholic has married a woman considerably older than he. She provides order and nurturing, but their sexual life is lacking, probably, we infer, because he brings too many unconscious, unresolved oedipal yearnings and resentments to it. Another participant – the daughter of a cold, narcissistic, rejecting mother and distant father – was an angry, rebellious, agoraphobic teenager. Her source of comfort was an aunt who lived with the family, and at 20 she eloped with the aunt's nephew, a brief marriage in which her affection for, and dependence on her aunt were displaced onto the boy. At 30 she was newly engaged but doubted she would have children because she feared treating them the way her parents treated her. On the one hand, her concern is realistic; on the other hand it is likely that her fear of parenting reflects a continuation of her adolescent phobic tendencies.

Common *primitive defenses* in the adults mistreated as children were *acting-out, denial, passive-aggression, identification with the aggressor, and apathetic withdrawal.* To illustrate, one participant was affable, articulate, and jovial, although his chain-smoking and nail-biting showed his tension. He recalled,

"Once when I was about eight my father asked me to get wood for the stove but when I came back with only one log because they were heavy he started beating me. An eight year old kid, can you imagine that. My mother attacked him to get him away from me and she took the beating instead [he starts sobbing]. This came over me like a wave. I didn't cry as a kid, not like I'm crying now. My father would say, 'I'll give you something to cry about. I'll give you a shot in the head.' I lived in fear of him and his criticism, and wanting to please him. I respected him because he was smart and well read. Strong as an ox physically. Sometimes he'd call me champ when he felt good about me, but if I didn't do something like throw a ball well he'd call me chump. Say I'd thrown the ball like a girl. But he wouldn't take time to teach me how to throw a ball. My parents divorced when I was ten, and when they sat us down to tell us they were breaking up my sister cried, but I thought it was the greatest thing in the world. He saw us a little after that and then just disappeared."

The subject's father's behavior, though inexcusable, is explainable since he lost his parents in World War II concentration camps, and spent much of his childhood in displaced persons' camps. The mother's physical protection of her son was admirable, but when she cared for him as a very young child she was awkward, lacked intimacy, and soothed him poorly. As a result of the family violence and the mother's limitations in infancy, it is likely that the child never developed effective emotional regulation, and the primitive defense mechanisms he evolved keep him in a state of struggle and at a chaotic level of functioning. He badly abused hallucinogens, stimulants, and alcohol as a youth (self-medication and the defense of *acting-out*) and dropped out of high school. He has become a skilled machinist, but when in conflict with himself or others he still turns to alcohol or to his hobbies such as sky-diving and motorcycle racing to calm himself (a continuation of his adolescent acting-out as well as a *counter-phobic* protection against anxiety). Usually feeling in a relatively good mood, he nonetheless has thoughts of suicide at times; but with the defense of strong *denial* he does not link his extreme sports to suicidal impulses. His greatest sadness is not having a father and the loss of his long-term girlfriend who left him when he wouldn't commit to her. His description made it sound as if his refusal to marry her despite loving her involved *passive-aggression* and *identification with his father as aggressor* as a way to control her, ultimately self-defeating unconscious mechanisms.

AGGRESSION

Civilization

Civilization is such a thin veneer –
Smiles mask a sneer
A proffered hand hides greed
Gentility covers savagery

Scarce removed from wilder beasts
That stalk alone or roam in packs,
Kill with speed and
Force the weaker to their knees

We form in tribes that
Make us strong, or wrong –
Our territory we call Nations
Our markings: the colors of our skins
Our flags, plumage raised above the din

Beliefs dissemble instincts
and tribalism lurks within civility
Ready to spring or avenge
Terror recycling endlessly
like seasons on a feral plain

Anonymous (2001)

The contemporary poet, writing of the first wars of the new millennium, catches the grim connection between mankind's sad history of violence and the human proclivity for forming tribal packs that hunt like animals. Additionally, however, the small, closely studied group of abusive families presented here, demonstrate aspects of aggression that are not inevitable, mysterious, or instinctual. Each abusive parent's hostility grew out of a psychological developmental disturbance that more propitious circumstances could have prevented. In some of the families the earlier generation of parents could have raised their children with more wisdom so that when they became parents they would have been less hobbled by pathological narcissism, obsessive-compulsive rigidity, or immaturity. War cast its fearsome, traumatic shadow on Ted's father's life when it orphaned him early and condemned him to the anomie of a childhood in displaced person's camps. Larry's father also was orphaned early and the relatives who stepped into the breach were neither tender nor supportive. Once damage was done in the abusive parents' childhoods, there were still opportunities to prevent abuse in the next generation. In each family in the generation the project studied, there was a non-abusive, or the least a less abusive parent. That parent (although in some instances unconsciously complicit in the violence) generally could have done more to safe-guard the child by setting limits earlier on the perpetrators, or enlisting help.

From an epidemiological point of view, the incidence of troubled parenting is very high in many societies, which magnifies the risk that child maltreatment will occur. In our study of 76 families, only one-third of the mothers rated "favorable" in their infant care; and when the project added the fathers to the study as the children reached age four, only one-third of the fathers met favorable criteria for pride, affection, and involvement with their children. Thus in approximately two-thirds of the families, parenting was troubled, although this incidence may be higher than that of families in the general population because our sample is volunteer, and vulnerable parents may have come to it seeking support. It is not a randomly chosen group in which the occurrence of troubled parenting may have been lower, nor a sample chosen from a clinical population in which perturbed parenting may be even more common.

Additional information about the high incidence of troubled parenting can be deduced from studies using the framework of psychological attachment. The Minnesota Child Development Study (Sroufe, Carlson, Shulman, 1993) of 267 families randomly selected from a poverty level population – with children at developmental risk because of the stresses of low income and frequent single parenthood – found that 39% of the children had Insecure attachments to their parents at one year of age using the Strange Situation test (Ainsworth, 1978). This laboratory procedure introduces the child to a stranger for a few minutes while the mother leaves the room. When the mother returns the child is classified as Secure or Insecure based on the child's ability to use and accept the mother's comforting to recover from the distress of separation. Ainsworth found a close correlation between children's Secure ratings on the laboratory-based Strange Situation and observations of the mothers' effectiveness with their children in the home, as have others (Main, 1995). Further, children securely attached on the Strange Situation are subsequently more effective academically and socially in school than children with Insecure ratings (Sroufe, Carlson, and Schulman, 1993) . Additionally, in the Minnesota study, children with Insecure-avoidant Strange Situation ratings at one year were more likely to become bullies later in childhood than securely attached children, and children who earlier had been Insecure-resistant/ambivalent were the likely targets of the victimizers (Troy and Sroufe, 1987). Meta-analyses of the Strange Situation in diverse cultures around the world (Main, 2000) find approximately 60% of children secure in their psychological attachment to their mothers.

Another source of insight into parenting comes from the Adult Attachment Interview (AAI) (George, Kaplan, and Main, 1985) which we incorporated into our 30-year followup of the Brody children. Providing a picture of an adult's internal emotional representation of security in childhood, the AAI rated only 2 of our 10 (20%) victims of child maltreatment as Secure at age 30, whereas 59% of the non-abused participants were Secure. Attachment status on the AAI connects directly with adults' working models of inner security in personal relationships and in the workplace. Individuals with Secure AAI ratings cope better than those with Insecure ratings, parent their own children more effectively, and are much more likely to have children who themselves become securely attached to their parents (Hesse, 1999; Main, 2000). In non-clinical settings around the world, 58% of 584 mothers have Secure representations of their childhood relationship to their parents (van Ijzendoorn, and Bakermans-Kranenburg, 1996), leaving 42% insecure and vulnerable to compromised parenting.

What forces conspire to impair parenting so frequently? Family histories of the kind reported here pinpoint potentially preventable and treatable psychiatric syndromes in the most troubled, dysfunctional families. Operating alongside internal emotional disorders are external, social forces that thwart mothers' innate desire to nurture, and innate capacity for nurturing young children. Among these social deterrents to effective parenting (elaborated in detail by Scheper-Hughes, [1992]) are, first, economic pressures that lead to anxious uncertainty about sufficient money for food, shelter, medicine and education for children, obstacles which also prevent parents from educating themselves about raising children. Second, the inconstancy of many fathers, whose support mothers need in order to have the time and emotional freedom to attend to children, often interferes with adequate mothering. Third, community violence and wars threaten death, privation and dislocation, traumatically interfering with nurturing.

The vise of psychopathology and destructive social forces inhibits parents; it constrains giving affection and inhibits mothers and fathers in seeing and feeling what children need. It breeds anger in parents that they may displace onto their children, as well as angry frustration with the neediness of children which some adults with few emotional reserves experience as insatiable. Some troubled parents project anger onto children, perceiving them for instance as ungiving when it is the parent who is withholding. In some parents, as we have seen, narcissistic self-centeredness blocks empathic sensitivity toward their youngsters.

Lessons learned from studying family violence may extend to social violence when we view humankind as one extremely large family, a genus whose members can't co-exist peacefully in too many parts of the world. Further, as a group we are a dysfunctional family that has not shown an ability to keep a roof over our heads or the water running clean; that is, we despoil the earth's atmosphere and pollute its waters, unable to nurture the natural environment that sustains us.

As in individual families, when violence erupts in communities or between nations it is almost invariably a man with a disordered mind who starts it. Often possessed of a charismatic vigor, that man seductively encourages his listeners to view themselves as a society or tribe separate from and in conflict with the larger family of mankind (identified by Erikson [1968] as the human propensity for dividing itself into "pseudospecies"). The top-man then urges his followers to suspend their normal, individual moral self-control against violence. Give that leader access to weapons and havoc follows. In *Thoughts for the Times on War and Death,* Freud (1915) wrote, "The history of the world which is taught to children is essentially a series of race murders." Like child abuse, war distorts and destroys lives full of promise, both coming about because emotionally troubled people create conflicts that their antagonists maintain – enmity which both sides try to solve with violence rather than by using the suppleness of reasoning and conciliation of which our species is capable. Too often in history, men who propel themselves into power are governed less by leaderships skills than by inner demons, infantile urges, and adolescent self-involvement. Perverting political institutions, moral codes, and their followers into anti-social agents of violence, such leaders do not heed the restraints that individual families and human culture can provide.

Historically, tribes and states have shown the same violent incivility towards each other as parents and children and brothers and sisters are capable of in families. The study of abusive families offers a partial catalogue of the psychodynamics of violence – human frailties linked to aggression when children are mistreated and when leaders mobilize one group to attack another: Hurt pride leads to the desire to repair pride by redressing grievances violently. Sometimes pride is over-weaning, sometimes its vulnerability lies in feelings of inferiority. Fear of being attacked (at times paranoid magnifications and distortions of the reality of danger) lead to pre-emptive attacks. Dreams and wishes for admiration, control, and power lead to clashes. Perception of others as inferior stirs hostility. Jealousy and envy of others spark anger. The need to test or prove manliness leads to aggression. When their will is opposed, people with rigid minds – lacking the flexibility for compromise and non-violent solutions to conflicts – counter with opposition. People who cannot retire old grudges face never-ending quarrels. Parent-child and sibling rivalry can breed rival camps and enmity. Nonetheless, the fact that violence arises from the weakness of individuals offers hope that addressing the vulnerability that lies within people may prevent hostility. On the other hand, the very ubiquity of human failings makes this a sobering, daunting challenge.

REFERENCES

Ainsworth, M., Blehar, M., Waters, E. and Wall, S. 1978). *Patterns of Attachment.* Hillsdale, NJ: Erlbaum.

American Psychiatric Association (1994). Global Assessment of Functioning Scale. *Diagnostic and Statistical Manual of Mental Disorders-IV*, p. 30-32. Washington, DC: American Psychiatric Press.

Anonymous (2001). *Civilization*. Monte Rio, CA: *Russian River Times*, Oct. 26.

Bahadur, M. (1998). Continuity and discontinuity of attachment from age 1 to age 30. Doctoral dissertation, New York University.

Bancroft, L. and Silverman, J. (2002). *The Batterer as Parent: Addressing the Impact of Domestic Violence on Family Dynamics*. Thousand Oaks, CA: Sage.

Bowlby, J. (1969). *Attachment and Loss, Vol. I: Attachment*. New York: Basic Books.

Brody, S. (1956). *Patterns of Mothering*. New York: International Universities Press.

Brody, S. and Axelrad, S. (1970). *Anxiety and Ego Formation in Infancy*. New York: International Universities Press.

Brody, S. and Axelrad, S. (1978). *Mothers, Fathers and Children: Explorations in the Formation of Character in the First Seven Years*. New York: International Universities Press.

Brody, S. and Siegel, M. (1992). *The Evolution of Character: Birth to 18 Years*. New York: International Universities Press.

Erikson, E. (1968). *Identity: Youth and Crisis*. New York: Norton, p. 41.

Freud, S. (1915). Thoughts for the times on war and death. *Standard Edition*, Vol. 14. London: Hogarth Press, p. 292.

George, C., Kaplan, N., and Main, M. (1985). *An Adult Attachment Interview*. Unpublished manuscript, Department of Psychology, University of California, Berkeley.

Green, A. (1978). Psychopathology of abused children. *J. American Acad. Child Psychiatry*, 17: 92-103.

Hawley, G. (1980). *Measures of Psychosocial Development*. Odessa, FL: Psychological Assessment Resources.

Heller, S., Larrieu, J., D'Imperio, R., and Boris, N. (1999). Research on resilience to child maltreatment: Empirical considerations. *Child Abuse and Neglect*, 23: 321-338.

Hesse, E. (1999). The Adult Attachment Interview: Historical and current perspectives. In J. Cassidy and P.R. Shaver, (Eds.), *Handbook of Attachment*. New York: Guilford Press, p. 395-433.

Khan, M. (1957). The concept of cumulative trauma. *Psychoanalytic Study of the Child*, 18: 286-306. New York: International Universities Press.

Kohut, H. (1972). Thoughts of narcissism and narcissistic rage. *Psychoanalytic Study of the Child*, 27: 360-400.

Luther, S., Cicchetti, D, and Becker, B. (2000). The concept of resilience: A critical evaluation and guidelines for future work. *Child Development*, 71: 543-562.

Main, M. (2000). The organized categories of infant, child, and adult attachment. *J. Am. Psychoanalytic Assoc.*, 48: 1055-1096.

_____ . (1995). Recent studies in attachment. In S. Goldberg, R. Muir, and J. Kerr (Eds.), *Attachment Theory*. Hillsdale, NJ: The Analytic Press, p. 407-474.

Massie, H. and Szajnberg, N. (2002). The relationship between mothering in infancy, childhood experience and adult mental health: Results of the Brody prospective longitudinal study from birth to age 30. *Int. J. Psychoanalysis*, 83: 35-55.l

McCloskey, L., Figueredo, A., and Koss, M. (1995). The effect of systemic family violence on children's mental health. *Child Development*, 66: 1239-1261.

McKay, M., Fanning, P., Paleg, K., and Landis, D. (1995). *When Anger Hurts Your Kids.* Oakland, CA: New Harbinger.

Milner, J. and Chilamkurti, C. (1991). Physical child abuse perpetrator characteristics: A review of the literature. *J. Interpersonal Violence,* 6: 345-366.

Scheper-Hughes, N. (1992). *Death Without Weeping: The Violence of Everyday Life in Brazil.* Berkeley, CA: University California Press.

Shaw, G. B. (1903/1951). *Man and Superman. Maxims for Revolutionists.* In *Seven Plays.* New York: Dodd, Mead, & Co., p. 731.

Steele, B. (1980). Psychodynamic factors in child abuse. In H. Kempe and R. Helfer (Eds.), *The Battered Child,* Chicago: University Chicago Press, p. 49-85.

Sroufe, A., Carlson, E., and Shulman, S. (1993). The development of individuals in relationships: From infancy through adolescence. In D. Funder, R. Parke, C. Tomlinson-Keesy, and K. Widaman (Eds.), *Studying Lives Through Time: Approaches to Personality and Development,* p. 315-342. Washington, DC: American Psychological Association.

Szajnberg, N. and Massie, H. (2003). Transition to young adulthood: A prospective study. *International Journal of Psychoanalysis,* 84: 1569-1586.

Troy, M., and Sroufe, L. A. (1987). Victimization among preschoolers: The role of attachment relationship history. *J. Am. Acad. Child and Adolescent Psychiatry,* 26: 166-172.

Vaillant, G. (1994). The defensive functioning scale. In *The Diagnostic and Statistical Manual of Mental Disorders-IV,* p. 751-757. Washington, DC: American Psychiatric Press.

van der Kolk, B., McFarlane, A., and Weisaeth, L. (1996). *Traumatic Stress.* New York: Guilford.

Van Ijzendoorn, M. and Bakermans-Kranenburg, M. (1996). Attachment representations in mothers, fathers, adolescents and clinical groups: A meta-analytic search for normative data. *J. Consulting and Clinical Psychology,* 64: 8-21.

Werner, E. and Smith, R. (1992). *Overcoming the Odds: High Risk Children from Birth to Adulthood.* Ithaca, NY: Cornell University Press.

In: *Focus on Aggression Research*
Editor: James P. Morgan, pp. 41-52

ISBN 1-59454-132-9
© 2004 Nova Science Publishers, Inc.

Chapter 3

DESTRUCTIVE COMMUNICATION IN STEPFAMILIES

Matthew M. Martin, Keith Weber
West Virginia University
Carolyn M. Anderson
University of Akron
Patricia A. Burant[*]
Cleveland State University

ABSTRACT

This study focused on destructive communication in stepfamilies. Specifically, this study investigated whether verbal aggression, criticism, and sarcasm were related to lower trust and satisfaction and whether stepchildren reported being similar to their stepparents in their use of these communication behaviors with each other. The results from this study further demonstrate the destructiveness of verbal aggressiveness, criticism, and sarcasm in interpersonal relationships. When people perceive their stepparents to be verbally aggressive, critical, and sarcastic, they are less satisfied and trustful. The results also show that people and their stepparents are similar in their use of verbal aggression, sarcasm, and criticism with each other.

INTRODUCTION

A family is "a group of intimates who generate a sense of home and group identity, complete with strong ties of loyalty and emotion, and experience a history and future" (Fitzpatrick & Badzinski, 1994, p. 730). In the 21st century, an increasing number of people

[*] Matthew M. Martin (Ph.D., Kent State University, 1992) is an Associate Professor of Communication Studies at West Virginia University (PO Box 6293, Department of Communication Studies, West Virginia University, Morgantown, WV, 26506, mmartin@wvu.edu). Carolyn M. Anderson (Ph.D., Kent State University, 1992) is a Professor at the University of Akron. Keith Weber (Ed.D., West Virginia University, 1998) is an Assistant Professor at West Virginia University. Patricia A. Burant (Ed.D., West Virginia University, 1999) is an Assistant Professor at Cleveland State University.

are members of a stepfamily. As Arliss (1993) noted, the prefix step signifies distance in a relationship. People clarify to others by using the prefix step that they are in a nonvoluntary relationship (Galvin & Brummel, 1996). At times, stepchildren see their stepparents less as serving in the role of a parent. Instead, they view stepparents as potential friends (Fine, Coleman, & Ganong, 1998). Stepparents themselves are often ambiguous about the role they play in the stepfamily (Golish, 2003). Golish argued that healthy stepfamily communication involves the members of the stepfamily willing to be open with each other, to establish and follow family rules, and to actively engage in problem solving.

While there are many stepfamilies that experience healthy communication (Coleman, Ganong, & Fine, 2000; Coleman, Ganong, & Weaver, 2001), conflicts do take place that are unique in stepfamilies, such as the uncertainty of roles and expectations when a new family unit is created (Fine, 2001; Kurdek & Fine, 1991). Coleman, Ganong, and Fine (2004) pointed out that communication may be awkward in the early stages of a stepfamily because while one of the relationships between the participants has developed over numerous years, such as the parent-child relationship, another relationship, the stepparent-stepchild relationship, is at the beginning stage. Often when a stepparent-stepchild relationship begins, conflict increases in the family (Barber & Lyons, 1994). However, stepfamilies are not the only families where destructive communication takes place. In the area of aggressive communication, researchers have consistently reported the presence and detrimental effects of verbal aggression in families. This study further explored destructive communication by focusing on verbal aggression, sarcasm, and criticism in the stepparent-stepchild relationship.

Verbally aggressive messages are messages that are sent with the intent of hurting the receiver (Infante & Wigley, 1986). Some verbally aggressive messages attack the competence (e.g., you are a moron, you drive like my great-grandmother) or character (e.g., you are a slut, you are spineless) of another individual. Other verbally aggressive messages include physical appearance attacks (e.g., four-eyes, Big Bird) or background attacks (e.g., what do you expect from someone who received a law degree from the University of Pitt, she is from the wrong side of the tracks). Other verbally aggressive messages include teasing, swearing, maledictions, and nonverbal emblems (e.g., giving someone the middle finger). Giving someone the middle finger is considered to be a verbally aggressive message because nonverbal emblems have literal meanings for members of a culture. As Wigley (1998) noted, "There seems to be no shortage of ways to cause other people to feel badly about themselves" (p. 192).

Research consistently suggests that being verbally aggressive in a relationship leads to negative relational outcomes (Infante, Myers, & Buerkel, 1994; Martin & Anderson, 1995a). In dating relationships, people are more like to end relationships when their partners are verbally aggressive (Venable & Martin, 1997). Anderson and Martin (1999) found that group members who reported a higher number of verbally aggressive messages in their groups also reported less group satisfaction and less cohesiveness to their groups. In the organizational setting, subordinates have lower satisfaction and organizational commitment when they perceive their superiors as being verbally aggressive (Infante, Anderson, Martin, Herington, & Kim, 1993; Infante & Gorden, 1985). Students report lower motivation and a more hostile learning environment when they perceive their instructors as being verbally aggressive. They also view their instructors as being lower in credibility and likeability (Myers, 2001; Myers & Knox, 2000; Myers & Rocca, 2001). To date, researchers have not identified a relationship or context where verbal aggression is related to any positive outcomes or consequences.

Infante, Myers, and Buerkel (1994) concluded that family situations are most likely where one will find verbal aggression because members of the family have a lower need for social desirability in that setting than in other environments. They reported that constructive disagreements involved higher levels of argumentativeness and lower levels of verbal aggressiveness. In contrast, verbal aggressiveness was much more common in destructive disagreements. The results have been overwhelming in that verbal aggression is linked to less satisfaction in the family relationship and often precedes or is concurrent with physical aggression (Sabourin, Infante, & Rudd, 1993; Sabourin & Stamp, 1995). Equally, if verbal aggression is directed toward one person regularly, it may constitute psychological abuse (Infante, 1995; Infante & Rancer, 1996). People that come from verbally aggressive households not only tend to be more verbally aggressive, but they also experience less satisfaction in their relationships with others (Beatty & Dobos, 1992b, 1993c). This study expected to support previous findings on the destructiveness of verbal aggressiveness in families.

In the sibling relationship, people perceived their siblings as being similar to themselves in their use of verbal aggression with each other (Martin, Anderson, Burant, & Weber, 1997). In that relationship, people's verbal aggressiveness and their siblings' verbal aggressiveness both were related to lower satisfaction and lower interpersonal trust. Additionally, Martin et al. reported that when siblings reported greater satisfaction with their siblings, they also noted a greater amount of hurt when their siblings were verbally aggressive. Similar to the findings of Martin, Anderson, and Horvath (1987), this finding adds further support that verbally aggressive messages are more hurtful when the source is either a friend or family member versus an acquaintance or stranger.

Martin and Anderson (1997) found that mothers and fathers who were high in trait verbal aggressiveness had sons and daughters who were high in trait verbal aggressiveness. While their study was a test of Social Cognitive Theory, the authors acknowledge that genetics may offer some explanation for the relationship between parents' verbal aggressiveness and their children's verbal aggressiveness (Beatty & McCroskey, 1997). Weber and Patterson (1997) investigated the effects of maternal verbal aggression on their children's current romantic relationships. They found that when mothers were verbally aggressive, children expressed having less solidarity in their romantic relationships.

Beatty and colleagues (Beatty & Dobos 1992a, 1992b, 1993a, 1993b, 1993c; Beatty, Dobos, Rudd, & Burant, 1994; Beatty, Zelley, Dobos, & Rudd, 1994; Burant, 1994) have focused on aggressive communication in the father-son relationship. Sons have lower satisfaction when they perceive their fathers as being critical, sarcastic, and communication apprehensive (Beatty & Dobos, 1992a, 1992b). Beatty and Dobos conceptualized sarcasm as being hypocritical, insulting, and snide; they defined criticism as being judgmental, disapproving, controlling, and evaluative. Beatty and Dobos concluded that fathers who were concerned about their sons' relational satisfaction should limit or avoid their own use of sarcasm and criticism. Additionally, Beatty and Dobos (1993a, 1993b, 1993c) found confirmation that sons feel from their fathers has an effect on sons' romantic relationships with their partners. Their results also supported that sons' perceptions of fathers' criticism and sarcasm may be contributing factors to female partners' perceptions of the disconfirming behavior that these sons display in their romantic relationships.

In studying situations where sons show defiance to their fathers, Beatty, Dobos, Rudd, and Burant (1994) and Burant (1994) found that fathers and sons were similar in their use of abusive and nonabusive strategies and that sons could predict which type their father would endorse using. Beatty, Zelley, Dobos, and Rudd (1994) posited that fathers' trait verbal aggressiveness and argumentativeness are predictors of adult sons' perceptions of fathers' sarcasm, criticism, and verbal aggressiveness. The results indicated that fathers who are verbally aggressive have sons that perceive their fathers to be verbally aggressive, critical, and sarcastic in their relational communication. In studying the use of verbal aggression, sarcasm, and criticism between members in a friendship, people reported reciprocating their friends use of destructive communication (Martin, Anderson, Burant, & Weber, 1996). Based on these previous findings, the following hypothesis was proposed:

H1: People's verbal aggressiveness, sarcasm, and criticism with their stepparents will be similar to their stepparents' verbal aggressiveness, sarcasm, and criticism.

In their overview of aggressive theory, Infante and Rancer (1996) stated that "Communication between parent and child is enhanced when parents are argumentative, affirming in communication style, and low in verbal aggressiveness" (p. 339). When stepfamilies cannot handle conflict constructively, satisfaction is lower (Baxter, Braithwaite, & Nicholson, 1999; Braithwaite, Olson, Golish, Soukup, & Turman, 2001). People who report being verbally aggressive with their stepparents would be expected to be less satisfied with the relationship; they would not enjoy communicating with their stepparents and would experience less trust with those individuals. Likewise, when people reported that their stepparents tended to be verbally aggressive, it would also be expected that there would be less satisfaction in the relationship. Crosbie-Burnett and Giles-Sims (1994) found that when stepparents attempted to use a control parenting style (e.g., supervision and discipline), stepchildren had lower satisfaction.

Along with verbal aggression, sarcasm and criticism in relationships are related negatively to relational outcomes (Beatty & Dobos, 1993b). People who use sarcasm or criticism are often unhappy or angry and intend for their communication to be perceived negatively (Gibbs, O'Brien, & Doolittle, 1995; Kassinove, Sukhodolsky, Tsytsarev, & Solovyova, 1997; Leggitt & Gibbs, 2000). Additionally, people often use sarcasm and criticism in conflict situations, especially when they have negative affect for the source (Canary, Cunningham, & Cody, 1988; Resnick, et al., 1981). Adolescents that receive criticism from parents tend to have lower self-esteem and be less likely to self-disclose (Felson & Zielinski, 1989; Harris & Howard, 1984; Martin, Anderson, & Mottet, 1999; Rosenthal, Efklides, & Demetriou, 1988).

In this study, we expected that stepchildren would view stepparent sarcasm and criticism negatively. Given what is known about verbal aggressiveness, sarcasm and criticism, the following two hypotheses were proposed:

H2:   People's verbal aggressiveness, sarcasm, and criticism toward their stepparents will be negatively related to their (a) trust and (b) satisfaction with those stepparents.

H3:   People's perceptions of their stepparents' verbal aggressiveness, sarcasm, and criticism towards them will be negatively related to their (a) trust and (b) satisfaction with those stepparents.

METHOD

Participants

Participants were 165 students enrolled in introductory communication courses at a large midwestern university. In order to participate in this study, individuals had to have at least one stepparent. Those that had more than one stepparent were asked to consider one of those stepparents in completing the questionnaire. Participation was voluntary. The sample was composed of 84 males and 79 females (1 unidentified). The mean age was 21.16 (SD = 4.53). The participants' stepparents consisted of 96 males and 68 females (1 unidentified), with an average age of 45.36 (SD = 7.68). Stepparents were married to the participants' parents for an average of 8.96 (SD = 5.68) years. When asked how often they communicate with their stepparents, 21 answered daily, 66 weekly, 62 monthly, 15 several times a year, 1 once or less a year. Only 13 participants currently lived with their stepparent, 89 had at one time, 61 had never lived with their stepparent (2 no report).

Procedure

Participants completed a questionnaire as one way of receiving extra credit. Individuals who did not have a stepparent were given an alternative opportunity. The questionnaire included measures of self and stepparent verbal aggressiveness, sarcasm, and criticism, and participants' interpersonal trust, and communication satisfaction with their stepparents. Self and stepparent verbal aggressiveness were measured using a 10-item version of Infante and Wigley's (1986) Verbal Aggressiveness Scale, with responses ranging from "almost never true" (1) to "almost always true" (5). Previous studies have found this 10-item version to be reliable and valid (Infante et al., 1993; Martin & Anderson, 1995b; Rudd, Burant, & Beatty, 1994). Participants completed the self-report of their verbal aggressiveness toward their stepparents, then their perceptions of their stepparents' verbal aggressiveness toward them. Coefficient alphas in this study were .88 (M = 2.37, SD = .83) for self verbal aggressiveness and .90 (M = 2.46, SD = .93) for stepparent verbal aggressiveness. Sample items included: My stepparent attacks my character when attempting to influence me. My stepparent loses her temper and says rather strong things to me when I do not agree with her. My stepparent yells and screams when nothing else seems to work in trying to influence me.

Sarcasm and criticism were measured using Beatty and Dobos' (1992b) seven-point bipolar adjective scales. The five sets of adjectives for sarcasm were: sarcastic-not sarcastic, insulting-praising, gentle-harsh, hostile-amiable, and hypocritical-consistent. The four sets of adjectives for criticism were: critical-noncritical, judgmental-nonjudgmental, evaluative-nonevaluative, and disapproving-approving. Participants completed reports of their own and their stepparents' use of sarcasm and criticism in their relationships. Coefficient alphas in this study were .77 (M = 3.35, SD = 1.07) for self sarcasm and .87 (M = 3.51, SD = 1.43) for stepparent sarcasm; .72 (M = 3.86, SD = 1.15) for self criticism and .73 (M = 4.12, SD = 1.32) for stepparent criticism.

Trust with stepparent was measured using Larzelere and Huston's (1980) 8-item Dyadic Trust Scale, with responses ranging from "strongly disagree" (1) to "strongly agree" (5). Coefficient alpha in this study was .93 (M = 3.40, SD = 1.07). Sample items included: I feel that I can trust my stepparent completely. My stepparent is truly sincere in her promises. I feel that my stepparent can be counted on to help me.

Communication satisfaction with stepparent was measured using Hecht's (1978) 16-item Communication Satisfaction Scale, with responses ranging from "strongly disagree" (1) to "strongly agree" (5). Coefficient alpha in this study was .96 (M = 3.34, SD = .97). Sample items included: My stepparent shows me that she understands what I say. I feel like I can talk about anything with my stepparent. My stepparent lets me know that I communicate effectively.

RESULTS

A canonical correlation analysis was used to test Hypothesis One. Since males are more verbally aggressive than females, and both males and females expect males to be more verbally aggressive (Martin & Anderson, 1996a, 1996b; Nicotera & Rancer, 1994), Hypotheses Two and Three were tested by partial correlations, controlling for the sex of participants and the sex of stepparents.

Hypothesis One involved the similarity between participants' and stepparents' use of verbal aggression, sarcasm, and criticism in their relationships together. The participants' communication behaviors served as one set of variables with the stepparents' communication behaviors as the second set of variables in the canonical correlation. The analysis resulted in two significant, interpretable roots (Wilks lambda = .36, $F(3,161)$ = 22.22, $p < .001$): Rc1 = .64 and Rc2 = .51. In the first root, participants who reported being verbally aggressive, sarcastic, and critical with their stepparents reported that their stepparents were verbally aggressive, sarcastic, and critical with them. The second root can be interpreted that participants who were critical with their stepparents had stepparents who were critical with them.

Table 1. Hypothesis One: Relationship between Participants' Aggressive
Communication with their Stepparents' Aggressive Communication

Aggressive Communication	Canonical Loadings	
	Root 1	Ro ot 2
Set 1: Participants		
Verbal Aggressiveness	.95	-.30
Criticism	.69	.66
Sarcasm	.83	.33
Redundancy coefficient	[.28]	[.05]
Set 2: Stepparents		
Verbal Aggressiveness	.96	-.23
Criticism	.72	.58
Sarcasm	.91	.29
Redundancy coefficient	[.31]	[.04]

Note: Wilks lambda = .36, $F(3,161)$ = 22.22, $p < .001$. Rc1 = .64 and Rc2 = .51.

Hypothesis Two stated that participants' verbal aggressiveness, sarcasm, and criticism would be negatively related to relational outcomes. This hypothesis was supported in that participants' verbal aggressiveness was negatively correlated to their satisfaction with stepparent ($r = -.63$ $p < .01$) and trust with stepparent ($r = -.60$, $p < .01$). Sarcasm ($r = -.50$, $p < .01$; $r = -.46$, $p < .01$) and criticism ($r = -.47$, $p < .01$; $r = -.41$, $p < .01$) were also significantly related.

Hypothesis Three stated that participants' perceptions of their stepparents' verbal aggressiveness, sarcasm, and criticism would be negatively related to relational outcomes. This hypothesis was also supported in that perceived stepparents' verbal aggressiveness was negatively correlated to participants' satisfaction with stepparent ($r = -.74$, $p < .01$) and trust with stepparent ($r = -.72$, $p < .01$). Sarcasm ($r = -.66$, $p < .01$; $r = -.63$, $p < .01$) and criticism ($r = -.55$, $p < .01$; $r = -.51$, $p < .01$) were also significantly related.

DISCUSSION

The results from this study further demonstrate the destructiveness of verbal aggressiveness, criticism, and sarcasm in interpersonal relationships. Whether people are reporting on their own or on their stepparents' verbal aggressiveness, criticism, and sarcasm, there is less satisfaction and trust when these communication tendencies are present in relationships.

People report that their stepparents are verbally aggressive, sarcastic, and critical with them, but they also admit to being verbally aggressive, sarcastic, and critical toward their stepparents. As noted by Claxton (2000), the image of the wicked stepparent may be more prevalent in the media versus reality. In fact, this study did not find a "wicked stepparent" effect taking place. Instead, results support previous findings; when there is verbal aggressiveness in a relationship, satisfaction and trust decrease. At the same time, when verbal aggression is low in a relationship, satisfaction and trust increase. The means for the verbal aggression scales show that people did not perceive their stepparents as necessarily using more verbal aggression than they themselves use in the relationship.

The results show that people and stepparents are similar in their use of verbal aggression, sarcasm, and criticism with each other and that when both members in a relationship are high in verbal aggressiveness, satisfaction and trust are low. Whether verbal aggression is the result of reciprocation, self-defense, or a lack of arguing skills, verbal aggression in this relationship appears to stimulate further use of verbal aggression, decreasing the relational attraction between stepparent and stepchild.

A future direction would be to look at verbal aggression at different times in the stepparent-stepchild relationship. Papernow (1993) argued that there are various stages of development in the stepfamily. Further research could demonstrate whether there is more verbal aggression in an early stage, such as Papernow's stage of immersion, where there is a clash of rules, social norms, and expectations, in comparison to the later stage of resolution, where there is mutual respect between the parties. Possibly as stepfamily relationships progress, the amount of verbal aggression decreases and the members of the stepfamily give and receive a greater amount of emotional support.

Emotional support involves expressions of concern, compassion, sympathy, and esteem for another individual (Buhrmester, Furman, Wittenberg, & Reis, 1988; Cohen & Wills, 1985; Hill, 1987). House (1981) wrote that the majority of emotional support that people receive is obtained from those that they form and maintain stable social relationships. When people receive emotional support, they report greater satisfaction and trust in their relationships and lower levels of conflict (Avtgis, 2002; Weber, Johnson, & Corrigan, 2004; Weber & Patterson, 1996). Additionally, Weber and Burant (1996) found that higher reports of parents' verbal aggression were related to a decrease in the amount of emotional support present in their children's current romantic relationships. Exploring emotional support in stepfamilies might be beneficial in identifying the type of communication necessary for healthy stepfamily communication (Golish, 2003).

The question of why people communicate might also help explain and decrease the amount of verbal aggression in stepfamilies. When family members report talking to their family in order to satisfy affection, pleasure, or inclusion needs, they report being more satisfied (Anderson & Martin, 1995a, Martin & Anderson, 1995b). However, when communication focuses on the needs of control and escape, satisfaction decreases in the relationship. Noncompetent communicators are more likely to communicate for control and escape (Anderson & Martin, 1995b). Noncompetent communicators are also more verbally aggressive (Martin & Anderson, 1996a). People may not perceive, or want, their stepfamily relationships to be constructive, and thus communicate accordingly. Golish and Caughlin (2002) argued that in stepfamilies people often use avoidance to create communication boundaries. Ganong, Coleman, Fine and Martin (1999) found that stepchildren often do not recognize when stepparents are using affinity-seeking behaviors. Finding out why people talk to their stepparents could be a way to improve stepfamily communication.

Future investigations will need to consider why people are verbally aggressive with their stepparents. The answer to that question would assist then in answering the question of whether stepparents' verbal aggressiveness leads to dissatisfaction in a relationship or whether dissatisfaction in relationships leads to stepparents' verbal aggressiveness. Most likely, there is an ongoing recursive relationship. One could conclude then that by reducing the amount of verbal aggression in a relationship, satisfaction will increase, and as satisfaction increases, the amount of verbal aggression will decrease.

People can be trained to decrease their use of verbal aggression (Infante, 1995; Infante & Rancer, 1996; Nelson & Leviant, 1991). Nelson and Leviant reported that training stepparents in communication skills increases positive communication with children and allows stepparents to better express their feelings and to empathize with their stepchildren. Stepparents who were not trained reported yelling and threatening their stepchildren more. As Lansford, Ceballo, Abbey, and Stewart (2001) concluded, what may be more important for a healthy family is effective and appropriate communication versus the structure of the family (e.g., two-parent biological, single parent, stepparent).

REFERENCES

Anderson, C. M., & Martin, M. M. (1995a, November). *Communication models of mothers and their adult children: The path from motives to self-disclosure to satisfaction.* Paper presented at the annual meeting of the Speech Communication Association, San Antonio.

_____ . (1995b). Communication motives of assertive and responsive communicators. *Communication Research Reports, 12,* 186-191.

_____ . (1999). The relationship of argumentativeness and verbal aggressiveness to cohesion, consensus and satisfaction in small groups. *Communication Reports, 12,* 21-31.

Arliss, L. P. (1993). *Contemporary family communication: Messages and meanings.* New York: St. Martin's Press.

Avtgis, T. A. (2002). Marital support giving as a function of attributional confidence. *Communication Research Reports, 17*, 357-365.

Barber, B. L., & Lyons, J. M. (1994). Family processes and adolescent adjustment in intact and remarried families. *Journal of Youth and Adolescence, 23*, 421-436.

Baxter, L. A., Braithwaite, D. O., & Nicholson, J. H. (1999). Turning points in the development of blended families. *Journal of Social and Personal Relationships, 16*, 291-313.

Beatty, M. J., & Dobos, J. A. (1992a). Adult sons' satisfaction with their relationships with fathers and person-group (father) communication apprehension. *Communication Quarterly, 40*, 162-176.

_____ . (1992b). Relationship between sons' perceptions of fathers' messages and satisfaction in adult son-father relationships. *Southern Communication Journal, 57*, 277-284.

_____ . (1993a). Adult males' perceptions of confirmation and relational partner communication apprehension: Indirect effects of fathers on sons' partners. *Communication Quarterly, 41*, 66-77.

_____ . (1993b). Direct and mediated effects of perceived father criticism and sarcasm on females' perceptions of relational partners' disconfirming behavior. *Communication Quarterly, 41*, 187-197.

_____ . (1993c). Mediated effects of adult males' perceived confirmation from father on relational partners' communication apprehension. *Southern Communication Journal, 58*, 207-214.

Beatty, M. J., Dobos, J. A., Rudd, J. E., & Burant, P. A. (1994, November). *Like father, like son: Interactive versus disciplinary responses to sons' oppositional messages.* Paper presented at the annual meeting of the Speech Communication Association, New Orleans.

Beatty, M. J., Zelley, J. R., Dobos, J. A., & Rudd, J. E. (1994). Fathers' trait verbal aggressiveness and argumentativeness as predictors of adult sons' perceptions of fathers' sarcasm, criticism, and verbal aggressiveness. *Communication Quarterly, 42*, 407-415.

Beatty, M. J., & McCroskey, J. C. (1997). It's in our nature: Verbal aggressiveness as temperamental expression. *Communication Quarterly, 45*, 446-460.

Braithwaite, D. O., Olson, L. N., Golish, T. D., Soukup, C., & Turman, P. (2001). Becoming a family: Developmental processes represented in blended family discourse. *Journal of Applied Communication Research, 29*, 221-247.

Buhrmester, D., Furman, W., Wittenberg, M. T., & Reis, H. T. (1988). Five domains of interpersonal competence in peer relationships. *Journal of Personality and Social Psychology, 55*, 991-1008.

Burant, P. A. (1994). *Correspondence between father and son responses to son's oppositional messages.* Unpublished Masters thesis, Cleveland State University.

Canary, D. J., Cunningham, E. M., & Cody, M. J. (1988). Goal types, gender, and locus of control in managing interpersonal conflict. *Communication Research, 15*, 426-446.

Claxton-Oldfield, S. (2000). Deconstructing the myth of the wicked stepparent. *Marriage and Family Review, 30*, 51-58.

Cohen, S., & Wills, T. A. (1985). Stress, social support, and the buffering hypothesis. *Psychological Bulletin, 98*, 310-357.

Coleman, M., Ganong, L., & Fine, M. (2000). Reinvestigating remarriage: Another decade of progress. *Journal of Marriage and the Family, 62*, 1288-1307.

_____. (2004). Communication in stepfamilies. In A. L. Vangelisti (Ed.), *Handbook of family communication* (pp. 215-232). Mahwah, NJ: Erlbaum.

Coleman, M., Ganong, L., & Weaver, S. (2001). Relationship maintenance and enhancement in remarried families. In J. Harvey & A. Wenzel (Eds.), *Close romantic relationships: Maintenance and enhancement* (pp. 255-276). Mahwah, NJ: Erlbaum.

Crosbie-Burnett, M., & Giles-Sims, J. (1994). Adolescent adjustment and stepparenting styles. *Family Relations: Interdisciplinary Journal of Applied Family Studies, 43*, 394-399.

Felson, R. B., & Zielinski, M. A. (1989). Children's self-esteem and parental support. *Journal of Marriage and the Family, 51*, 727-735.

Fine, M. A. (2001). Marital conflict in stepfamilies. In J. H. Grych & F. D. Fincham (Eds.), *Interparental conflict and child development: Theory, research, and applications* (pp. 363-383). New York: Cambridge University Press.

Fine, M. A., Coleman, M., & Ganong, L. H. (1998). Consistency in perceptions of the step-parent role among step-parents, parents, and stepchildren. *Journal of Social and Personal Relationships, 15*, 810-828.

Fitzpatrick, M. A., & Badzinski, D. M. (1994). All in the family: Interpersonal communication in kin relationships. In M. L. Knapp & G. R. Miller (Eds.), *Handbook of interpersonal communication 2nd edition* (pp. 726-771). Thousand Oaks, CA: Sage.

Galvin, K. M., & Brommel, B. J. (1996). *Family communication: Cohesion and change.* New York: HarperCollins.

Ganong, L., Coleman, M., Fine, M., & Martin, P. (1999). Stepparents' affinity-seeking and affinity-maintaining strategies with stepchildren. *Journal of Family Issues, 20*, 299-327.

Gibbs, R. W., O'Brien, J. E., & Doolittle, S. (1995). Inferring meanings that are not intended: Speakers' intentions and irony comprehension. *Discourse Processes, 20*, 187-203.

Golish, T. D. (2003). Stepfamily communication strengths: Understanding the ties that bind. *Human Communication Research, 29*, 41-80.

Golish, T. D., & Caughlin, J. P. (2002). "I'd rather not talk about it": Adolescents' and young adults use of topic avoidance in stepfamilies. *Journal of Applied Communication Research, 30*, 78-106.

Harris, I. D., & Howard, K. I. (1984). Parental criticism and the adolescent experience. *Journal of Youth and Adolescence, 13*, 113-121.

Hecht, M. L. (1978). The conceptualization and measurement of interpersonal communication satisfaction. *Human Communication Research, 4*, 253-264.

Hill, C. A. (1987). Affiliation motivation: People who need people but in different ways. *Journal of Personality and Social Psychology, 5*, 321-333.

House, J. S. (1981). *Work stress and social support.* Reading, MA: Addison-Wesley.

Infante, D. A. (1995). Teaching students to understand and control verbal aggression. *Communication Education, 44*, 51-63.

Infante, D. A., Anderson, C. M., Martin, M. M., Herington, A. D., & Kim, J. K. (1993). Subordinates' satisfaction and perceptions of superiors' compliance-gaining tactics, argumentativeness, verbal aggressiveness, and style. *Management Communication Quarterly, 6*, 307-326.

Infante, D. A., & Gorden, W. I. (1985). Superiors' argumentativeness and verbal aggressiveness as predictors of subordinates' satisfaction. *Human Communication Research, 12*, 117-125.

Infante, D. A., Myers, S. A., & Buerkel, R. A. (1994). Argument and verbal aggression in constructive and destructive family and organizational disagreements. *Western Journal of Communication, 58*, 73-84.

Infante, D. A., & Rancer, A. S. (1996). Argumentativeness and verbal aggressiveness: A review of recent theory and research. *Communication Yearbook, 19*, 319-351.

Infante, D. A., & Wigley, C. J. (1986). Verbal aggressiveness: An interpersonal model and measure. *Communication Monographs, 53*, 61-69.

Kassinove, H., Sukhodolsky, D. G., Tsytsarev, S. V., & Solovyova, S. (1997). Self-reported anger episodes in Russia and America. *Journal of Social Behavior and Personality, 12*, 301-324.

Kurdek, L. A., & Fine, M. A. (1991). Cognitive correlates of satisfaction for mothers and stepfathers in stepfather families. *Journal of Marriage and the Family, 53*, 565-572.

Lansford, J. E., Ceballo, R., Abbey, A., & Stewart, A. J. (2001). Does family structure matter? A comparison of adoptive, two-parent biological, single-mother, stepfather, and stepmother households. *Journal of Marriage and the Family, 63*, 840-851.

Larzelere, R. E., & Huston, T. L. (1980). The Dyadic Trust Scale: Toward understanding interpersonal trust in close relationships. *Journal of Marriage and the Family, 42*, 595-604.

Leggitt, J. S., & Gibbs, R. W., Jr. (2000). Emotional reactions to verbal irony. *Discourse Processes, 29*, 1-24.

Martin, M. M., & Anderson, C. M. (1997). Aggressive communication traits: How similar are young adults and their parents in argumentativeness, assertiveness, and verbal aggressiveness. *Western Journal of Communication, 61*, 299-314.

_____ . (1996a). Argumentativeness and verbal aggressiveness. *Journal of Social Behavior and Personality, 11*, 547-554.

_____ . (1996b). Communication traits: A cross-generational investigation. *Communication Research Reports, 13*, 58-67.

_____ . (1995a). Roommate similarity: Are roommates who are similar in their communication traits more satisfied? *Communication Research Reports, 12*, 46-52.

_____ . (1995b). The father-young adult relationship: Interpersonal motives, self-disclosure, and satisfaction. *Communication Quarterly, 43*, 119-130.

Martin, M. M., Anderson, C. M., Burant, P. A., & Weber, K. (1996, November). *Verbal aggression in friendships*. Paper presented at the Speech Communication Association Convention, San Diego.

Martin, M. M., Anderson, C. M., Burant, P. A., & Weber, K. (1997). Verbal aggression in sibling relationships. *Communication Quarterly, 45*, 304-317.

Martin, M. M., Anderson, C. M., & Horvath, C. L. (1996). Feelings about verbal aggression: Justifications for sending and hurt from receiving verbally aggressive messages. *Communication Research Reports, 13*, 19-26.

Martin, M. M., Anderson, C. M., & Mottet, T. P. (1999). Perceived understanding and self-disclosure in the stepparent-stepchild relationship. *Journal of Psychology, 133*, 281-290.

Myers, S. A. (2001). Perceived instructor credibility and verbal aggressiveness in the college classroom. *Communication Research Reports, 18*, 354-364.

Myers, S. A., & Knox, R. L. (2000). Perceived instructor argumentativeness and verbal aggressiveness and student outcomes. *Communication Research Reports, 17*, 299-309.

Myers, S. A., & Rocca, K. A. (2001). Perceived instructor argumentativeness and verbal aggressiveness in the college classroom: Effects on student perceptions of climate, apprehension, and state motivation. *Western Journal of Communication, 65*, 113-137.

Nelson, W. P., & Levant, R. F. (1991). An evaluation of a skills training program for parents in stepfamilies. *Family Relations, 40*, 291-296.

Nicotera, A. M., & Rancer, A. S. (1994). The influence of sex on self-perceptions and social stereotyping of aggressive communication predispositions. *Western Journal of Communication, 58*, 283-307.

Papernow, P. L. (1993). *Becoming a stepfamily*. San Francisco: Jossey-Bass.

Resick, P. A., Barr, P. K., Sweet, J. J., Kieffer, D. M., Ruby, N. L., & Spiegel, D. K. (1981). Perceived and actual discriminators of conflict from accord in marital communication. *American Journal of Family Therapy, 9*, 58-68.

Rosenthal, D. A., Efklides, A., & Demetriou, A. (1988). Parental criticism and young adolescent self-disclosure: A cross-cultural study. *Journal of Youth and Adolescence, 17*, 25-39.

Rudd, J. E., Burant, P. A., & Beatty, M. J. (1994). Battered women's compliance-gaining strategies as a function of argumentativeness and verbal aggression. *Communication Research Reports, 11*, 13-22.

Sabourin, T. C., Infante, D. A., & Rudd, J. E. (1993). Verbal aggression in marriages: A comparison of violent, distressed but nonviolent, and nondistressed couples. *Human Communication Research, 20*, 245-267.

Sabourin, T. C., & Stamp, G. H. (1995). Communication and the experience of dialectical tensions in family life: An examination of abusive and nonabusive families. *Communication Monographs, 62*, 213-242.

Venable, K. V., & Martin, M. M. (1997). Argumentativeness and verbal aggressiveness in dating relationships. *Journal of Social Behavior & Personality, 12*, 955-964.

Vuchinich, S., Hetherington, E. M., Vuchinich, R. A., & Clingempeel, W. G. (1991). Parent-child interaction and gender differences in early adolescents' adaptation to stepfamilies. *Developmental Psychology, 27*, 618-626.

Weber, K., & Burant, P. A. (1996). *Parents and their adult children: Parental verbal aggression and the adult-child's communication apprehension and self-esteem*. Paper presented at the Speech Communication Association Convention, San Diego.

Weber, K., Johnson, A., & Corrigan, M. W. (2004). *Communicating emotional support and its relationship to feelings of being understood, trust, and self-disclosure*. Paper submitted for publication.

Weber, K., & Patterson, B. P. (1996). Construction and validation of a communication based emotional support scale. *Communication Research Reports, 13*, 68-76.

_____ . (1997). The effects of maternal verbal aggression on the adult child's future romantic relationships. *Communication Research Reports, 14*, 221-230.

Wigley, C. J. (1998). Verbal aggressiveness. In J. C. McCroskey, J. A. Daly, M. M. Martin, & M. J. Beatty (Eds.) *Communication and personality: Trait perspectives* (pp. 191-214). Cresskill, NJ: Hampton Press.

In: *Focus on Aggression Research*
Editor: James P. Morgan, pp. 53-57

ISBN 1-59454-132-9
© 2004 Nova Science Publishers, Inc.

Chapter 4

THE MEASUREMENT OF
MEMORIES FOR CHILDHOOD TEASING

Deborah A. Roth[*] and Eric A. Storch

INTRODUCTION

Many experiences during childhood can contribute to later psychological difficulties. One such experience, which has recently been the focus of considerable empirical attention, is bullying (see Hawker & Boulton, 2000 for a review). Bullying has been defined as being exposed "repeatedly and over time, to negative actions on the part of one or more other students" (Olweus, 1993, p. 9). Olweus further defines "negative actions" as occurring when "someone intentionally inflicts, or attempts to inflict, injury or discomfort upon another" (Olweus, 1993, p. 9). Teasing is a specific form of bullying in which "negative actions" are verbal in nature. Although bullying via physical contact is much more common in boys than in girls (Crick & Bigbee, 1998; Crick & Grotpeter, 1996; Storch, Nock, Masia-Warner, & Barlas, 2003; Storch, Masia-Warner, & Brassard, 2003), bullying with non-physical means, including verbal teasing, is the most common form of peer victimization in children of both sexes (Olweus, 1993). Further, an estimated one in five youth is chronically exposed to ongoing teasing (Storch & Masia-Warner, in press). Although the majority of children are teased at some point during youth, it is widely recognized that chronic peer torment may escalate into more serious forms of violence (Galdston, 1984).

When patients present for psychological treatment, many recall teasing experiences that they believe were pivotal in the development of their specific problems. For example, patients with eating disorders often recall being teased about their weight as they grew up. Similarly, patients with social anxiety disorder often remember being teased about a particular physical symptom, such as blushing (e.g., see Hackmann, Clark, & McManus, 2000). While the experience of being teased is only one potential contributing factor to later psychological

---

[*] Author for correspondence: Deborah A. Roth, Ph.D., Center for the Treatment and Study of Anxiety, University of Pennsylvania School of Medicine, 3535 Market St., 6th Floor, Philadelphia, PA, 19104. Fax: 215-746-3311. E-mail: droth3@mail.med.upenn.edu.

difficulties, it is an important one to explore nonetheless. Finding that teasing during childhood plays a role in the development of later difficulties can inform prevention efforts, either by trying to decrease the incidence of teasing among children, or more realistically, helping children who are victims of teasing to deal with the experience in a more adaptive, healthy way.

In order to learn more about childhood teasing, it is essential that instruments are available to measure the experience. Instruments to measure bullying experiences among children are available (e.g., Peer Victimization Scale; Neary & Joseph, 1994), but instruments to measure adults' memories of childhood teasing experiences are limited. Most research on this topic has focused on the relationship between recalled childhood teasing and later difficulties with eating and body image, and as such, available measures are limited in scope to teasing about weight and physical appearance.

Thompson and colleagues (Thompson, Fabian, Moulton, Dunn, & Altabe, 1991) developed the Physical Appearance Related Teasing Scale (PARTS), an 18-item scale that consisted of two factors: Weight/Size Teasing (WST) and General Appearance Teasing (GAT). In the initial report on this scale, participants who recalled more frequent WST reported greater eating and body image disturbance, higher levels of depression, and lower self-esteem. In contrast, being teased about general appearance was found to be unrelated to any of these later difficulties. With these findings in mind, Thompson and colleagues (1995) revised and extended the PARTS, calling their new 11-item scale the Perception of Teasing Scale (POTS, Thompson, Cattarin, Fowler, & Fisher, 1995). This scale diverges in three significant ways from the earlier PARTS. First, the scale only inquires about teasing related to weight (the General Weight Teasing subscale) since the earlier study suggested that General Appearance teasing was not associated with later difficulties with eating and body image. Second, the item content of the POTS is slightly broader than the earlier scale, including five items about Competency (e.g., "people made fun of you by repeating something you said because they thought it was dumb;" "people made fun of you because you were afraid to do something;" "people said you acted dumb;" "people laughed at you because you didn't understand something;" and "people teased you because you didn't get a joke"). Finally, whereas the PARTS asked only about frequency of teasing, the POTS also asked participants to report how upset they were about being teased.

Recently, Vessey, Duffy, O'Sullivan, and Swanson (2003) further revised the PARTS, creating the Physical Appearance Related Teasing Scale – Revised (PARTS-R). Three of the PARTS 17 items were deleted due to low item-total correlations (< .40). Principal components analysis identified three components, namely Harassment (six items), Appearance Teasing (four items), and Physical Teasing (four items). Cronbach's alpha for each component and the PARTS-R total score were adequate. No other reliability and validity data were reported.

Despite the addition of the competency scale to the POTS and Vessey et al.'s (2003) revision, these measures have a number of shortcomings as tools for assessing the range of issues about which children are teased. Clearly, this is because the original scale was developed specifically to examine teasing in domains thought to be related to later body image and eating disturbances. However, teasing can be related to other later difficulties as well and as such, a scale must be available to assess for teasing experiences in multiple domains. On a related note, the POTS has only been standardized in female undergraduates and limited psychometric data on the PARTS-R have been reported, leaving no established measure for assessing teasing experiences, broadly defined.

The Teasing Questionnaire – Revised (TQ-R; Storch et al., in press) is a 29-item scale designed to assess memories of teasing experiences during childhood. The scale was empirically derived from questions in the original TQ (Roth, Coles, & Heimberg, 2002), as well as new items generated with the goal of creating teasing domains. Responses to the TQ-R are made on a 5-point Likert-type scale (0 = "I was never teased about this," 1 = "I was rarely teased about this," 2 = "I was sometimes teased about this," 3 = "I was often teased about this," and 4 = "I was always teased about this").

TQ-R items were generated by carefully reviewing the existing literature to identify topics about which children are commonly teased (e.g., "I was teased about my height," "I was teased about particular aspects of my appearance such as the way that I dressed, wearing glasses, the color of my hair"). In addition, colleagues with expertise in anxiety and depression were asked to report topics that their patients recalled having been teased about or that they themselves might have been teased about as children. This proved to be beneficial, with these professionals gleaning items from characteristics associated with people who are anxious or depressed (e.g., "I was teased because I wasn't good at initiating and maintaining conversations with other kids," "I was teased because I wasn't a very cheerful kid") and from other experiences that their patients or they themselves had (e.g., "I was teased because I excelled at school," "I was teased for being a tomboy or a feminine boy"). Visual inspection of the TQ-R revealed that items assessed five relatively unique constructs, namely teasing about performance, academic characteristics, social behavior, family background, and appearance.

Initial psychometric investigation of the TQ-R was promising. Using structural equation modeling, the proposed five-factor model was confirmed. The moderate relations among the factors suggested that the TQ-R subscales assessed related, but conceptually unique dimensions of teasing. Internal consistency of the TQ-R total score was .87. Cronbach's α for the Performance (3-items), Academic (6-items), Social Behavior (7-items), Family (3-items), and Appearance (8-items) factors were .58, .84, .70, .48, and .78, respectively. Finally, convergent validity was supported vis-à-vis positive and meaningful relations between the TQ-R total score and depressive symptoms, anxiety, fear of negative evaluation, and loneliness (Storch et al., in press).

Currently, a second psychometric investigation is underway. The goals of this study are to: (1) confirm the five-factor model found by Storch et al. (in press); (2) examine the internal consistency and interscale correlations; (3) examine the test-retest reliability of the TQ-R over two weeks; and (4) attempt to replicate findings that the TQ-R Total score was meaningfully related to depressive symptoms, anxiety, fear of negative evaluation, and loneliness in a second sample of young adults.

Since we developed our TQ-R, two other means of assessing recalled childhood teasing in adults have been reported. Similar to the focus on weight-related teasing in the POTS, a Racial Teasing Scale (RTS) was recently developed (Iyer & Haslam, 2003). The RTS is an 8-item measure, based on the POTS, that assesses the frequency and impact of teasing on the basis of race or ethnicity. Items include, "People called you names because of your ethnicity" and "People excluded you from participating in activities because of your ethnicity." This scale is a positive development because it takes into account the fact that children can be teased about attributes besides their weight, but is clearly also limited in scope.

McCabe et al. (2003), in a study looking at the relationship between childhood teasing and later anxiety disorders, simply asked patients whether or not they had a "history of severe teasing." This single question yielded very interesting findings – patients with social anxiety disorder were more likely than patients with other anxiety disorders to recall being severely teased as children. While using a single question to assess for recalled teasing certainly gets around the issue of the multiple domains about which children can be teased, it prevents an examination of whether specific domains of teasing are uniquely related to specific psychological difficulties later in life.

Having available retrospective measures of childhood teasing can be beneficial in various ways. Identifying a link between childhood teasing and later anxiety and depression will help inform investigators in devising prevention and intervention strategies aimed at helping children and adolescents at the time they are teased. Such efforts could not only ward off the immediate impact of teasing, but also help build resiliency that is important during psychosocial development. This might be particularly true for anxious, withdrawn children who are often the targets of teasing and probably less likely than more outgoing children to go to adults for help when they are teased. In addition, having a comprehensive understanding about negative childhood experiences that may have shaped patients' pathological beliefs will assist in addressing dysfunctional beliefs that contribute to distress and impairment. For example, the inability of teased children to reduce the frequency of victimization might make them believe that they are unable to cope in the social world. Such beliefs can be targeted in treatment, both through cognitive restructuring and through direct experiences in which patients can come to see that they have a greater ability to cope with the social world than they had thought.

Given the importance of intervening as teasing occurs, having a good measure of teasing experiences for children is also important. While measures of peer victimization for children exist, none capture the domains of teasing included in the TQ-R. Since we have found that specific domains of teasing are related to specific psychological difficulties later in life, it is important to be able to do this fine-grained level of analysis at the time that teasing happens and to the implement targeted interventions. For example, children who are teased in the social domain might benefit specifically from social skills and assertiveness training. To this end, we have set about developing a child version of the TQ-R. Although this version will maintain the factor structure of the TQ-R, the measure will be developmentally appropriate for children between the ages of 8 and 18 years.

REFERENCES

Crick, N. R., & Bigbee, M. A. (1998). Relational and overt forms of peer victimization: A multi-informant approach. *Journal of Consulting and Clinical Psychology, 66,* 337-347.

Crick, N. R., & Grotpeter, J. K. (1996). Children's treatment by peers: Victims of relational and overt aggression. *Development and Psychopathology, 8,* 367-380.

Galdston, R. (1984). Teasing as an inducer of violence. In J. D. Call, E. Galenson, & R. R. Tyson (Eds.), *Frontiers of infant psychiatry* (pp. 237-243). New York: Basic Books.

Hackmann, A., Clark, D.M., & McManus, F. (2000). Recurrent images and early memories in social phobia. *Behaviour Research & Therapy, 38,* 601-610.

Hawker, D. S., & Boulton, M. J. (2000). Twenty years' research on peer victimization and psychosocial adjustment: A meta-analytic review of cross-sectional studies. *Journal of Child Psychology and Psychiatry and Allied Disciplines, 41,* 441-455.

Iyer, D.S. & Haslam, N. (2003). Body image and eating disturbance among South Asian-American women: The role of racial teasing. *International Journal of Eating Disorders, 34,* 142-147.

McCabe, R.E., Antony, M.M., Summerfeldt, L.J., Liss, A. & Swinson, R.P. (2003). Preliminary examination of the relationship between anxiety disorders in adults and self-reported history of teasing or bullying experiences. *Cognitive Behaviour Therapy, 32,* 187-193.

Neary, A. & Joseph, S. (1994). Peer victimization and its relationship to self-concept and depression among schoolgirls. *Personality and Individual Differences, 16,* 183-186.

Olweus, D. (1993). *Bullying at school: What we know and what we can do.* Oxford, England: Blackwell Publishers.

Roth, D., Coles, M. & Heimberg, R.G. (2002). The relationship between memories for childhood teasing and anxiety and depression in adulthood. *Journal of Anxiety Disorders, 16, 151-166.*

Storch, E. A., & Masia-Warner, C. L. (in press). The relationship of peer victimization to social anxiety and loneliness in adolescent females. *Journal of Adolescence.*

Storch, E. A., Masia-Warner, C., & Brassard, M. R. (2003). The relationship of peer victimization to social anxiety and loneliness in adolescence. *Child Study Journal, 33,* 1-18.

Storch, E. A., Nock, M. K., Masia-Warner, C., & Barlas, M. E. (2003). Peer victimization and social-psychological adjustment in Hispanic-American and African-American children. *Journal of Child and Family Studies, 12,* 439-452.

Storch, E. A., Roth, D. A., Coles, M. E., Heimberg, R. G., Bravata, E. A., & Moser, J. (in press). The measurement and impact of childhood teasing in a sample of young adults. *Journal of Anxiety Disorders.*

Thompson, J.K., Cattarin, J., Fowler, B., & Fisher, E. (1995). The Perception of Teasing Scale (POTS): A revision and extension of the Physical Appearance Related Teasing Scale (PARTS). *Journal of Personality Assessment, 65,* 146-157.

Thompson, J.K., Fabian, L.J., Moulton, D.O., Dunn, M.E. & Altabe, M.N. (1991). Development and validation of the Physical Appearance Related Teasing Scale. *Journal of Personality Assessment, 56,* 513-521.

Vessey, J. A., Duffy, M., O'Sullivan P., & Swanson, M. (2003). Assessing teasing in school-age youth. *Issues in Comprehensive Pediatric Nursing, 26,* 1-11.

In: *Focus on Aggression Research*
Editor: James P. Morgan, pp. 59-74

Chapter 5

WHEN BAD DEEDS ARE FORGIVEN: JUDGMENTS OF MORALITY AND FORGIVENESS FOR INTERGROUP AGGRESSION[*]

Michael J. A. Wohl
Carleton University
Glenn D. Reeder
Illinois State University

INTRODUCTION

In general, aggression tends to be frowned upon. Mummendey and colleagues (Mummendey & Otten, 1993; Otten, Mummendey, & Wenzel, 1995) have convincingly argued, however, that not all aggressive acts are created equal. For example, negative judgments will be minimized if the harmful act was committed accidentally (Lysak, Rule, & Dobbs, 1989). Yet even when aggression is intentional, perceivers may react differently depending on the motives that are attributed to the perpetrator (Reeder, Kumar, Hesson-McInnis, & Trafimow, 2002). The present research extended this line of inquiry by asking the following question: How are perceivers' judgments influenced by the group membership of the aggressor (Brewer, 1979; Tajfel & Turner, 1986)? Participants in the current research were asked to judge an aggressor who was described as either a member of their own group or as a member of a rival group. We explored the possibility that group membership may affect inferences about the perpetrator's level of morality and the extent to which the perpetrator could be forgiven for the aggression.

Before reviewing social psychological theories that bear on the effect of group membership, we will offer a brief introduction to the two main dependent variables under

---

[*] The research was supported in part by a Social Sciences and Humanities Research Council of Canada Doctoral Fellowship (#752-2000-1333) to the first author while completing his doctorate at the University of Alberta. Address correspondence to Michael J. A. Wohl, Department of Psychology, Carleton University, 1125 Colonel By Drive, B550 Loeb Building, Ottawa, Ontario, Canada K1S 5B6. Email: michael_wohl@carleton.ca

study—judgments of morality and forgiveness. Judgments about morality are of central importance in person perception (Wojciszke, 1994; Wojciszke, Bazinska, & Jaworski, 1998). In fact, such judgments dominate the global evaluative judgments we make about others. Like judgments of morality, judgments of forgiveness have a strong evaluative tone and are important for a number of reasons. First and foremost, forgiveness is functional. When one person transgresses against another damage is done to the relationship. The act of forgiveness allows the relationship to move forward following the occurrence of a transgression (Minow, 1998). That is, forgiveness provides the opportunity for reconciliation and the possibility for the relationship to return to its pre-transgression state. Perhaps more importantly, a transgressed party may choose the path of forgiveness in order to let go of the negative feelings associated with the transgression. Doing so enables a movement towards a normal life without the weight of the transgression as an impediment (Dorff, 1998; Rowe & Halling, 1998). When aggression occurs between groups of people, forgiveness precludes harboring negative feelings toward members of the group that committed the harmful behaviors and more generally to the perpetrator group as a whole (Tutu, 1999; Wohl & Branscombe, 2004).

We suspect that there is a distinction between willingness to forgive and inferences of morality. Inferences of morality tend to be relatively rule-bound and objective (Shafer-Landau, 1997). Perceivers may hold relatively clear guidelines about the morality of different forms of aggression and, consequently, the group membership of the perpetrator may have a limited effect on morality judgments. In contrast, willingness to forgive may be more personal and biased by self-interest. As described below, the present research allowed us to explore differences in judgments concerning morality and forgiveness.

The participants in our research read about a target person who engaged in one of several different forms of aggression. In one case the aggression was accidental, or unintentional (the target accidentally stepped on another person's reading glasses). In two additional conditions, however, the aggression was intentional. In the case of hostile aggression (Bushman & Anderson, 2001), or what we will call reactive aggression, the target person had earlier been provoked by the victim of aggression (e.g., the victim insulted the target). In contrast, in the instrumental aggression condition, the target aggressed against the victim in order to gain a reward for his own group (e.g., success in a classroom competition), at the expense of a rival group. For our purposes, the most important manipulation in the study involved the group membership variable: Participants were asked to imagine that the aggressor was a member of their own classroom group or a member of a rival group. Below we will discuss three theoretical perspectives that are relevant to the potential impact of group membership as it may affect judgments about morality and forgiveness.

THEORETICAL PERSPECTIVES ON GROUP MEMBERSHIP AS A DETERMINANT OF SOCIAL JUDGMENTS

Social Identity Theory

A fundamental premise of social identity theory (SIT) is that people tend to separate their social world into discrete categories and then situate themselves into one of these categories (Tajfel & Turner 1986). The process of categorization results in the creation of *ingroups* and *outgroups*. The effects of this process of self-categorization into social groups are well documented. Once a person views him or herself as a member of the ingroup, judgments and behavior toward ingroup members are biased in a positive direction (Brewer, 1979; Hogg & Turner 1987; Judd, Ryan & Park 1991; Schaller 1991). Tajfel and Turner (1986) have suggested that this bias is triggered by self-serving motives. In order to maintain and enhance a positive self-regard, individuals dispose themselves positively toward members of their own group and discriminate against members of other groups.

The group is also a tool for personal survival (Stevens & Fiske, 1995) because it enhances the likelihood of reaching desired goals for the individual members (Baumeister & Leary, 1995). Thus, anyone who threatens the efficacy of the group also threatens each individual member (Caporael, 2001; Caporael & Brewer, 1991; Darby & Schlenker, 1989). It follows, that within the context of intergroup conflict, when outgroup members threaten the efficacy of the ingroup, those outgroup members should be judged in a relatively harsh manner. According to this logic, moral judgments about an aggressor from the outgroup should be more negative than those for an aggressor from the ingroup. Moreover, perceivers should be less willing to forgive an aggressor from the outgroup.

Within the context of our research, it is useful to distinguish between a strong version of SIT predictions and a weaker version. The strong version of SIT predicts that inferences of morality and forgiveness should be more negative for an outgroup aggressor (relative to an ingroup aggressor), regardless of the type of aggression committed. In contrast, a weak version of SIT would predict that discriminatory judgments about an outgroup aggressor should depend on the type of aggression and the type of judgment involved. First, judgments about the outgroup should be relatively more negative (compared to the ingroup) in the case of instrumental aggression, as opposed to accidental aggression or reactive aggression. This should occur because an outgroup member's instrumental aggression puts the ingroup at a competitive disadvantage, which should be particularly threatening. Second, discriminatory perceptions of the outgroup aggressor should be most evident on the measure of forgiveness, as opposed to morality. This should occur because judgments of forgiveness may be less objective, and presumably more subject to bias, compared to judgments of morality.

The Black Sheep Effect

According to research on the so-called black sheep effect, a misbehaving ingroup member can be considered a serious threat to the group (Marques, Abrams, & Serodio, 2001; Marques & Yzerbyt, 1988; Marques, Yzerbyt, & Leyens, 1988). The group strives to see itself as moral and just. A deviant member of the ingroup, whose behavior crosses clear moral boundaries, could threaten the group's identity. Findings from this research suggest that social perceivers sometimes judge misbehaving ingroup members more extremely than they do equally misbehaving outgroup members. Because aggression is ordinarily considered deviant (at least in a classroom setting), this perspective suggests that perceivers might react more negatively to an aggressor from the ingroup, as opposed to an aggressor from the outgroup. Moreover, given that instrumental aggression tends to be perceived more negatively than other forms of aggression (Reeder et al., 2002), instrumental aggression by an ingroup member might lead to particularly harsh judgments about the aggressor.

Note, however, the black sheep effect is not inconsistent with a broad view of social identity theory. According to both perspectives, the members of the group are motivated to protect and enhance the ingroup. Yet, the black sheep perspective emphasizes that such ends are sometimes best served by rejecting a deviant ingroup member. That is, in order to maintain a positive social identity, at times, it is important to distance the group from certain misbehaving ingroup members.

The Perceived Motives Perspective

Even the most casual observer of human nature is aware of the importance of perceived motives in social interaction. Was your girlfriend intentionally trying to upset you by being late? Did your classmate cheat because he needed a passing grade to stay on the school football team? Not surprisingly, concepts related to the perception of intention and motive play an important role within fields such as developmental psychology (Lillard, 1998; Piaget, 1932) and language comprehension (Zwaan & Radvansky, 1998). Yet within social psychology, the study of perceived motives has received relatively little attention (Malle, 1999; 2001; McClure, 2002; Read & Miller, 1993; Reeder, Vonk, Ronk, Ham, & Lawrence, 2004). The difference between intentionality and motive is subtle (Malle, 1999). Intentionality concerns whether an act was voluntary (as opposed to accidental). In contrast, a motive describes the specific aim of an intentional act. For instance, if your fiancé deliberately left the wedding party standing at the altar for over an hour, you would want to know her motives. In turn, inferences about motive can be important for inferring the dispositional characteristics of the target person (Reeder et al., 2004). In our research, we were particularly interested in the possibility that perceived motives may mediate perceivers' judgments concerning morality and forgiveness the target.

Perceivers may infer different motives as underlying reactive aggression and instrumental aggression, both of which are intentional forms of aggression (Reeder et al., 2002). Reactive aggression involves a response to provocation. For example, suppose a boy named Vince insults John by calling him names and preventing him from joining a baseball game on the playground. John might retaliate with his fists in a state of frustration. Perceivers are likely to focus on self-defense and revenge as possible motives for the aggression. In contrast, instrumental aggression involves aggression that is committed as a means of obtaining a reward. For instance, imagine that John punched Vince in the arm so as to prevent Vince from being an effective pitcher on the opposing baseball team. Perceivers are likely to focus on the fact that John could gain from his aggression toward Vince.

With regard to the group membership variable, the predictions of the motives perspective are not in conflict with the predictions of SIT or the black sheep perspective. Rather, the motives perspective directs attention to the possibility that group membership may lead perceivers to attribute different motives to an aggressor. Indirect evidence for this possibility comes from studies of the perceptions held by the victims of transgressions versus the perpetrators of those transgressions. Compared to the perpetrators, the victims tend to cite self-serving motives as underlying the perpetrator's acts (Baumeister, Stillwell, & Wotman, 1990; Stillwell & Baumeister, 1997). More generally, perceivers tend to be especially attentive to the motive of self-interest in others (Miller, 1999), perhaps seeing that motive as a more important explanation for other's behavior than their own behavior (Ross & Ward, 1996). The motives perspective suggests that to the extent ingroup and outgroup members attribute aggression to different motives, judgments of morality and forgiveness should vary accordingly.

AN EMPIRICAL TEST

In order to test our hypotheses, we had participants read a short vignette about a student who broke another student's glasses either accidentally (e.g., the target person stepped on the glasses by mistake) or intentionally (e.g., the target deliberately stepped on the glasses) during a chemistry class. When the act was intentional, the aggression was portrayed as either an instance of reactive aggression or instrumental aggression. Participants (N = 134) were told to imagine how they would feel if the events described actually happened during one of their own classes.

Participants read that the professor announced that he would split the class into two teams. He then told the class that each team would be given some substances in both solid and liquid form and that they were to perform an experiment in which each team was to distill all substances and identify the chemicals. He said the team that completed the experiment first would receive 10 bonus marks and be given the next class off. In contrast, the slower team would be required to redo the experiment.

Participants in the reactive aggression conditions read that, during the course of the class, a member of your team [the other team] named Shawn and a member of the other team [your team] named Jason found themselves going for the same chemistry instrument. Shawn then pushed Jason with both hands and verbally degraded the other team. Participants in the instrumental aggression condition were told that Shawn, the smartest student in class, was assigned to your team [the other team]. In all six conditions, the participants then read that Shawn (who was either a member of the participant's team or the other team) splashed some chemicals on his chin by accident and went to the restroom to wash his face leaving his glasses on a table by the door. In instrumental and reactive aggressive conditions, participants read that Jason left his team and walked quietly over to where Shawn had left his glasses. When no one was looking, Jason nudged the glasses off the table and deliberately stepped on them, breaking the lenses. The accidental condition, in contrast, described Jason as walking over to the table where Shawn's glasses were, but failing to notice them. He attempted to move the table, which was in his way. In the process, the glasses fall to the floor and Jason stepped on them unintentionally.

Perceived Motives

One of our primary concerns was to determine the kinds of motives that are perceived to underlie reactive and instrumental aggression (means and standard deviations for all motive measures reported in Table 1). We asked participants to rate the extent to which the aggressive behavior was due to several motivating factors (revenge, self-defense, better chance to win). These items included the following: "Jason was seeking revenge when he broke Shawn's glasses" anchored at (1) *strongly disagree* and (10) *strongly agree*; "Jason was motivated by self-defense when he broke Shawn's glasses" anchored at (1) *strongly disagree* and (10) *strongly agree*; and "Jason stood to gain by breaking Shawn's glasses" anchored at

(1) *strongly disagree* and (10) *strongly agree*. A series of ANOVAs revealed only a main effect of aggression for the first two items, $Fs < .001$. We anticipated that participants would perceive the motives of revenge and self-defense as most relevant to the reactive aggression condition. As expected, Tukey's HSD post-hoc t-tests revealed that participants perceived Jason as acting out of revenge more in the reactive aggression condition ($M = 8.85$) than in either the instrumental ($M = 4.31$) or accidental aggression ($M = 1.66$) conditions, $ps < .001$ (there was also a significant difference between instrumental and accidental aggression conditions, $p < .001$). In addition, participants gave stronger ratings to the motive of self-defense in the reactive aggression condition ($M = 3.98$) than the instrumental ($M = 2.79$) or accidental aggression ($M = 1.68$) conditions, $ps < .02$ (there was also a significant difference between instrumental and accidental aggression conditions, $p < .03$).

Table 1. Perceived Motive for the Aggressive Act as a
Function of Aggression and Group Membership: Experiment 1

Measure	Accidental Aggression		Reactive Aggression		Instrumental Aggression	
	Ingroup	Outgroup	Ingroup	Outgroup	Ingroup	Outgroup
Revenge						
M	1.95	1.38	8.75	8.96	4.95	3.67
SD	1.16	0.65	2.31	1.85	3.24	1.96
Self-Defense						
M	1.86	1.50	4.17	3.78	2.33	3.24
SD	1.24	0.93	2.25	2.17	2.39	2.39
Selfish Gain						
M	4.38	3.75	3.88	3.74	5.05	7.67
SD	2.58	2.79	3.21	3.26	3.57	2.12

Note: Higher numbers on each item signify greater attribution to that attribute on a scale of 1 to 10.

We anticipated that perceived motivation to gain would be most relevant to the instrumental aggression condition. Analysis of variance revealed a significant main affect of aggressive scenario, $F(2, 128) = 9.69$, $p < .001$. Participants in the instrumental aggression conditions believed that Jason was motivated by gain more ($M = 6.36$) than did those participants in either the reactive ($M = 3.81$) or accidental aggression conditions ($M = 4.04$), $ps > .001$. The latter two conditions did not differ significantly from one another, $p > .90$. Of greater interest, a significant aggressive scenario by team interaction emerged, $F(2, 128) = 3.75$, $p < .03$. This interaction is produced by the combination of Jason committing an act of instrumental aggression and being on the other team. In this situation, participants perceived Jason as having a lot to gain from acting aggressively toward Shawn. This is confirmed by post-hoc tests using one-way ANOVAs performed at each level of aggressive scenario. Participants in the instrumental aggression condition indicated that Jason had more to gain when he was on the other team ($M = 7.67$) than when he was on the participants' own team ($M = 5.05$), $F(1, 40) = 8.34$, $p < .007$. Ratings of harm did not differ between the reactive or accidental aggression conditions regardless of which team Jason was on, $ps > .43$. Implications for this interaction will be addressed in the discussion.

Perceived Morality and Willingness to Forgive

Two items measured inferences of morality: "How moral do you think Jason is?" anchored at (1) *very immoral* and (10) *very moral*; and "I think that Jason is a moral person" (1) *strongly disagree* and (10) *strongly agree*. The items were significantly correlated, $p < .001$, and were thus combined into an overall morality score. A two-way ANOVA yielded only a main effect of aggressive scenario, $F(2, 127) = 48.46$, $p < .001$(see Table 2 for means and standard deviations). Tukey's HSD post-hoc test revealed that Jason was rated more moral in the accidental condition ($M = 6.97$) than in either the reactive aggression ($M = 4.28$) or instrumental aggression ($M = 3.04$) conditions, $ps < .001$. Also as expected, Jason was perceived to be more moral in the reactive aggression conditions than in the instrumental aggression condition, $p < .007$. Finally, the group membership variable produced no significant effects on the measure of perceived morality.

Table 2. Judgments of Morality and Willingness to Forgive an Aggressive Target Person as a Function of Aggression and Group Membership: Study 1

Measure	Accidental Aggression		Reactive Aggression		Instrumental Aggression	
	Ingroup	**Outgroup**	**Ingroup**	**Outgroup**	**Ingroup**	**Outgroup**
Morality						
M	6.81	7.11	4.17	4.39	2.79	3.29
SD	2.08	1.53	2.18	2.19	1.62	1.60
Forgiveness						
M	7.90	8.33	6.21	6.14	6.71	4.80
SD	1.80	1.50	2.03	2.38	1.39	2.37

Note: Higher numbers on each item signify greater attribution to that attribute on a scale of 1 to 10.

In addition to perceptions of morality, the two items that were included to test participant's willingness to forgive Jason for his aggressive act were highly correlated, $p <.001$, and thus combined: "How willing would you be to forgive Jason for breaking Shawn's glasses?" anchored at (1) *Not at all willing* and (10) *very willing*; and "Jason should be forgiven for his actions" anchored at (1) *strongly disagree* and (10) *strongly agree*. ANOVA revealed a significant aggressive scenario main effect, $F(2, 126) = 18.47$, $p < .001$ (see Table 2 for means and standard deviations). Tukey's HSD post-hoc test revealed that participants were more willing to forgive in the accidental aggression condition ($M = 8.12$) than in the reactive ($M = 6.17$) or instrumental aggression ($M = 5.76$) conditions, $p < .001$. Of greater interest, this effect, was qualified by an aggressive scenario by team interaction, $F(2, 126) = 4.27$, $p < .02$. This interaction was driven by the condition in which instrumental aggression was committed by a member of the outgroup. In this situation, participants were unforgiving of the aggressor ($M = 4.80$), as compared to the other conditions ($M = 7.06$), $p < .001$. In particular, it appears that although instrumental aggression by an ingroup member was forgiven ($M = 6.71$), comparable aggression by an out group member was not forgiven ($M = 4.80$), $F(1, 39) = 10.10$, $p < .001$. When the aggression was reactive or by accident, willingness to forgive did not differ by group membership, $ps > .38$.

In the introduction of this article, we noted that perceivers may be highly attuned to the motive of self-interest in others (Miller, 1999; Ross & Ward, 1996). Likewise, the social identity perspective suggests that perceivers may be very sensitive to information about an outsider taking advantage of the group (cheating). As a result, they may find it hard to forgive an outsider who directed instrumental aggression at one of their own, thereby putting their group at a disadvantage. One of our measures of perceived motives is relevant to this issue. As described earlier, participants rated the extent that Jason (and presumably his group) was motivated by gain. We conducted an analysis to determine if perceived gain mediated the effect of group membership on forgiveness for instrumental aggression. We used the procedure described by Baron and Kenny (1986). Separate regression equations revealed that the team manipulation was predictive of both willingness to forgive, $B = 0.45$, $t(39) = 3.18$, $p < .004$, and perceptions of gain, $B = -0.42$, $t(40) = -2.89$, $p < .007$, respectively. However, when the team manipulation and perceptions of gain were examined simultaneously as predictors of willingness to forgive, the effect of perceptions of gain remained significant, $B = -.40$, $t(38) = -2.78$, $p < .003$, whereas the effect of the team manipulation was reduced to nonsignificance, $B = 0.29$, $t(38) = 2.00$, $p > .05$. This pattern suggests that perceptions of gain mediated the effect of group membership on willingness to forgive for acts of instrumental aggression.

DISCUSSION

Perhaps the most interesting of the above findings involve the effect of group membership within the instrumental aggression condition. In this condition, perceivers demonstrated a high level of objectivity when offering judgments about the morality of the aggressor. That is, ratings of the morality of the ingroup aggressor were low and quite similar to ratings for the outgroup aggressor. But willingness to forgive proved to be less objective. Perceivers were willing to forgive instrumental aggression at the hands of a member of the ingroup, but they were relatively unforgiving of comparable aggression by an outgroup member. Inferences about motives apparently underlie these patterns of judgment. Most tellingly, perceivers were quick to spot the motive of self-interest in the outgroup aggressor and inferences about this motive mediated the different levels of forgiveness felt for the ingroup aggressor and outgroup aggressor.

Overall, the results tend to support both the perceived motives perspective and the weak version of SIT. In particular, inferences about perceived intentions and motives explain many of the findings of Study 1. First, participants provided higher ratings of morality and were more willing to forgive accidental aggression than intentional aggression. Second, within the category of intentional aggressive behavior, perceivers reacted more positively to reactive aggression than to instrumental aggression. Third, inferences about motive appear to underlie the different reactions to reactive aggression and instrumental aggression. Reactive aggression was attributed to the motives of revenge and self-defense, whereas instrumental aggression was attributed to the motive of personal gain. Finally, inferences about motives tended to mediate judgments about morality and willingness to forgive the perpetrator.

The weak version of SIT implies that discrimination toward the outgroup should be selective and most apparent for judgments of forgiveness as it pertains to instrumental aggression. This model also received support. Rather than demonstrating a blanket level of discrimination toward the outgroup, perceivers discriminated only against an outgroup member who committed instrumental aggression. That is, relative to their ratings of an ingroup member, perceivers inferred greater self-interest on the part of the outgroup aggressor and found it harder to forgive the aggression. But ratings of other motives and ratings of morality showed no evidence of differing as a function of the aggressor's group membership. Taken as a whole, these findings are less supportive of the strong version of SIT (which predicts more widespread discrimination toward the outgroup) and the black sheep effect (which predicts that ratings should be more negative for the ingroup aggressor than the outgroup aggressor).

A SECOND EMPIRICAL TEST

Although the findings of Study 1 are clear-cut, we are hesitant to generalize the results to other situations without further investigation. Perhaps instrumental aggression by an outgroup aggressor is more forgivable in other situational contexts. In order to investigate this issue, Study 2 introduces a new context for the aggressive behavior. The scenarios described in Study 2 reflect aggression in the context of a sporting event as opposed to a classroom setting. The scenarios in Study 2 described a soccer game in which one of the players was spiked by an opposing player's cleat. Once again, the harmdoer was described as being a member of the ingroup or a member of the outgroup. Instrumental aggression in the context of sports is relatively common, even when it is against the rules of the game. It is possible, therefore, that perceivers may be more objective in their feelings of forgiveness in this context and less likely to favor the ingroup.

One of our aims was to compare the explanatory power of the strong SIT, weak SIT, and black sheep perspectives. Once again, the strong SIT predicts a broad level of discrimination in favor of the ingroup. The weak form of SIT, in contrast, predicts a more selective pattern of discrimination that occurs for judgments of forgivenesss only within the instrumental aggression condition. Finally, recall that the black sheep perspective implies that deviant aggression by an ingroup member should lead to harsher judgments than similar behavior by an outgroup member.

To provide a stronger test of our hypotheses, we replaced the accidental aggression with a new condition in which the aggression was gratuitous, being neither reactive nor instrumental in any obvious sense. Rather, in the gratuitous aggression condition, there appeared to be no good reason for the aggression. Within the context of the gratuitous aggression condition, the black sheep effect might receive more support. In our original test, perhaps the aggression in the instrumental and reactive aggression conditions was not deviant enough to justify derogating an ingroup member. If, however, the aggression is truly deviant, perceivers may be more likely to judge a misbehaving ingroup member harshly. Indeed, gratuitous aggression would seem to be deviant, regardless of the group membership of the perpetrator.

To assess perceiver's reactions to an aggressor who was described as an ingroup member or an outgroup member, we asked undergraduate students enrolled in introductory psychology at the University of Alberta ($N = 122$) to read about a target person (Jason) who deliberately hurt another player (Shawn). The transgression occurred when Jason spiked Shawn with his cleat during a particular soccer match. Once again, an important manipulation was whether Jason was described as a member of the participant's team or as a member of the opposing team.

In the reactive aggression conditions participants read that during a soccer match, Shawn, a player from the opposing team [your team], intentionally bumped into Jason causing Jason to cry out in pain. Shawn then made a rude sign at Jason. Conversely, in the instrumental aggression conditions Shawn was playing exceptionally well. It was clear that your team [the opponent's team member] could not win with Shawn in the game. Participants in the Gratuitous aggression condition where not given a context for the aggression.

In all conditions participants were told, later in the game Jason and Shawn where both going for the soccer ball when Jason lost his footing. He found himself in the air coming down on Shawn. Jason could either hurt Shawn by spiking him with his cleat or turn away and avoid hurting him, but instead decided to spike Shawn. Immediately following the description of the situation and behavior, participants rated Jason on a series of 10 point scale items.

Perceived Motives

We expected that the harmdoer in the reactive aggression condition would be perceived as strongly motivated by revenge and self-defense. Indeed, participants perceived these motives as strong in the reactive aggression condition. That is, participants indicated that Jason was motivated by revenge more in the reactive aggression condition ($M = 6.38$) than in either the instrumental ($M = 2.25$) or gratuitous aggression ($M = 2.80$) conditions, $ps < .001$ (there was no significant difference between instrumental and gratuitous aggression, $p > .42$). In addition, participants reported that Jason was acting in self-defense more in the reactive aggression condition ($M = 7.12$) than in either the instrumental ($M = 5.28$) or gratuitous aggression ($M = 4.30$) conditions, $ps < .002$ (there was no significant difference between instrumental and gratuitous aggression, $p < .11$).

Once gain, we expected that the harmdoer in the instrumental condition would be perceived as strongly motivated by personal (or team) gain. ANOVA revealed a significant main affect of aggressive scenario, $F(2, 116) = 19.52$, $p < .001$ (see Table 3 for means and standard deviations). Participants in the instrumental aggression conditions believed that Jason stood more to gain by harming Shawn ($M = 8.03$) than did those participants in either the reactive aggression ($M = 5.62$) or the gratuitous aggression conditions ($M = 5.55$), $ps > .001$, with the latter two conditions not differing from one another. There was also a main effect of team, $F(1, 116) = 6.55$, $p < .02$, and an aggressive scenario by team interaction, $F(2, 116) = 3.09$, $p < .05$. When Jason was a member of the outgroup participants believed that he stood more to gain from hurting Shawn ($M = 6.87$) than when Jason was a member of the ingroup ($M = 5.93$). The main effects, of course, are qualified by the interaction. The interaction was produced by two changes across team and aggressive scenario. Once again, participants in the instrumental aggression condition indicated that Jason had more to gain when he was on the other team ($M = 8.65$) than when he was on the participants' own team ($M = 7.40$), $F(1, 38) = 4.66$, $p < .04$. Second, participants in the reactive aggression condition also reported that Jason had more to gain when he was on the other team ($M = 6.55$) than when he was on the participant's own team ($M = 4.68$), $F(1, 40) = 11.10$, $p < .003$. Ratings of perceived gain did not differ in the two gratuitous aggression conditions, $F < 1$.

Table 3. Perceived Motive for the Aggressive Act as a
Function of Aggression and Group Membership: Study 2

Measure	Reactive Aggression		Instrumental Aggression		Gratuitous Aggression	
	Ingroup	Outgroup	Ingroup	Outgroup	Ingroup	Outgroup
Revenge						
M	6.41	6.35	1.75	2.75	2.90	2.70
SD	1.14	1.04	1.37	2.84	2.29	2.23
Self-Defense						
M	7.05	7.20	5.20	5.35	4.60	4.00
SD	1.53	0.89	1.88	2.25	3.00	2.88
Selfish Gain						
M	4.68	6.55	7.40	8.65	5.70	5.40
SD	1.67	1.96	2.37	1.04	2.45	2.32

Note: Higher numbers on each item signify greater attribution to that attribute on a scale of 1 to 10.

Perceived Morality and Willingness to Forgive

Jason's morality was perceived to be higher in the reactive aggression conditions ($M = 7.37$) than in either the instrumental aggression ($M = 5.29$) or gratuitous aggression conditions ($M = 2.71$), $ps < .001$ (see table 4 for means and standard deviations). Also as expected, Jason's morality was perceived to be higher in the instrumental aggression conditions than in the gratuitous aggression conditions, $p < .001$. Participants were also more willing to forgive in both the reactive ($M = 4.24$) and instrumental aggression conditions ($M = 4.43$) than in the gratuitous aggression conditions ($M = 2.44$), $ps < .001$ (see Table 3 for means and standard deviations). As in our first empirical test, this effect was qualified, however, by an aggressive scenario by team interaction, $F(2, 116) = 4.94$, $p < .01$. The interaction was produced by the condition in which Jason committed an act of instrumental aggression. Jason's instrumental aggression was forgiven more when he was on the perceivers own team ($M = 5.25$) than when he was on the other team ($M = 3.60$), $F(1, 38) = 9.36$, $p < .005$. When the aggression was reactive or gratuitous, willingness to forgive did not differ by Jason's team, $ps > .1$. At a descriptive level, it is worth noting that the lowest level of forgiveness in the design occurred when Jason committed gratuitous aggression as an ingroup member. Although the direction of this trend is certainly consistent with the predictions of the black sheep effect, the effect of group membership fell short of statistical significance in the gratuitous aggression condition, $F(1,38) = 2.60$, $p > .11$.

Once again, we sought to determine if perceptions of personal gain mediated willingness to forgive in the instrumental aggression condition. Separate regression equations revealed that the team manipulation was predictive of both willingness to forgive, $B = -0.44$, $t(38) = -3.06$, $p < .005$, and perceptions of gain, $B = 0.33$, $t(38) = 2.16$, $p < .04$, respectively. However, when the team manipulation and perceptions of gain were examined simultaneously as predictors of willingness to forgive, the effect of perceptions of gain remained significant, $B = -0.68$, $t(37) = -6.29$, $p < .001$, whereas the effect of the team manipulation was reduced to nonsignificance, $B = -0.22$, $t(37) = -2.02$, $p > .05$. Thus, perceived gain mediated the effect of our team manipulation on willingness to forgive (Baron & Kenny, 1986). As in Study 1, our evidence suggests that perceptions of gain mediated the effect of group membership on willingness to forgive for acts of instrumental aggression.

Table 4. Judgments of Morality and Willingness to Forgive an Aggressive
Target Person as a Function of Aggression and Group Membership: Study 2

Measure	Reactive Aggression		Instrumental Aggression		Gratuitous Aggression	
	Ingroup	Outgroup	Ingroup	Outgroup	Ingroup	Outgroup
Morality						
M	7.07	7.70	5.32	5.26	2.65	2.78
SD	0.92	0.97	1.64	1.82	1.61	1.48
Forgiveness						
M	4.36	4.10	5.25	3.60	2.00	2.88
SD	1.98	1.92	1.71	1.70	1.08	2.18

Note: Higher numbers on each item signify greater attribution to that attribute on a scale of 1 to 10.

Understanding Emotional Responses to Intergroup Aggression

A classic study by Hastorf and Cantril (1954) demonstrated bias relevant to the perception of aggression by ingroup and outgroup members. The researchers studied reactions to a particularly contentious football game between the universities of Dartmouth and Princeton. After the game, the researchers asked students from both schools to view films of the action on the field in an effort to identify rule infractions. The students' reports demonstrated an ingroup serving bias: Princeton students saw twice as many infractions by Dartmouth players as the Dartmouth students did. Subsequent research suggests that bias in favor of the ingroup can take many forms (Brewer, 1979; Tajfel & Turner, 1986). The present results contribute to this literature in two respects. First, group-biased reactions to an aggressor can be quite selective. For example, perceivers were more willing to forgive instrumental aggression by an ingroup member than by an outgroup member, yet reactions to other forms of aggression did not vary according to group membership. Related to this selectivity, judgments about the morality of the aggressor showed more objectivity, being unaffected by group membership. Second, inferences about the motives that underlie aggression played a crucial role in these reactions.

The importance of perceived motives is evident in several aspects of the research. In our first study, the target aggressor was judged more moral when the aggression was accidental then when the aggression was intentional. However, within the category of intentional aggression, participants judged the aggressor as being more moral if the aggression was reactive in nature as opposed to instrumental. Furthermore, participants evaluated the morality of an aggressor by considering the underlying motives for aggression. That is, an aggressor was judged as relatively moral if the behavior was perceived as motivated by revenge or self-defense (motives which were associated with reactive aggression). If, however, the behavior was perceived as motivated by selfish reasons (a motive which was associated with instrumental aggression), the aggressor was judged as relatively immoral. In our second study, we eliminated the accidental aggression condition and replaced it with a gratuitous aggression condition. In this gratuitous aggression condition there was no obvious motive for committing the aggressive act. The results of our second study closely resembled those of our first study. Participants once again judged an aggressor who committed reactive aggression as being more moral than an aggressor who committed instrumental aggression and, not surprisingly, the target person in the gratuitous aggression condition was judged most harshly.

The Influence of Group Membership on Judgments of Morality and Forgiveness

The results of our two studies clearly suggest that judgments of morality and willingness to forgive an aggressor are not symmetrical. A judgment of morality is apparently more objective than is the willingness to forgive. In other words, there appears to be a loose connection between these two types of judgments. In our second study, one could imagine an ingroup member saying, "Sure what my teammate did was wrong, but he did it for the good of the team." When Jason hurt the other team's best player, his ingroup benefited by improving their odds of winning the soccer match. Thus, perhaps participants understood that the aggressive act was immoral, but because it benefited their team, they were willing to forgive the act. An alternative angle on the results is that participants were particularly upset by aggression from the outgroup because it placed their own team at a disadvantage. Supporting this latter line of reasoning, participants cited personal gain as a more important motive for the outgroup aggressor than the ingroup aggressor (Miller, 1999; Ross & Ward, 1996). When reacting to an aggressor from the outgroup, then, participants seem to be saying, "That guy took advantage of us. I can't forgive him for it".

We have drawn a distinction between strong and weak versions of SIT. The strong version of SIT predicts that inferences of morality and forgiveness should be more negative for an outgroup aggressor than an ingroup aggressor, regardless of the type of aggression committed. Conversely, the weak version of SIT predicts that discriminatory judgments about an outgroup aggressor should depend on the type of aggression and the type of judgment involved. Results from our two studies support the weak version over the strong version of SIT. In our scenarios, people were willing to forgive outgroup members if their aggressive acts were seen as being the result of an accident or the result of prior provocation.

Finally, there is little evidence for the black sheep effect (Marques & Yzerbyt, 1988) in these studies. Although we investigated reactions to a variety of different types of aggression, there was no clear evidence that participants were particularly upset over the aggression of an ingroup member. In fact, even when aggression was clearly deviant, as in the gratuitous aggression condition of Study 2, participant ratings of neither morality nor forgiveness varied significantly for the ingroup and outgroup aggressor.

Caveat

In our studies, as in any studies using vignettes, one has to introduce a note of caustion when discussing the findings. The vignettes we employed represent hypothetical situations designed to elicit judgments of an aggressive target. It is conceivable there may be a difference between the judgments made by members of a real group and those who role-play. In particular, the perceptions of real group members may be more emotionally-driven and display greater support for the strong version of SIT. It is also conceivable that the vignettes may have elicited a random response from participants. Responses to our vignettes were influenced by some of the same factors as have been shown in other studies (Reeder et al., 2002). This pattern suggests that the responses reported here are far from random.

CONCLUSION

Stevens and Fiske (1995) noted that the group is a tool for personal survival because it helps us to achieve our goals (Baumeister & Leary, 1995). Therefore, when an outgroup threatens ingroup efficacy, the outgroup is judged harshly (cf., Wohl & Branscombe, 2004). Conversely, when an ingroup member aggresses to aid group efficacy, the ingroup member should be lauded. That is, if people perceive an outgroup to be trying to gain a competitive advantage over the ingroup, judgments of morality and forgiveness will be relatively harsh. People don't like to see a competing group make gains (i.e., through instrumental aggression) at the expense of the ingroup. In contrast, when the ingroup gains an unfair advantage over an outgroup, people may realize the immorality of the actions, but forgive nonetheless. Why? We view the world through the lens of our group membership. If the actions of ingroup members help their group succeed, all will be perceived as "fair in love and war."

REFERENCES

Baumeister, R. F., & Leary, M. R. (1995). The need to belong: Desire for interpersonal attachments as a fundamental human motivation. *Psychological Bulletin, 117,* 497-529.

Baumeister, R. F., Sillwell, A., & Wotman, S. R. (1990). Victim and perpetrator accounts of interpersonal conflict: Autobiographical narratives about anger. *Journal of Personality and Social Psychology, 59,* 994-1005.

Brewer, M. B. (1979). In-group bias in the minimal intergroup situation: A cognitive-motivational analysis. *Psychological Bulletin, 86,* 307-324.

Bushman, B. J., & Anderson, C. A. (2001). Is it time to pull the plug on hostile versus instrumental aggression dichotomy? *Psychological Review, 108,* 273-279.

Caporael, L. R. (2001). Parts and wholes: The evolutionary importance of groups. In C. Sedikides & M. B. Brewer (Eds.). *Individual self, relational self, collective self* (pp. 241-258). Philadelphia, PA: Psychology Press/Taylor & Francis.

Caporael, L. R., & Brewer, M. B. (1991). The quest for human nature: Social and scientific issues in evolutionary psychology. *Journal of Social Issues, 47,* 1-9.

Darby, B. W., & Schlenker, B. R. (1989). Children's reactions to transgressions: Effects of the actor's apology, reputation and remorse. *British Journal of Social Psychology, 28,* 353-364.

Dorff, E. N. (1998). The elements of forgiveness: a Jewish approach. In E. L. Worthington, Jr. (Ed.), *Dimensions of Forgiveness: Psychological Research and Theological Perspectives* (pp. 29-55). Radnor, PA: Templeton Foundation Press.

Hastorf, A., & Cantril, H. (1954). They saw a game: A case study. *Journal of Abnormal and Social Psychology, 49,* 129-134,

Hogg, M. A., & Turner, J. C. (1987). Intergroup behaviour, self-stereotyping and the salience of social categories. *British Journal of Social Psychology, 26,* 325-340.

Judd, C. M., Ryan, C. S., & Park, B. (1991). Accuracy in the judgment of ingroup and outgroupvariability. *Journal of Personality and Social Psychology, 61*, 366-79.

Levine, L. J. (1996). The anatomy of disappointment: A naturalistic test of appraisal models of sadness, anger, and hope. *Cognition and Emotion, 10*, 337-359

Lillard, A. (1998). Ethnopsychologies: Cultural variations in theories of the mind. *Psychological Bulletin, 123*, 3-32.

Lysak, H., Rule, B. G., & Dobbs, A. R. (1989). Conceptions of aggression: Prototype or defining features? *Personality & Social Psychology Bulletin, 15*, 233-243.

Malle, B. F. (1999). How people explain behavior: A new theoretical framework. *Personality and Social Psychology Review, 3*, 21-43.

Malle, B. F. (2001). Folk explanations of intentional action. In B. F. Malle, L. J. Moses, & D. A. Baldwin (Eds). *Intentions and intentionality: Foundations of social cognition* (pp.265-286). Cambridge, MA: The MIT Press.

Marques, J. M., Abrams, D., & Serodio, R. G. (2001). Being better by being right: Subjective dynamics and derogation of in-group deviants when generic norms are undermined. *Journal of Personality and Social Psychology, 81*, 436-447.

Marques, J. M., & Yzerbyt, V. Y. (1988). The black sheep effect: Judgemental extremity towards ingroup members in inter-group situations. *European Journal of Social Psychology, 18*, 287-292.

Marques, J. M, Yzerbyt, V. Y. & Leyens, J. P. (1988). The "Black Sheep Effect": Extremity of judgments towards ingroup members as a function of group identification. *European Journal of Social Psychology, 18*, 1-16.

McClure, J. (2002). Goal-based explanations of actions and outcomes. In W. Stroebe & M. Hewstone (Eds.), *European Review of Social Psychology, 12*, 201-235.

McCullough, M. E., Hoyt, W. T., & Rachel, K. C. (2000). What we know (and need to know) about assessing forgiveness constructs. In M. E. McCullough, K. I. Pargament, & C. E. Thoresen (Eds.) *Forgiveness: Theory, research, and practice* (pp. 65-68). New York: Guilford.

Miller, D. T. (1999). The norm of self-interest. *American Psychologist, 54*, 1053–1060.

Minow, M. (1998). *Between vengeance and forgiveness: Facing history after genocide and mass violence.* Boston: Beacon Press.

Mummendey, A., & Otten, S. (1993). Aggression: Interaction between individuals and social groups. In R. B. Felson & J. T. Tedeschi (Eds). *Aggression and violence: Social interactionist perspectives* (pp. 145-167). Washington, DC: American Psychological Association.

Otten, S., Mummendey, A., & Wenzel, M. (1995). Evaluation of aggressive interactions in interpersonal and intergroup contexts. *Aggressive Behavior, 21*, 205-224.

Piaget, J. (1932). *The moral judgement of the child.* New York: Free Press.

Read, S. J., & Miller, L. C. (1993). Rapist or "regular guy": Explanatory coherence in the construction of mental models of others. *Personality & Social Psychology Bulletin, 19*, 526-540.

Reeder, G. D., Kumar, S., Hesson-McInnis, M. S., & Trafimow, D. (2002). Inferences about the morality of an aggressor: The role of perceived motive. *Journal of Personality and Social Psychology, 83*, 789-803.

Reeder, G. D., Vonk, R., Ronk, M. J., Ham, J., & Lawrence, M. (2004). Dispositional Attribution: Multiple Inferences About Motive-Related Traits. *Journal of Personality and Social Psychology, 86,* 530-544.

Ross, L., & Ward, A. (1996). Naïve realism in everyday life: Implications for social conflict and misunderstanding. In E. E., Reed, E. Turiel, & T. Brown (Eds.) *Values and knowledge* (pp. 103-135). Mahwah, N.J.: Erlbaum.

Rowe, J. O., & Halling, S. (1998). Psychology of forgiveness: implications for psychotherapy. In R. Valle (Ed.) *Phenomenological Inquiry in Psychology: Existential and Transpersonal Dimensions* (pp. 227-246). New York, NY: Plenum Press.

Schaller, M. (1991). Social categorization and the formation of group stereotypes: Further evidence of biased information processing in the perception of group-behavior correlations. *European Journal of Social Psychology, 21,* 25-35.

Shafer-Landau, R. (1997). Moral rules. *Ethics, 107,* 584-611.

Stevens, L. E., & Fiske, S. T. (1995). Motivation and cognition in social life: A social survival perspective. *Social Cognition, 13,* 189-214.

Stillwell, A. M., & Baumeister, R. F. (1997). The construction of victim and perpetrator memories: Accuracy and distortion in role-based accounts. *Personality and Social Psychology Bulletin, 23,* 1157-1172.

Tajfel, H., & Turner, J. C. (1986). The social identity theory of intergroup behavior. In S. Worchel and W. G. Austin (Eds.) *Psychology of intergroup relations* (pp. 7-24). Chicago: Nelson-Hall.

Tutu, D. M. (1999). *No future without forgiveness.* New York: Doubleday.

Wohl, M. J. A., & Branscombe, N. R. (2004). Importance of social categorization for forgiveness and collective guilt assignment for the Holocaust. In N. R. Branscombe & B. Doosje (Eds.) *Collective guilt: International perspectives* (pp. 248-305). New York: Cambridge University Press.

Wojciszke, B. (1994). Multiple meanings of behavior: Construing actions in terms of competence or morality. *Journal of Personality and Social Psychology, 67,* 222-232.

Wojciszke, B., Bazinska, R., & Jaworski, M. (1998). On the dominance of moral categories in impression formation. *Personality and Social Psychology Bulletin, 24,* 1251-1263.

Zwann, R. A., & Radvansky, G. A. (1998). Situation models in language comprehension and memory. *Psychological Bulletin, 123,* 162-185.

In: *Focus on Aggression Research*
Editor: James P. Morgan, pp. 75-90

ISBN 1-59454-132-9
© 2004 Nova Science Publishers, Inc.

Chapter 6

DIMINISHED SENSE OF SELF-EXISTENCE AND AGGRESSION: THE PSYCHOLOGY OF MODERN JAPANESE YOUTHS[2]

Shintaro Yukawa
Graduate School of Comprehensive Human Sciences
University of Tsukuba

BACKGROUND

Self and Aggression of Modern Japanese Youths

The problem of children and adolescents suddenly and impulsively expressing their anger at school, known in Japanese as "*kireru*" (breaking out), has been frequently discussed in recent years in Japan (Miyashita & Ohno, 2002; Tokyo Metropolis, 1999). Together with the related juvenile delinquency problems, the "youth aggression and violence" issue has assumed major significance in Japanese society. Although there is a strong pressure to deal with the problem quickly and effectively, there are innumerable factors from the biological through to the social level that may facilitate or restrain aggression and violence. Youth aggression and violence have long been recognized as a social problem in the West, especially in the United States of America, and numerous studies and literature on aggression and violence (e.g., Moeller, 2001)have been conducted within a Western context. In contrast, empirical research on aggression in Japan remains extremely sparse. This might be due to weaker public concern about youth aggression and violence, because Japan is a comparatively non-violent society in terms of violent crime rate. For instance, Japan's annual homicide rate (i.e., the number of homicides for every 100,000 people) is about 10 times less than that of

---

[2] This paper is the revised version of the author's paper in Japanese, "Sense of Self-existence and Aggressiveness: Development of the Diminished Sense of Self-existence Scale," which appeared in the Japanese Journal of Counseling Science (Yukawa, 2002b) with permission by the Japanese Association of Counseling Science. Correspondence concerning this chapter should be addressed to Shintaro Yukawa, who is now at the Institute of Psychology, University of Tsukuba, 3-29-1 Otsuka, Bunkyo-ku, Tokyo, 112-0012 Japan. Electronic mail may be sent to Shintaro Yukawa at s-yukawa@human.tsukuba.ac.jp.

the United States, and the number of young people arrested for homicide in Japan has been steadily decreasing since the end of World War II (Research and Training Institute of the Ministry of Justice, 2001). However, as modern Japanese society has become materially prosperous and advanced information technology has spread, more diverse values have emerged, with certain social standards, functions, and norms becoming subject to change. As a consequence, it is probably extremely difficult to cope with the youth issues within an education system because of the multiplicity of values and norms. In brief, youth aggression and violence have gained public attention as a major new social problem, without any viable solutions on the horizon.

Some observers of Japanese society posit that the sense of self-existence may be diminishing among adolescents (Kageyama, 1999; Kiyonaga, 1999). They describe this phenomenon as "loss of self" (Kiyonaga, 1999) or "empty self." From a criminal sociological perspective, Kiyonaga (1999) explains that, although survival and defiance were considered as the underlying cause of juvenile delinquency between World War II and the 1980's in Japan, in the 1990's "impulse" began to be seen as the root of the problem. According to Kiyonaga, youths impulsively engage in sudden violence to express their personal emotions directly against indiscriminate targets, because they feel hollow inside: They have lost their sense of self, as well as their sense of others and of (formerly restraining) social norms. On the other hand, from a criminal psychological stance, Kageyama (1999) argues that, due to their empty and diminished self-existence, youths commit crime in order to confirm their existence. Thus, in a society where traditional values and norms are crumbling, a diminished sense of self-existence is likely to be a common psychological factor among most adolescents, with youth crime driven by a quest for self-confirmation.

In this chapter, the study conducted by the author will be presented. The main aim of the study is to examine how a diminished sense of self-existence may be empirically related to aggression and violence. Before examining the relationship between the diminished sense of self-existence and aggression, we will take a closer look at the concept of the sense of self-existence, which, hitherto, has never been clearly conceptualized in psychology.

Sense of Self-existence

It goes without saying that we perceive, experience, or discern a certain existence, a phenomenon, or an object in our daily lives on the basis of space and time (Kant, 1787/1962). If perceiving the existence of self is the same as perceiving other things and phenomena, we can presume that preserving the self also involves the temporal and spatial dimensions. To begin with, self-perception on the temporal dimension originates in the fact that we are historical beings. Specifically, we perceive or experience ourselves along a temporal dimension consisting of our past, present, and future selves. The past self is recalled from memory, the present self is perceived as alive (here and now), and the future self is the self imagined in terms of the future. Markus and Nurius (1986) also propose the concept of "the possible self." This includes our past and future selves and motivates the present real self. Thus, the perception of self-existence in terms of the *Time* dimension is related to how we understand our self on the basis of past, present, and future selves. On the other hand, perceiving the existing self from a spatial perspective can be divided into the two dimensions of internal perception and (perception of) external perception. This division is parallel to

James's (1892/1993) concepts of "pure ego - self as knower or I" and "empirical ego - self as known or me", and Buss's (1980) "private self" and "public self" in his self-consciousness theory. Internal perception is an internal, subjective and private self-perception based on focus and thoughts about one's own personal and internal world i.e., a self-understanding along the dimension of *Self*. In contrast, external perception is an external, objective and public self-perception based on one's own relation to surroundings, people, and society, i.e., a self-understanding along the dimension of *Others*. Interestingly, these three dimensions of Self, Others, and Time correspond with the negative cognitive triad (i.e., self, world, and future) characteristic as the thinking mode of depressive patients and the focus of treatment in Beck's cognitive therapy (Beck, Rush, Shaw, & Emery, 1979).

Although it is possible to consider the "perception" of our own self-existence on these three dimensions, what kind of "sense" or feeling is involved in the sense of self-existence? "*Sonzaikan*" (sense of existence) can be defined as (1) a feeling of existence that a person distinctly exists by his/her unique personality and ability, or (2) a realization that something is certainly at present (exists) (*Daijirin*; Matsumura, 1995). Based on these definitions, we can assume that the sense of self-existence is the realization of one's existence through one's unique personality and ability. We should also note here that unique personality and ability, "*mochiaji*" in Japanese, are further codified as unique abilities and good qualities in a standard Japanese dictionary (e.g., *Koujien*; Niimura, 1998). That is, the sense of existence indicates a positive realization of reasons or values for one's existence. In sum, we have good grounds for defining the sense of self-existence as "a positive sense about one's own reasons or values for existing."

We can further conjecture that the senses of self-existence on the dimensions of Self, Others, and Time are interrelated. For instance, the sense of self-existence on the Self dimension may be based on recollections of the past self and visions of the future self, and the relations and evaluations of others and the society. In addition, the feeling of existence on the Others dimension is likely to be supported by the past self and a sense of personal self-worth. External appraisals by others and one's own internal estimation are also assumed to shape individual perspectives on the present and the future. It is therefore possible to posit that these three dimensions are interconnected. If this is the case, it would be difficult to divide the sense of self-existence into the three dimensions clearly.[3] However, it is necessary to divide the sense of self-existence into the three aspects conceptually and theoretically (Beck et al., 1979; Buss, 1980; James, 1892/1993; Kant 1787/1962; Markus & Nurius, 1986) in order to reach a comprehensive theoretical understanding of the sense of self-existence.

---

[3] After gathering data, the factor analysis was performed for all items on the Diminished Sense of Self-existence Scale. On the basis of the results, it is acceptable to interpret that the scale has a one-factor structure that consists of intermingled items on each dimension, Self, Others, and Time. After the development of subscales for Self, Others, and Time dimensions, the Pearson correlation coefficients between each subscale were calculated. High correlations among subscales were observed ($r = .63$ between Self and Others, $r = .73$ between Self and Time, and $r = .59$ between Others and Time). Hence, the three dimensions, Self, Others, and Time, are likely to be closely correlated and co-vary with each other. For subsequent analysis, the principle component analyses for the 3 subscales of Self, Others, and Time will be separately performed to attach more importance to the conceptual and theoretical significance and to develop a more comprehensive framework.

The Sense of Self-existence and Identity

If we define the sense of self-existence as above, the (diminished) sense of self-existence appears to be analogous to the (diffusion of) *ego-identity* (Erikson, 1959, 1968). It is an irrefutable fact that the concept of "identity" can be interpreted in manifold ways and covers similar concepts in a complicated manner (e.g., Tatara & Yamashita, 1999). Although this indicates the ubiquity and utility of the construct of identity, it also means that the construct can obscure the focal issue. Erikson (1959, 1968) originally defined identity as a subjective sense of self-uniformity and self-continuity. Specifically, the uniformity and continuity of self consist of the internal uniformity (i.e., "I am me"), the consistency between the primary self and the self seen by others, and the temporal continuity of their selves (Erikson, 1959, 1968). If we realign Erikson's concept of identity with the argument of this paper, identity can be understood as a sense of uniformity, consistency, and continuity of self-perception on the dimensions of Self, Others, and Time. In contrast, the sense of self-existence is "a positive sense about one's reasons or values for existing on the dimensions of Self, Others, and Time." This makes it possible to assume that identity is a concept that can be defined at the level of self-perception, whereas the sense of self-existence is a construct that can be understood in terms of values related to self. In other words, the sense of self-existence is not mere self-perception, but is also comprised of reasons or values for one's own presence. However, we can further hypothesize that the sense of self-existence would be diminished if the identity were not sufficiently established. That is, if self-perception lacks a sense of unity, the sense of self-existence will be reduced. Based on this hypothesis, we can predict that a diminished sense of self-existence will be negatively correlated with the establishment of identity.

Unstable and Vulnerable Self

As diffusion and confusion are recognized as a problem related to identity (Erikson, 1968), diminution can also be considered as a problem for the sense of self-existence. We seldom question the existence of our own selves. We adapt to our reasons and values for our existence and feel content. Conversely, we contemplate the reasons or values for our existence when we feel discontented. In this case, the diminished sense of self-existence becomes a significant problem.

Although the diminished sense of self-existence is subject to individual difference, most people feel it more or less sometimes. Particularly a diminished sense of self-existence immediately follows a feeling of unstable and vulnerable self (i.e., "loss of self", Kiyonaga, 1999; or "empty self", Kageyama, 1999). That is, a person may become intensely aware of their diminished sense of self-existence as if his/her unstable and vulnerable self directly appeared outside. On the other hand, suppose an individual has an extremely strong sense of self-existence, i.e., he/she feels excessively positive about his/her own values and ability. In such cases, the sense approaches *narcissism*. We can thus infer that a diminished sense of self-existence will be negatively related with a narcissistic disposition. However, it is also possible to contend that, for a narcissistic person, an inflated self-image and excessive sense of self-existence are a psychological defense mechanism toward an unstable and vulnerable self (Kohut, 1971; Kernberg, 1975). Hence, it is important to note that the pathology of the unstable and vulnerable self can be expressed in opposing and conflicting phenomena, namely a diminished sense of self-existence and narcissistic personality.

Emotional Experience and Mental Health

Contentment and satisfaction in our daily existence depend on how rich and healthy the emotional experiences of our daily lives are. In order to achieve *mental health*, it is necessary to have the ability to perceive adequately and express (verbalize) internal affective experience, and to maintain a stable affective experience (Goldman, 1995; Pennebaker, 1997). For instance, *alexithymia* (a poor ability to perceive and express one's own state of emotion) and *emotionality* (inadequate emotional control) can lead to an unhealthy mental state and a poor feeling of self-existence. Hence, we can postulate that a diminished sense of self-existence will be positively related to alexithymia, emotionality, and mental unhealthiness.

RESEARCH ON DIMINISHED SENSE OF SELF-EXISTENCE AND AGGRESSION

In this study, the sense of self-existence is defined as "a positive sense about one's own reason or value for existing." Three scales were developed to measure the diminished senses of self-existence on the *Self*, *Others*, and *Time* dimensions. To verify the construct validity of these three scales, the relationships between the scales and establishment of identity, narcissism, alexithymia, emotionality, and mental healthiness are examined. This study also considers how the diminished sense of self-existence is connected with aggression among young people in present-day Japan.

Preliminary Research

To develop the Diminished Sense of Self-existence Scale (DSSS), preliminary research was conducted to establish items for the scale (Yukawa, 2002a). Three dimensions were set up as the standards for gathering and selecting items prior to development of the questionnaire: (a) the dimension of Self (thoughts about one's personal and internal world); (b) the dimension of Others (relationship with surroundings, other people, and society); (c) the dimension of Time (perspectives on one's past, present, and future).

Items from previous measures on self and psychology of youth that appear to be associated with the (diminished) sense of self-existence were modified to suit the scale. After adding some original items, a total of 81 items was developed for the scale (38 items for the dimension of Self, 21 items for the dimension of Others, and 22 items for the dimensions of Time)(DSSS ver.1).

This DSSS ver.1 was administered to 286 Japanese undergraduate students (115 men and 171 women) during class. The mean age of the respondents was 20.03 ($SD = 1.70$). Based on the results of the analysis of DSSS ver.1, the content and formulation of items showing response bias were re-examined and rephrased. One item was deleted from the scale. The revised scale consists of 80 items (DSSS ver.2), with 37 items for the Self dimension, 21 items for the Others dimension, and 22 items for the Time dimension.

Main Research

A total of 569 Japanese undergraduate students (337 men and 230 women, 2 of unknown sex; mean age = 19.94 and SD = 1.34) from a national university in Ibaraki Prefecture and a private university in Tokyo metropolis area voluntarily participated in the present research. The participants were asked to complete a questionnaire consisting of the group of scales shown below. The questionnaire was distributed to the participants during class, and collected unsigned so that anonymity was guaranteed.

Diminished Sense of Self-existence

The DSSS ver.2 developed in the preliminary research was used to measure the diminished sense of self-existence. As mentioned above, the scale consists of 80 items: 37 items in the Self dimension, 21 items in the Others dimension, and 22 items in the Time dimension. The items were rated on a 5-point scale (1 = *strongly disagree* to 5 = *strongly agree*).

Establishment of Identity

In order to measure an achieved level of identity, the establishment of identity scale, a subscale contained in an identity scale originally developed by Shimoyama (1992), was utilized. The scale consists of 10 items, such as "I choose to live in my own way" and "I trust myself very much." The items were rated on a 5-point scale as in the DSSS. For further analysis, the mean rating of all 10 items was calculated to obtain a composite averaged score.

Narcissism

Based on Raskin and Hall's (1979) Narcissistic Personality Inventory (NPI), Oshio (1999) developed a shorter version of the scale in Japanese to measure narcissism (Narcissistic Personality Inventory–Short Version; NPI-S). Through factor analysis, Oshio found that the NPI-S is comprised of three subscales, *a sense of superiority and competence*, *a need for attention and praise*, and *self-assertion*. For the present study, three items with the highest factor loadings were selected from each subscale. The total number of items employed was 9 (3 x 3). The items were rated on a 5-point scale as in the DSSS. The mean ratings of the items on each subscale were calculated to obtain 3 types of composite averaged scores.

Alexithymia

Goto, Kodama, and Sasaki (1999) originally developed a Japanese scale for measuring alexithymia based on the TAS (Toronto Alexithymia Scale; Taylor, Ryan, & Bagby, 1985) and SSPS (Schalling-Sifneos Personality Scale; Apfel & Sifneos, 1979). One of the two subscales from the alexithymia questionnaire, *deficit in identifying and expressing one's own affect and physical sensations* scale, was utilized in the present study. The subscale consists of 8 items, such as "I am often confused because I don't understand my feelings" and "I have difficulty expressing my own feelings verbally." The items were rated as in the DSSS. The mean rating of all 8 items was calculated to obtain a composite averaged score.

Emotionality

A Japanese version of the emotionality scale (Buss, 1986/1991) was employed. The scale contains 4 items. The items were rated as in the DSSS. The mean rating of all 4 items was calculated to obtain a composite averaged score.

Mental Healthiness

Nakagawa and Daibo (1985) translated the General Health Questionnaire developed by Goldberg (1972) into Japanese. The short version of their (GHQ-12) questionnaire in Japanese was employed in the present research. The items were rated on a 4-point scale. The mean rating of all 12 items was calculated to obtain a composite averaged score.

Aggression

Ando, Soga, Yamasaki, Shimai, Shimada, Utsuki, Oashi, and Sakai (1999) developed a Japanese scale of aggression based on the Buss-Perry Aggression Questionnaire (AQ; Buss & Perry, 1992). The Japanese version contains 22 items and the same 4 subscales as the original AQ: *physical aggression* (tendency to react violently, impulsive nature toward violence, justification of violence), *anger* (easily angered, quick-tempered, low control of anger), *hostility* (negative perception and attitudes toward others, suspicion and distrust such as malice and disregard), and *verbal aggression* (verbally aggressive reactions such as insistence and argumentativeness). Three items with the highest factor loadings from each subscale were selected for use in the present study. The total number of items employed was 12 (4 x 3). The items were rated on a 5-point scale as in the DSSS. The mean ratings of items on each subscale were calculated to obtain 4 kinds of composite averaged scores.

Development of DSSS

Reliability

Principal component analyses were performed for each dimension of the DSSS: Self(37 items), Others(21 items), and Time (22 items). The proportions of the first principal component for each subscale were 17.96%, 25.36%, and 30.86% respectively. After removing the items with factor loadings under .50 at the first principal component, 13 items were retained for the Self dimension, 11 items for Others, and 11 items for Time. Principal component analyses were repeated for all subscales. As a result, the proportions of the first principal component of each subscale were 38.60% (Self), 41.04% (Others), and 42.16% (Time). The absolute values of the factor loadings were .50 or more (Table 1, 2, and 3). Thus, every subscale was concluded to have a one-factor structure. The subscales were then used for further analyses in the present study.

Table 1. Result of Principle Component Analysis for the Self Dimension of DSSS

Self Dimension (α = .86)		Loadings	M	SD
I always suffer a sense of inferiority.		-.72	3.08	1.22
I have a positive attitude toward myself.	(-)	.70	3.25	1.01
I often dislike myself.		-.69	3.45	1.16
I have strong belief in myself.	(-)	.66	3.19	1.02
I am a valueable human being.	(-)	.66	3.30	1.00
I can hardly be proud of myself.		-.63	2.99	1.12
I sometimes feel that I can't be successful in whatever I do.		-.63	2.89	1.22
I am satisfied with what I am doing.	(-)	.59	3.09	.94
I have a clear sense of myself.	(-)	.58	2.88	.96
I don't quite understand who I am.		-.57	2.78	1.22
I live my life the way I believe in.	(-)	.56	3.54	.93
I don't really know what I want to do.		-.53	3.17	1.25
I know myself very well.	(-)	.50	3.30	.94
Eigen Value		5.02		

(-) indicates reverse item. Before using this English version of the Self dimension of DSSS above, you must confirm its reliability and validity, because the English version was merely translated from the Japanese version by the author himself and the standalization was performed only for the Japanese version.

Table 2. Result of Principle Component Analysis for the Others Dimension of DSSS

Others Dimension (α = .85)		Loadings	M	SD
I feel that other people require me.	(-)	.75	3.12	.89
There are few people who respect me.		-.71	2.74	.96
People trust me.	(-)	.71	3.23	.85
People understand me.	(-)	.69	3.14	.86
I am not needed by anyone.		-.68	2.24	1.02
I am indispensable among my close friends.	(-)	.63	3.14	.87
Other people don't listen to me seriously.		-.62	2.44	.87
I have close friends who I can open myself to.	(-)	.59	4.14	.91
I only have superficial social relationships.		-.57	2.84	1.06
I fulfill the expectations of my family and friends well.	(-)	.54	3.06	.99
People treat me like a child.		-.51	2.64	.92
Eigen Value		4.51		

(-) indicates reverse item. Before using this English version of the Others dimension of DSSS above, you must confirm its reliability and validity, because the English version was merely translated from the Japanese version by the author himself and the standalization was performed only for the Japanese version.

Cronbach's coefficient alphas were .86 for Self, .85 for Others, and .88 for Time. Thus, the internal consistency of every subscale was considered to be sufficiently high. The mean ratings of items on each subscale were calculated to obtain 3 kinds of composite averaged scores. The scores indicate that the higher the score, the more diminished the sense of self-existence is.

Table 3. Result of Principle Component Analysis for the Time Dimension of DSSS

Time Dimension ($\alpha = .88$)		Loadings	M	SD
I feel like living vaguely every day.		-.74	3.29	1.18
I have some aim in my present life.	(-)	.72	3.40	1.12
I have my goal to live for.	(-)	.70	3.53	1.11
Prospects for my future are bright.	(-)	.69	3.31	.99
I am leading a full life every day.	(-)	.68	3.21	1.06
My future is full of hope.	(-)	.66	3.10	1.08
I have nothing to devote my life to.		-.65	2.79	1.41
I believe that I will attain something I wish for even if I don't now.	(-)	.62	3.50	1.04
I believe "I am living fully" from my heart.	(-)	.62	3.29	1.08
I'm not sure what I want to do in the future.		-.61	3.25	1.35
I have no confidence in the way I have lived until now.		-.59	2.60	1.07
I am proud of what I have done so far.	(-)	.57	3.22	1.01
Every day is very boring, repeating the same routine.		-.56	2.91	1.26
Eigen Value		5.48		

(-) indicates reverse item. Before using this English version of the Time dimension of DSSS above, you must confirm its reliability and validity, because the English version was merely translated from the Japanese version by the author himself and the standalization was performed only for the Japanese version

Validity

Pearson correlation coefficients between DSSS and other variables are shown in Table 4. As expected, the results show that a diminished sense of self-existence in each dimension (Self, Others, and Time) is negatively associated with the establishment of identity, and positively related to alexithymia, emotionality, and mental unhealthiness. All correlations were statistically significant. In other words, the findings indicate that the less satisfactory the establishment of identity and the lower and unstable the emotional experience are, the more diminished the sense of self-existence and the poorer the mental health state will be.

Table 4. Pearson Correlation Coefficients between DSSS and Other Variables

	DSSS		
	Self	Others	Time
Establishment of Identity	-.74[*]	-.52[*]	-.68[*]
Sense of Superiority and Competence	-.47[*]	-.36[*]	-.33[*]
Need for Attention and Praise	-.05	-.18[*]	-.06
Self-assertion	-.40[*]	-.33[*]	-.35[*]
Alexithymia	.53[*]	.40[*]	.34[*]
Emotionality	.58[*]	.44[*]	.42[*]
Mental Unhealthiness (GHQ)	.52[*]	.47[*]	.48[*]

[*] $p < .01$.

In addition, Table 4 shows that the diminished sense of self-existence on every dimension was negatively related to the sense of superiority-competence, and self-assertion in narcissism. This indicates that the more diminished the positive sense of one's reasons and values for existing are, the weaker the narcissistic inclination of a strong positive feeling regarding oneself will be. However, the need for attention and praise was negatively correlated with the diminished sense of self-existence only on the dimension of Others. That is, regardless of the evaluation of oneself in internal private world and the meaning of one's presence in historical and temporal terms, an individual's disposition to seek more admiration from others becomes stronger only when he/she clearly becomes aware that the reasons and values for existence are fundamental to his/her relation with surroundings, people, and society.

In sum, the results indicate the relationships between DSSS and most of variables support the predictions made prior to the study. Thus, the construct validity of DSSS was mostly confirmed on the basis of the results. In the future, it will be necessary to validate this scale comprehensively by investigating criterion-related validity.

Sex Differences

Sex differences regarding the diminished senses of self-existence on each dimension (Self, Others, and Time) were examined. The results show that only on the dimension of Others did men ($M = 2.72$, $SD = .59$) feel more diminished about their self-existence significantly than women ($M = 2.52$, $SD = .56$)($t(556) = 3.93$, $p < .01$). There was no significant sex difference on the dimension of Self ($M = 2.89$, $SD = .68$ for men; $M = 2.93$, $SD = .65$ for women) and Time ($M = 2.82$, $SD = .77$ for men; $M = 2.73$. $SD = .69$ for women).

Although there was no difference between men and women regarding the sense of self-existence based on the inner self-knowledge and the temporal perspective, women were found to have a relatively higher sense than men of self-existence gained through external evaluation. This may result from women trusting and depending on others more than men. This result corresponds to the findings reported by Sugihara and Amagai's (1996) finding of Japanese youths from junior high school students to graduate students. Although the researchers did not find gender difference regarding trusting oneself, women were found to have greater trust in others than men.

Relationship between the Diminished Sense of Self-existence and Aggression

Pearson correlation coefficients between the diminished sense of self-existence and aggressiveness are presented in Table 5. First, these results indicate that the diminished senses of self-existence in each dimension (Self, Others, and Time) positively correlated with hostility in both men and women. Second, regardless of sex, the diminished senses of self-existence in Self and Others dimensions were positively related with anger, whereas the diminished sense of self-existence in Time dimension was related to a tendency to get angry only for women. Third, the diminished senses of self-existence in Self and Time dimensions were negatively associated with verbal aggression for both sex. In addition, men who had more diminished sense of self-existence on the Others dimension are found to be less inclined to be verbally aggressive. Lastly, we should note that the diminished sense of self-existence on Self and Others dimensions was positively correlated with physical aggression only for women. All correlations were statistically significant.

Table 5. Pearson Correlation Coefficients between DSSS and Aggressiveness

	DSSS	Physical Aggression	Anger	Hostility	Verbal Aggression
			AQ		
Self					
	Men	-.05	.14*	.37**	-.38**
	Women	.15*	.25**	.44**	-.25**
Others					
	Men	.00	.13*	.44**	-.28**
	Women	.21**	.23**	.50**	-.12
Time					
	Men	-.01	.07	.32**	-.26**
	Women	.10	.21**	.29**	-.19**

* $p < .05$.
** $p < .01$.

In general, the diminished sense of self-existence was positively related to covert (internal, latent) aggressiveness such as hostility and anger, whereas it was negatively or insignificantly related to overt (external, manifest) aggressiveness such as verbal and physical aggression. However, depending on the dimension, the results show some sex differences. For instance, the diminished sense of self-existence was positively related to physical aggression in women.

GENERAL DISCUSSION AND FUTURE PROSPECTS

In the present study, (1) a new scale to measure the diminished sense of self-existence (DSSS) was developed, and the reliability and validity of the scale were examined, and (2) the relationship between the diminished sense measured by the DSSS and aggressiveness measured by AQ was examined. In this section, we will mainly focus on the relationship between the diminished sense of self-existence and aggression.

The Diminished Sense of Self-existence and Hostility

The results show that the diminished senses of self-existence measured on Self, Others, and Time were related positively to hostility in both sex. This suggests that the more diminished we feel our reasons or values to exist, the more likely we hold negative attitudes and suspicion toward others regardless of the dimension. If we take into consideration the association between a diminished sense of existing and poor unstable emotional experience, the feeling of maladjustment generated by little satisfaction and contentment in social life and human relations is likely to lead youths to judge others negatively. In fact, a complex interrelated causal relationship seems to exist between poor emotional experience, diminished self-existence, and hostile cognition. Thus, we can extensively and dynamically examine a general negativity on the emotive and cognitive levels by focusing on the diminished sense of self-existence.

The Diminished Sense of Self-existence and Anger

The present study demonstrates that the diminished senses of self-existence on Self and Others dimensions are positively linked with anger. Thus, we can infer that youths tend to get angry when they perceive their existence diminished on their internal and external evaluation. One plausible interpretation is that individuals with a negative sense of self-existence interact with others and get angry in a defensive manner when they think others are hostile or negatively evaluative toward them. To put it in extreme terms, an individual may well feel as if he/she is on the verge of extinction when his/her sense of self-existence is both internally and externally diminished. That is, he/she no longer exists anywhere in the present space formed by self and others. If this is the case, we can easily imagine that he/she would be sensitive to others' evaluation of himself/herself. According to the theory of evolution or adaptation, an angry feeling is a warning toward self and others for self-preservation and self-defense (e.g., Izard, 1991; Toda, 1992). It is highly probable that this warning signal achieves an incessant force if the self-existence teeters on the brink.

Only in women was the diminished sense of self-existence on Time dimension found to be related to the tendency toward anger. This indicates that women have a greater tendency than men to become more sensitive to others and get angry in a defensive manner when their historical and temporal sense of self-existence is threatened. Because women tend to trust others more than men (Sugihara & Amagai, 1996), they also tend to rely more on others' appraisal in attaining values for their existence. Consequently, they rely heavily on others for the meaning of their own entity even in temporal terms - the past, the present, and the future. Since women's sense of trust toward others and their sense of self-existence are closely related, they are likely to get easily angry with others when their sense of self-existence is diminished than men.

The Diminished Sense of Self-existence and Verbal Aggression

This study revealed that the diminished sense of self-existence on the Self and Time dimensions was negatively correlated with verbal aggression. In other words, young people are less prone to assert their opinions or object to others' ideas as they lose both the sense of value for existing at a personal level and a positive outlook on their past, present, and future lives. Under such conditions, they may find it difficult to insist on advocating their ideas and counter-arguing with others. In reverse, this implies that if the individual possesses abundance experience of expressing their thinking and opinions verbally in order to counter-argue others' views in an appropriate manner, this experience is likely to be linked with a positive sense of self-existence.

Moreover, men were found to show less verbal aggression when their diminished sense of existence was based on relationships with others and society, whereas, in women, there was no significant relationship between the low sense of self-existence on the Others dimension and verbal aggression. That is, for men whether they argue with others or not will depend on whether they do or do not receive social approval generally. On the other hand, women may show verbal aggression regardless of others' evaluation. For Japanese young men, the reluctance to receive disapproval from others probably leads them to being hesitant in expressing themselves or their thinking. This is because, compared to women, men distrust others more (Sugihara & Amagai, 1996) and have a more diminished sense of self-existence on the Others dimension.

The Diminished Sense of Self-existence and Physical Aggression

In this study, we should note that the diminished senses of self-existence on Self and Others dimensions were positively related to physical aggression in women only. This suggests that, for women, the more diminished the senses of self-existence on the Self and Others dimensions are, the stronger the inclination to justify or perform physical violence will be. On the other hand, there was no significant relation between a diminished sense of self-existence on each dimension and physical aggression in men. This finding contradicts the prevailing opinion that violent crime and delinquency, which is believed among a lot of causes to be led by a diminished sense of self-existence, is mainly committed by men in Japan. The items employed to measure physical aggression in the AQ in the present study are not concerned with frequency and seriousness of actual aggressive behavior, but with the tendency and intention to engage in physical violence. So, whether the aggressive motive will be put into action remains a problem that is worth further consideration.

The present study demonstrates the relationship between the diminished sense of self-existence and physical aggression (motive) in women but not in men. It is highly probable that women tend to be unsettled by society and others' negative views and images toward themselves, and are likely to feel strongly motivated to counterattack defensively to eliminate such negative values at all costs. One reason is that women are more sensitive to their public evaluations and images (Sugawara, 1984), and have a stronger trust in others (Sugihara & Amagai, 1996) than men. This study also reveals that women feel a more positive sense of self-existence in terms of others' evaluations and interpersonal relations than men. Moreover, we see from the results that the diminished sense of self-existence on the Others dimension is more strongly related to physical aggression than that on the Self dimension. Hence, negative evaluations and images are likely to lead to physical aggression more in women than men.

CONCLUSIONS AND PROSPECTS

Summing up the findings of the present study on modern Japanese youths, we arrive at the conclusion that the diminished sense of self-existence is positively correlated with covert and latent aggression (i.e., hostility and anger), but negatively or insignificantly correlated with overt and manifest aggression (i.e., verbal and physical aggression). In Yukawa's (2003) study of Japanese young people, it was found that high evaluation of one's own value and ability (i.e., narcissism) was related not only to anger and hostility, but also to verbal and physical aggression, i.e., overt behavior. We can infer from this finding that a sense of one's reasons or values for existing is likely to play an essential role in whether an individual holds anger and hostility internally or expresses them in an aggressive manner.

Baumeister and his colleagues (Baumeister & Boden, 1998; Baumeister, Bushman, & Campbell, 2000; Baumeister, Smart, & Boden, 1996) developed the "Threatened Egotism Model" to explain the relationship between narcissism and aggression. According to their model, excessive self-confidence and self-worth lead to a sensitivity toward others' evaluation, where the evaluation becomes an ego-threat to the person as well. In turn, the threat drives the person to exhibit aggressive behavior as a defensive denial to maintain his/her highly-positive self-evaluation. In this way, an unstable and vulnerable self becomes the root of narcissism. This pathology of self is likely to be the same as the origin of the diminished sense of self-existence. Although the phenomenon of narcissism appears to be different from the phenomenon of the diminished sense of self-existence, both are based on the same unstable and vulnerable self. Further research is necessary to achieve a better understanding of the relationship between narcissism and the sense of diminished sense of self-existence.

In addition, sex differences can be observed in different dimensions of the diminished sense of self-existence. The results of the present research indicate that a diminished sense of self-existence on the Self and Others dimensions were positively related to physical aggression only in women. While the diminished sense on Time dimension was positively associated with anger in women, the sense on the Others dimension was negatively linked with verbal aggression in men. In the future, the reason for these sex differences on each dimension and the mechanisms of sex differences will need to be examined in more detail.

In conclusion, I would like to add three points. First, although the respondents of this study are Japanese youths, there is a room for examining whether the general findings and sex differences in this research are applicable to adolescents in other Asian countries and the West. With the remarkable economic growth in Asian countries today, it would be interesting to explore how young people perceive their self-existence in changing social situations, and how their perceptions are connected with various social problems such as aggression and violence. To predict future social trends in Japan, it would also be interesting to examine how the sense of existence in young adults is associated with social problems in the West, where the problems of youth aggression and violence are more serious and deeper than those in Japan at present. Finally, although this study employed undergraduate respondents, the diminished sense of self-existence observed in this study is likely to be relevant to the mental and psychological problems of teenagers and people in their later 20s. Given that in resent years, the problem of identity has been discussed in terms of life-span development (Tatara & Yamashita, 1999), we need to regard the crisis of the diminished sense of self-existence also as a problem for middle and old age.

REFERENCES

Ando, A., Soga, S., Yamasaki, K., Shimai, S., Shimada, H., Utsuki, N., Oashi, O., & Sakai, A. (1999). Nihon-ban Buss-perry kougekisei shitsumonshi (BAQ) no sakusei to datousei, shinraisei no kentou [Development of the Japanese version of the Buss-Perry Aggression Questionnaire (BAQ)]. *Japanese Journal of Psychology, 70*, 384-392.

Apfel, R. J., & Sifneos, P. E. (1979). Alexithymia: Concept and measurement. *Psychotherapy and Psychosomatics, 32*, 180-190.

Baumeister, R. F., & Boden, J. M. (1998). Aggression and the self: High self-esteem, low self-control, and ego threat. In R. G. Geen & E. Donnerstein (Eds.), *Human Aggression: Theories, research, and implications for social policy* (pp.111-137). San Diego: Academic Press.

Baumeister, R. F., Bushman, B. J., & Campbell, W. K. (2000). Self-esteem, narcissism, and aggression: Does violence result from low self-esteem or from threatened egotism? *Current Directions in Psychological Science, 9*, 26-29.

Baumeister, R. F., Smart, L., & Boden, J. M. (1996). Relation of threatened egotism to violence and aggression: The dark side of high self-esteem. *Psychological Review, 103*, 5-33.

Beck, A. T., Rush, A. J., Shaw, B. F., & Emery, G. (1979). *Cognitive Therapy of Depression.* New York□Guilford Press.

Buss, A. H. (1980). *Self-consciousness and social anxiety.* San Francisco: Freeman.

_____ . (1986). *Social behavior and personality.* Hillsdale, New Jersey: Lawrence Erlbaum Associates.

_____ . (1991). *Taijin koudou to pahsonarithi* [Social behavior and personality](K. Ohbuchi, Trans.). Kyoto, Japan: Kitaohji.

Buss, A. H., & Perry, M. P. (1992) The Aggression Questionnaire. *Journal of Personality and Social Psychology, 63*, 452-459.

Erikson, E. H. (1959). *Identity and the life cycle.* New York: W.W.Norton & Company.

_____ . (1968). *Identity: Youth and crisis.* New York: W.W.Norton & Company.

Goldberg, D. P. (1972). *The detection of psychiatric illness by questionnaire□A technique for the identification and assessment of non-psychiatric illness.* London: Oxford University Press.

Goleman, D. (1995). *Emotional intelligence: Why it can matter more than IQ.* New York: Bantam Books.

Gotow, K., Kodama, M., & Sasaki, Y. (1999). Arekishisaimia wa itijigenteki tokusei nanoka?: 2 inshi moderu arekishisaimia sitsumonshi no sakusei [Is alexithymia unidimensional?: Development of a 2-factor model alexithymia questionnaire]. *Tsukuba Psychological Research, 21*, 163-172.

Research and Training Institute of the Ministry of Justice. (2001). *Heisei 13 nen-ban hanzai hakusyo* [Criminal white book, 2001]. Tokyo, Japan: Printing Bureau of the Ministry of Finance.

Izard, C. E. (1991). *The psychology of emotions.* New York: Plenum Press.

James, W. (1993). *Shinrigaku* [Psychology; The briefer course](H. Imada, Trans.). Tokyo, Japan: Iwanami.□Original work published 1892□

Kageyama, J. (1999). *Kuukyo na jiko no jidai* [Age of empty self]. Tokyo, Japan: NHK Books.

Kant, I. (1962). *Junsui risei hihan* [Kritik der Reinen Vernunft] (H. Shinoda, Trans.). Tokyo, Japan: Iwanami. (Original work published 1787)

Kernberg, O. (1975). *Borderline conditions and pathological narcissism.* New York: Jason Aronson.

Kohut, H. (1971). *The analysis of the self.* New York: International University Press.

Kiyonaga, K. (1999). *Gendai syounen hikou no sekai* [World of modern juvenile delinquency]. Tokyo, Japan: Yuuhikaku.

Matsumura, A. (Ed.). (1995). *Daijirin* (2nd ed.). Tokyo, Japan: Sanseido.

Moeller, T. G. (2001). *Youth aggression and violence: A psychological approach.* Mahwah, NJ: Lawrence Erlbaum Associates.

Markus, H. & Nurius, P. (1986). Possible selves. *American Psychologist, 41*, 954-969.

Miyashita, K., & Ohno, H. (2002). *Kireru seisyounen no kokoro* [Psychology of breaking-out-youths]. Kyoto, Japan: Kitaohji.

Nakagawa, Y., & Daibo, I. (1985) *Nihon-ban GHQ seishin kenkou tyousahyou tebiki* [Manual for GHQ in the Japanese version]. Tokyo, Japan: Nihon Bunka Kagaku Sya.

Niimura, I. (Ed.). (1998). *Koujien* (5th ed.). Tokyo, Japan: Iwanami.

Oshio, A. (1999). Koukousei niokeru jikoaikeikou to yuhjinkankei no arikata tono kanren [Relationships among narcissistic personality, self-esteem, and friendship in adolescence]. *Japanese Journal of Educational Psychology, 46*, 291-299.

Pennebaker, J. W. (1997). *Opening up: The healing power of expressing emotions*. New York: The Guilford Press.

Raskin, R., & Hall, C. S. (1979). A narcissistic personality inventory. *Psychological Reports, 45*, 590.

Shimoyama, H. (1992). Daigakusei no moratoriamu no kaibunrui no kenkyuu: Aidenthithi no hattatsu tono kanren de [A study on the subclassification of moratorium of university students: In relation to the identity development]. *Japanese Journal of Educational Psychology, 40*, 121-129.

Sugawara, K. (1984). Jiishiki syakudo (self-consciousness scale) nihongo-ban sakusei no Kokoromi [An attempting to construct the self-consciousness scale for Japanese]. *Japanese Journal of Psychology, 55*, 184-188.

Sugihara, K., & Amagai, Y. (1996). Tokuseiteki oyobi ruikeiteki kanten kara mita shinraikan no hattatsu [A study on development of trust from the point of its traits and types]. *Tsukuba Psychological Research, 18*, 129-133.

Tatara, M., & Yamashita, I. (1999). *Aidenthithi* [Identity]. Tokyo, Japan: Nippon Hyoron Sya.

Taylor, G. J., Ryan, D., & Bagby, M. (1985) Toward the development of a new self-report alexithymia scale. *Psychotherapy and Psychosomatics, 44*, 191-199.

Toda, M. (1992). *Kanjyou* [Emotions]. Tokyo, Japan: University of Tokyo Press.

Tokyo Metropolis. (1999). *Kireru* [Breaking out]. Tokyo, Japan: Brain.

Yukawa, S. (2002a) Diminished sense of self-existence and self-reported aggression among Japanese students. *Psychological Reports, 90*, 634-638.

Yukawa, S. (2002b) Jiko-sonzaikan to kougekisei: Jiko-sonzaikan no kihakusa syakudo no shinraisei to datousei no kentou [Sense of Self-existence and Aggressiveness: Development of the Diminished Sense of Self-existence Scale]. *Japanese Journal of Counseling Science, 35*, 219-228.

_____ . (2003). Seinenki niokeru jikoai to kougekisei: Genjitsu heno futekiou to kyokou heno botsunyuu wo fumaete [Narcissism and aggression in young adults: Relationship with maladjustment to reality and absorption in fiction]. *Japanese Journal of Criminal Psychology, 41(2)*, 27-36.

In: *Focus on Aggression Research*
Editor: James P. Morgan, pp. 91-113

ISBN 1-59454-132-9
© 2004 Nova Science Publishers, Inc.

Chapter 7

Neurobehavioral Aspects of Aggression

E. Kim
University of Medicine and Dentistry of New Jersey

Abstract

Aggression is a complex neurobehavioral phenomenon that may be elicited by a variety of internal and external triggers. Studies of individuals with acquired brain injuries and dementia demonstrate common neuropathological findings of frontal lobe dysfunction, which support both disinhibition and kindling models of TBI-induced aggression. In addition, there is a substantial body of literature describing neurochemical alterations that are associated with increased aggressive behavior. The substantial syndromal variability of aggressive behaviors make classification a difficult task, and this creates challenges in testing the efficacy of strategies to reduce such behaviors. The management of aggressive syndromes may involve pharmacological, environmental, and psychotherapeutic strategies.

Introduction

Traumatic brain injuries (TBI) are frequently complicated by changes in personality, cognition, and impulse control that may lead to behavioral disturbances. These disturbances may present a substantial obstacle to community integration following recovery from the acute neurological symptoms of TBI. These neurobehavioral changes may be either transient and self-limited, or chronic and persistent. More chronic syndromes may lead to treatment within public mental health delivery systems lacking awareness or expertise in the management of TBI-related neuropsychiatric disorders [93]. Suboptimal treatment of these symptoms may lead to substantial psychosocial morbidity and a failure to access or benefit from neurorehabilitation services [43]. Moreover, families are adversely affected by these behavioral disturbances [54]. Despite the deleterious impact on outcomes resulting from these syndromes, most treatment data consists of retrospective case series or small prospective studies. The totality of the literature, however, supports general principles of management. This paper will review the existing data on agitation and aggressive syndromes following

TBI, proposed mechanisms, and treatments. Limitations of the available data and recommendations for future research will also be discussed.

SYNDROME DEFINITION, PREVALENCE, AND RISK FACTORS

The type of agitation syndrome often depends on the clinical status of the patient. In the acute recovery period, agitated behavior may occur in 35-96% of patients [89,111]. Risk factors for acute agitation include frontotemporal injury [138], disorientation, comorbid medical complications, and use of anticonvulsant medications [49]. Acute agitation generally resolves prior to resolution of post-traumatic amnesia (PTA) [26, 138] and has been conceptualized as a form of delirium in the coma-emerging patient [116]. A Rancho Los Amigos Scale score of 4 (Confused, Agitated) would correspond to acute post-traumatic agitation [69].

More persistent changes in behavior have been described in the literature since the classical case of Phineas Gage [33, 70]. Agitation in post-acute TBI patients may occur in 31-71% of cases of severe TBI, while studies of milder TBIs have yielded rates of 5-71% [121]. Individuals who sustain more than one TBI during their lifetime may develop increasing irritability following each subsequent injury, particularly when associated with loss of consciousness [18]. Up to two-thirds of TBI patients develop significant changes in character traits that cause difficulty with interpersonal relationships, irrespective of severity of injury or age at injury [72, 110]. Pre-morbid risk factors for aggression include a history of impulsive aggression [63], arrest [86] and substance abuse [40]. In such cases it is difficult to determine whether the post-injury behavioral disturbances are related to the TBI or merely an extension of pre-morbid character pathology. Again, there is limited systematic data allowing clinicians to clarify the role of TBI in exacerbating or ameliorating pre-morbid character pathology. While a prior history of substance abuse is also associated with poorer cognitive and functional outcome [80, 127], it is unclear whether this is due to direct neurotoxic effects of chronic substance use or an increased vulnerability to the effects of cerebral trauma in this population.

The DSM-IV classification system can be used to diagnose Personality Change Secondary to a General Medical Condition [1], with several subclassifications to clarify the type of behavior changes manifested. The Aggressive type is characterized by predominantly aggressive behavior. The Disinhibited type is characterized primarily by disinhibition and sexual indiscretions, but may lead to aggression when redirected for frustrated. Patients with the Labile type primarily demonstrate affective lability, which may include verbal outbursts with minimal provocation, but without substantial threatening or violent behaviors. Alternatively, impulsive aggression may occur in the context of a mixed bipolar syndrome. Bipolar symptoms secondary to TBI are frequently characterized by irritability and dysphoria [146]. In the absence of pre-injury bipolar symptoms, the appropriate diagnosis for this type of aggressive, dysphoric syndrome is Mood Disorder Secondary to a General Medical Condition, Mixed Type [1]. There may be considerable overlap between the personality and mood syndromes associated with impulsive aggression. Certain distinguishing symptoms of mania such as increased energy, reduced need for sleep, pressured speech and racing thoughts may assist in distinguishing personality from mood symptoms. Table 1 summarizes the range of syndromal clusters that may result in agitation and aggression following TBI.

Table 1. Syndromal Clusters Associated with Aggression

Syndrome	Core Features
– Delirium	– Disorientation
	– Fluctuating level of consciousness
	– Sleep-wake disturbance
	– Increased non-directed activity
– Personality Change due to a General Medical Condition	– Stable, predictable character style
	– Absence of manic symptoms
– Aggressive Type	
– Labile Type	
– Impulsive Type	
– Mood Disorder due to a General Medical Condition, Mixed Type	– Irritability, dysphoria
	– Increased energy
	– Racing thoughts
	– Increased directed activity
– Episodic Dyscontrol	– Brief outbursts
	– No identifiable provocation
	– Primitive, semi-directed aggression
– Catastrophic Reaction	– Escalating tension
	– Patient confronted with overwhelming task
	– Awareness of and frustration with deficits

NEUROANATOMICAL FACTORS

Aggression is a phenomenon that can occur naturally or be experimentally induced in both humans and animals. The central nervous system component of aggression in mammals involves complex interconnections between cortical and subcortical nuclei in the limbic system, which mediates emotional and motivational states. The precise structures that comprise this system are somewhat variable depending on the investigator, but general include the orbitofrontal cortex, hippocampus, parahippocampal gyrus, insula, temporal pole, olfactory cortex, cingulate cortex, amygdala, septal nuclei, hypothalamus, and select thalamic nuclei [30, 95]. Projections from the orbitofrontal cortex extend to subcortical nuclei in a circuit that is completed by projections back to the orbitofrontal cortex. The prefrontal cortex is involved in executive cognitive functioning such as planning, initiative, and evaluation, but also in regulation of behaviors and impulses [71, 95]. Decreased metabolism in the orbitofrontal cortex has been associated with increased aggression in subjects with personality disorders [58, 126] as well as in healthy subjects imagining aggressive behavior [106].

The biomechanical characteristics of closed head injuries result most commonly in damage to the orbitofrontal and anterior temporal cortex [27, 77]. Additional diffuse axonal injury occurs at the white-gray matter junction and diffusely throughout connecting pathways in the brain [92]. Damage to the prefrontal cortex, particularly the orbitofrontal and ventromedial regions, has been associated with increased hostility, impulsivity, and aggression [33, 59, 131, 132]. In functional neuroimaging studies of TBI survivors, agitation is associated with hypoperfusion in the orbitofrontal and basotemporal regions [103, 138].

These findings suggest that deactivation of orbitofrontal structures or their associated circuitry may lead to a failure of impulse control and affect regulation. This deactivation may be mediated by a number of mechanisms from acquired brain injury to self-induced imaginal aggressive states.

The neuroanatomical mechanism mediating TBI-induced aggression is unclear, but may result from loss of tonic balance between inhibitory pathways in the orbitofrontal cortex and limbic structures that mediate impulse and drive expression [132]. Alternatively, orbitofrontal injury may disrupt efferent projections to limbic structures, leading to denervation hypersensitivity and limbic kindling. The resulting hyperactivity or kindling of these structures may lead to an increase in aggression [78].

NEUROCHEMICAL FACTORS

While the neural circuitry of aggression in TBI is important with respect to the mechanisms of injury and affected brain regions, pharmacological interventions will largely be driven by our understanding the neurochemistry of aggression in TBI. Animal and human models provide evidence for multiple influences. The neurochemical changes associated with TBI may represent protective reactions to trauma. Traumatic injury causes an abrupt and significant release of many neurotransmitters in the brain, including those associated with the cholinergic, serotonergic, and catecholaminergic systems. The increases in cholinergic transmission may contribute to excitotoxic injury, while an increase in serotonergic and catecholaminergic activity appears to reduce cerebral metabolism and may serve a neuroprotective role [9, 105]. Chronic neurochemical changes are less well-understood, but may contribute to behavioral syndromes. It may be helpful to extrapolate available neurochemical data in idiopathic psychiatric conditions in order to develop treatment hypotheses that may help guide the selection of medications.

Acetylcholine

Cholinergic transmission occurs diffusely throughout the entire brain. A major site of central cholinergic neurons is the nucleus basalis of Meynert, located in the basal forebrain and possessing axonal projections throughout the cortex. The mechanics of closed head injuries may disrupt these long axonal pathways, leading to cholinergic deficits [36, 115]. Cholinergic dysfunction has been associated with an increased risk for behavioral disturbances in Alzheimer's disease [98]. Currently there is no available data regarding the implications of cholinergic dysfunction on behavioral disturbances in TBI.

Serotonin

The role of serotonin in aggression is well-documented in non-brain-injured patients. Impaired serotonergic functioning is a common marker in individuals with impulsive aggression. Aggression and impulsivity are associated with decreased serotonin metabolites in the cerebrospinal fluid (CSF) as well as blunted neuroendocrine response to serotonin agonists [25]. Decreased CSF levels of the serotonin metabolite 5-hydroxyindoleacetic acid

(5-HIAA) are associated with increased levels of aggression [13]. These aggressive symptoms are substantially reduced by treatment with selective serotonin reuptake inhibitors in personality-disordered patients [24].

Catecholamines

Dopaminergic mechanisms facilitate aggression in animal models involving electrical stimulation of the ventral tegmentum or substantia nigra [28, 90, 120]. Increases in dopamine and norepinephrine may be associated with increased aggression in animal models [41]. Stanislav [128] compared aggressive brain-injured patients with non-aggressive brain-injured controls. There were no significant differences between the two groups in CSF levels of 5-HIAA or the dopamine metabolite homovanillic acid (HVA). There was a trend toward significantly higher levels of the norepinephrine metabolite 3-methoxy-4-hydroxymethylphenylglycol (MHPG) within the aggressive group. Thus far, the role of dopamine and norepinephrine in post-TBI aggression is unclear.

PSYCHOSOCIAL AND ENVIRONMENTAL FACTORS

The multitude of neurochemical and neuroanatomical disturbances associated with TBI may at times distract clinicians from considering interpersonal and environmental factors. Family support and an intact family structure play a vital role in functional and psychosocial outcomes of TBI (84, 88). Moreover, the environment and quality of therapeutic relationships may play a role in reducing agitation and aggression (85). It is therefore incumbent upon the clinician to the role of neurobiological substrates in the larger context of how they influence the patient's interactions to his or her environment. Additionally, the role of the patient's behavior in influence adaptive or maladaptive interactions with the patient is equally important in understanding the etiology of agitation and aggression.

PRINCIPLES OF ASSESSMENT

Clinical Assessment

A comprehensive, multidisciplinary assessment of the behavioral disturbance will assist in the development of appropriate pharmacological, environmental, and psychotherapeutic interventions. Given the complexity and variability of TBI, each patient requires thoughtful consideration of all factors that may lead to agitation and aggression. Pre-injury risk factors for agitation and aggression may be reviewed as described above. This will include a history of psychiatric illness, attention deficit disorder, and prior behavioral disturbances may be useful in determine the contribution of the acquired injury to a new pattern of neurobehavioral disturbances. Collateral sources of information such as family and friends are particularly important in that brain-injured patients often have little or no awareness of the extent of their post-injury changes [46].

Symptom presentation will also assist in developing a treatment plan. Three general syndromes of post-TBI aggression have been described: 1) episodic dyscontrol consisting of brief, aggressive outbursts with no identified provocation; 2) disinhibition leading to easily provoked aggression and temper tantrums; and 3) exacerbation of pre-morbid antisocial traits [97]. These distinctions carry an implicit identification of precipitating factors; episodic dyscontrol appears to be predominantly modulated through internal factors, while disinhibition syndromes are modulated via enhanced environmental reactivity. An increase in pre-morbid antisocial behavior reflects predatory rather than reactive aggression. Irritability, disinhibition, mixed mania and apathy may all coexist simultaneously or at different periods within a single individual. There is significant syndromal overlap between patients with disinhibition and those who develop secondary mania. In TBI, mania is more dysphoric and is associated with more frequent aggression. Agitation and aggression accompanied by fragmented sleep, restless energy, may suggest a mixed bipolar picture. The author has encountered numerous patients presenting with a mixed bipolar syndrome that became emerged after they were treated with antidepressants for "depressed" mood associated with irritability and fragmented sleep.

Irritability and negativism may result from post-TBI depression that, when combined with reduced frustration tolerance and diminished impulse control, may lead to agitation or aggression. This irritable presentation of depression has also been reported following stroke, another form of acquired brain injury [32]. Careful assessment for evidence of anhedonia and vegetative signs of depression are important to ensure accurate diagnosis and management of depressive syndromes, particularly when patients present primarily with irritability and affective lability. Anxiety may also be a source of restlessness and agitation in patients with TBI. This is supported by the finding that patients with Alzheimer's disease who experience anxiety are at increased risk for behavioral disturbances [45]. In summary, the challenge in reviewing the clinical history of the brain injury and behavioral disturbance is to clarify the nature of the syndrome (depressive, impulsive, bipolar), as well as precipitants and underlying neural substrates.

Neuropsychological Assessment

Neuropsychological testing is warranted in any patient presenting with post-TBI behavioral disturbances in order identify the patient's cognitive resources and deficits, which may not be evident during a diagnostic interview. In particular, neuropsychological testing can detect subtle deficits in executive functioning and impulse regulation necessary for behavioral control. The results of such assessment will assist providers in structuring treatments that match the patient's cognitive capacity and compensate for deficits. The role of neuropsychological deficits in predicting risk of aggressive behavior is complex. While orbitofrontal damage is generally associated with such behaviors, traditional neuropsychological tests may not be sensitive for dysfunction in this region [23. 43]. Some studies have noted that TBI patients with impulsive aggression demonstrate more cognitive dysfunction and impaired electrophysiological markers of cognitive efficiency than those without such behaviors [3, 48]. Moreover, deficits in executive cognitive functioning have been reported in non-brain-injured children with aggressive behaviors [50, 51] and young men without neurological or behavioral problems [52]. These data suggest that impulsive aggression, both in brain-injured and non-brain-injured patients, represents a form of cognitive deficit that may be detected by neuropsychological testing.

Neuroimaging

Structural neuroimaging studies such as computed tomography (CT) and magnetic resonance imaging (MRI) may help identify areas of damage, atrophy, and, in the case of MRI, evidence of diffuse axonal injury [5]. However, structural studies yield little information regarding the viability of morphologically intact brain tissue. Functional neuroimaging techniques such as regional cerebral blood flow (rCBF) and single photon emission computed tomography (SPECT) are clinically available nuclear scans that provide useful information regarding perfusion of various brain structures. In TBI, the number and size of identified lesions is substantially increased using SPECT compared to CT or MRI, though the difference is diminished in severe injuries [61, 91]. One study using SPECT noted hypoperfusion in orbitofrontal and basotemporal perfusion in TBI patients with post-acute aggression [63]. This is consistent with structural imaging studies. Thus, neuroimaging may complement the clinical examination and formal neuropsychological testing of patients. A rational and cost-effective approach to neuroimaging would begin with structural neuroimaging for all cases in order to rule out gross pathology. In the absence of significant structural findings or the presence of findings that are inconsistent with the clinical presentation, a SPECT scan will help clarify regional cerebral functioning. In cases where patients have already undergone structural imaging, SPECT scanning is preferable.

TREATMENT

Management of aggression and disinhibition due to TBI is a multi-disciplinary process that begins with comprehensive assessment to determine the various factors contributing to the problematic behaviors [142]. In the acute coma-emerging phase, delirium-induced agitation may be managed both pharmacologically and by minimizing the use of agents known to impair cognition. Additionally, environmental stimuli may be optimized to reduce over stimulation and assist the patient in reorientation [102]. The use of medications must be weighed against potential side effects and drug-drug interactions. Persistent post-acute behavioral disturbances require even more coordination of care, given the complexity of leaving institutional settings in the process of community re-entry. Given their combination of dysphoria, irritability, and increased energy and impulsivity, such patients may require aggressive pharmacological management and/or brief psychiatric hospitalization for rapid stabilization. Outpatient management of such symptoms may be difficult if the patient lacks the insight or organizational capacity to adhere to recommended treatment. However, a supportive caregiver or structured day program may reduce the need for more restrictive inpatient treatment.

Pharmacological Treatment

General principles of pharmacological treatment include attention to the heightened sensitivity of TBI patients to medication side effects [122]. In particular, sedating or anticholinergic medications may lead to substantial cognitive and functional impairment. Lower starting dosages and slower titration is a generally accepted principle of psychopharmacological management of TBI-induced aggression.

Antipsychotic Medications

Antipsychotic medications consist of a wide range of compounds that may be classified into conventional and atypical agents. The conventional antipsychotic medications act primarily through blockade of dopamine D2 receptors. Atypical antipsychotic medications may weakly block dopamine D2 receptors but also block dopamine D1 and serotonin 5-HT2 receptors [68]. Conventional antipsychotic medications have been used effectively for agitation and aggression in TBI patients [111]. However, animal and human studies suggest that the effects of dopamine blockade may impair motor recovery from brain injury [44, 57]. However, these studies were isolated to the acute post-injury phase. There is no clear data regarding the effects of antipsychotic medications on postacute neurorehabilitation. Conventional antipsychotics may impair cognition in patients with TBI, with the more anticholinergic low potency agents potentially causing the greatest impairment [130]. Other side effects of the conventional antipsychotics include parkinsonian symptoms and tardive dyskinesia, an involuntary movement disorder. An expanding literature suggests that atypical antipsychotic medications may exert beneficial effects on impaired executive functioning and memory in schizophrenia [72, 100]. The potential cognitive benefits of such medications in TBI have not been assessed, but these medications may have a more benign side effect profile in this population than conventional antipsychotics. Risperidone, an atypical antipsychotic medication, has been shown to preferentially reduce hostility and aggression in schizophrenic patients independent of its antipsychotic properties [31]. Whether this selective anti-aggressive is applicable to TBI-induced behavioral disorders is unclear. Additionally, newer antipsychotics such as risperidone and olanzapine have demonstrated efficacy in reducing agitation and aggression in elderly patients with dementia [79, 133]. The only published report of atypical antipsychotic medications for agitation and aggression in TBI found that clozapine appears to reduce aggression but is associated with significant side effects [96]. The newer atypical medications may be better tolerated and efficacious, but thus far no reports have been published.

Mood Stabilizers

Mood stabilizers represent a broad class of compounds with primary indications for bipolar disorder. The three medications approved by the U.S. Food and Drug Administration (FDA) for the treatment of acute mania are lithium, valproic acid, and olanzapine. Additionally, there is increasing interest in the role of anticonvulsants as mood stabilizers. However, the term "mood stabilizer" is somewhat narrow, since anticonvulsants have a wide range of other uses, including migraine headaches peripheral neuropathy [34]. Acute mania may be associated with irritability and aggression; this phenomenon has led clinicians to use mood stabilizers manage post-traumatic agitation in acute and post-acute patients.

Lithium is a salt with an unclear mechanism of action. While it has also been reported to reduce aggressive behaviors in brain-injured patients [4, 55], treatment may be limited by tremor, nausea, and cognitive impairment. Brain-injured patients appear to be more vulnerable to the neurotoxic effects of lithium even at therapeutic serum levels [75, 101]. However, the author has at times used low doses of lithium as an adjunct to other mood stabilizers with few side effects and some benefit. Because lithium is renally excreted, it is particularly useful in patients with liver dysfunction.

Carbamazepine is an anticonvulsant that stabilizes voltage-dependent sodium channels. It has been used to reduce post-traumatic agitation and aggression in acute and post-acute patients [2, 22, 47]. However, chronic administration of carbamazepine leads to increased clearance of hepatically metabolized medications. In patients treated with multiple medications this may complicate treatment. Additional side effects include nausea, rash, and rare hepatotoxicity and agranulocytosis. Additionally, carbamazepine has been reported to cause cognitive impairment in brain-injured patients [124]. Despite these caveats, carbamazepine has a long history of usage and, in the absence of these adverse effects, can be both safe and effective.

Valproic acid, another anticonvulsant, inhibits degradation of GABA and facilitates post-synaptic GABA transmission. It is available in immediate release and extended release preparations and is the only anticonvulsant with FDA approval for a psychiatric indication (acute mania). The extended release version may be taken once daily. Valproic acid has been used effectively to reduce agitation and aggression in both acute and post-acute patients [21, 141]. Valproic acid appears to be well-tolerated with respect to cognitive functioning [38], but may cause weight gain, thrombocytopenia, alopecia, and, more rarely, pancreatitis and hepatotoxicity. Nevertheless, the availability of convenient once-daily dosing and a long history of usage for psychiatric and neuropsychiatric conditions make valproic acid a first line agent in the absence of contraindications.

The mood stabilizing properties of novel anticonvulsants has received increasing attention in both open label and placebo-controlled studies. Lamotrigine has demonstrated efficacy in treated both mania and bipolar depression in randomized controlled trials [8, 14, 15, 76]. Moreover, in brain injured patients, the use of lamotrigine for seizure control was associated with more rapid rehabilitative progress, suggesting some treatment-associated cognitive enhancement [119]. Lamotrigine has low potential to cause significant weight gain, in contrast to valproic acid [6]. The most notable adverse reaction to this drug is a skin rash that may evolve into the more serious Stevens - Johnson syndrome. However, the occurrence of this serious condition appears to be less than 0.3% of cases and may be even less common if the medication is titrated slowly in increments of no more than 25mg/d every 2 weeks [94]. This, however, may lead to unacceptably slow rates of titration for acute agitation, necessitating adjunctive medication for patients with more acute behavioral disturbances. Lamotrigine may be beneficial as an adjunctive medication for partial response, or in cases where the degree of agitation is such that slow titration is an acceptable approach.

Topiramate has demonstrated antimanic efficacy in monotherapy and as an adjunctive treatment for partial response [16, 64, 65]. Its tendency to induce weight loss through dulling of the appetite may be a beneficial side effect in patients prone to gain weight on other anticonvulsants such as valproic acid [53]. However, topiramate treatment has been associated with the emergence of psychotic symptoms [81] and, more commonly, cognitive impairment [134]. The latter reaction is partly dose-related, but when present can be particularly problematic in the context of TBI, where cognitive deficits already exist. The author has noted substantial cognitive improvements following discontinuation of topiramate therapy in TBI patients, consistent with the experience reported in the epilepsy literature. However, if cognitive side effects do not emerge, this medication may be advantageous for patients with a tendency to gain weight on other psychotropic medications.

Gabapentin demonstrated effectiveness in reducing manic symptoms in two open label studies [19, 125], but note in a double-blind study [104]. The author has observed substantial reductions in agitation and affective lability in TBI patients treated with gabapentin 900-3600mg/d in both inpatient and outpatient settings. Gabapentin is minimally processed in the liver and excreted in urine, making it particularly suitable for patients with liver disease due to alcohol abuse or hepatitis.

Oxcarbazepine is a keto-analog of carbamazepine with similar anticonvulsant and antimanic efficacy [42]. Although hepatically metabolized, oxcarbazepine leads to much less autoinduction of cytochrome enzymes and therefore does not substantially influence the metabolism of other hepatically-excreted medications. Agranulocytosis has not been reported, though there is some increased incidence of hyponatremia that is usually not clinically significant [60]. The side effect profile is similar to that of carbamazepine, though in the author's experience, these symptoms are much milder and less common. The author has noted efficacy and tolerability of oxcarbazepine for TBI-related agitation and aggression at doses of 600-2400 mg/d.

The selection of a mood stabilizer may be determined by the side effect profile of each medication. In some cases, the author has noted therapeutic benefits and reduced incidence of side effects by using somewhat lower doses of several medications. However, there is no systematic data regarding the efficacy and tolerability of medication combinations.

Table 2 summarizes the plethora of mood-stabilizers and putative mood stabilizers that may reduce TBI-induced aggression.

Beta Blockers

The beta blockers are antihypertensive antagonists of beta-adrenergic receptors, and have been used to reduce aggression in patients with a wide variety of patients that were refractory to conventional treatments such as antipsychotics, benzodiazepines, and mood stabilizers [144]. Propranolol in doses ranging from 60-520mg daily has been reported to reduce aggressive behaviors in brain-injured patients [10, 62, 143]. Treatment is limited by cardiovascular effects of this medication such as hypotension and bradycardia. Moreover, patients with asthma or emphysema may experience bronchospasm in response to beta receptor blockade. The role of beta blockers in causing depression is controversial, with mixed findings in the literature (113). However, the generally high doses used in the treatment of TBI-induced agitation are not typical of the available reports. Therefore, patients may be at an increased risk for developing depression.

Table 2. Mood Stabilizers

Medication	Dose Range/ Serum Level	Clinical Comments
Carbamazepine	200-800mg/d 6-12 mg/ml	– Bone marrow suppression – Hepatotoxicity – Rash – Increases metabolism of other medications
Valproic Acid	500-3500mg/d 50-125mg/ml	– Weight gain – Thrombocytopenia – Hepatotoxicity – Pancreatitis
Lithium	600-1800mg/d 0.5-1.5mEq/l	– Tremor, cognitive impairment – Weight gain – Thyroid suppression
Lamotrigine	100-400mg/d NA	– Rash may be avoided by slow titration – Minimal weight gain
Topiramate	100-500mg/d NA	– Weight loss – Cognitive impairment – Renal stones
Gabapentin	900-3600mg/d NA	– Renally excreted – Possibly less effective in acute mania
Oxcarbazepine	900-2400mg/d NA	– Minimal influence on other medications – No bone marrow suppression – Rare hyponatremia

Antianxiety Medications

Benzodiazepines are a closely related class of compounds that have sedative, antianxiety, and anticonvulsant effects. They interact with receptors for gamma-aminobutyric acid (GABA), the primary inhibitory neurotransmitter in the brain [68]. Benzodiazepines may be useful in reducing anxiety and irritability that contribute to some forms of aggression in TBI. However, the use of benzodiazepines may be associated with sedation, cognitive impairment, paradoxical agitation, and increasing tolerance to medication necessitating dose escalation [68]. Chronic use of this class of medications is therefore not recommended. The short-term benefits obtained may provide clinicians with the opportunity to titrate other medications to therapeutic effect. A particular concern when using sedative hypnotic medications in brain-injured patients is the potential to develop paradoxical reactions that actually exacerbate agitation and aggression (118Shafer).

Buspirone, a partial agonist of post-synaptic serotonin 5-HT1a receptors, is primarily indicated for the treatment of anxiety. Unlike benzodiazepines, it does not interact with GABA receptors or cause sedation. Other uses of buspirone include adjunctive treatment of depression and obsessive-compulsive disorder [68]. In brain-injured patients buspirone has been reported to reduce agitation and aggression [67, 112, 129]. Because patients may transiently experience worsening of aggression, dosing should start as low as 5mg bid and slowly titrated to a maximum of 60mg/day [121]. A limitation of buspirone is that it may take several weeks before beneficial effects are observed. In more acutely agitated patients other medications may be necessary in the interim.

Antidepressant Medications

Serotonin reuptake inhibitors such as fluoxetine, sertraline, paroxetine, and citalopram may also be helpful in reducing agitation and aggression. Citalopram has demonstrated efficacy in reducing agitation in elderly patients with Alzheimer's disease [82, 108]. Kim et al [83] reported reductions in aggressive behaviors in three brain-injured patients treated with selective serotonin reuptake inhibitors (SSRIs). Trazodone, an older SSRI with partial serotonin 5-HT2 agonist properties, is frequently used for agitation in geriatric and brain-injured patients [113, 123]. Its sedative properties appear to exert a beneficial anxiolytic and serenic effect. Typical doses range from 25-50mg as needed up to a total daily dose of 400mg.

Sympathomimetic Medications

Sympathomimetic agents such as methylphenidate have been used to improve alertness and reduce agitation in patients with frontal lobe dysfunction and impaired attention, concentration, and executive functioning. A particularly robust response has been reported in coma-emerging patients [99]. Typical doses of methylphenidate range from 10-60mg per day. Amantadine indirectly acts upon the dopaminergic system by inhibiting presynaptic reuptake of dopamine. In dosages of 50-400mg/day, amantadine has been used to decrease aggressive behavior in coma-emerging patients, though at higher doses memory disturbances may develop [20, 66]. The hypothesized mechanism of action of these medications is through increased arousal and awareness in confused patients. However, adverse reactions to sympathomimetic agents may include irritability, agitation, psychosis and anorexia.

Cholinesterase Inhibitors

Acetylcholine is primarily degraded by the enzyme acetylcholinesterase. Several inhibitors of this enzyme are available for the management of cognitive deficits associated with Alzheimer's disease. These medications include tacrine, donepezil, rivastigmine, and galantamine. Cholinesterase inhibitors have demonstrated efficacy in reducing agitation and psychosis in elderly demented patients [29]. Moreover, cholinergic dysfunction has been linked to behavioral disturbances in demented patients [98]. There is, therefore, some theoretical basis for the use of cholinesterase inhibitors for behavioral problems in TBI, though to date, the literature has only reported cognitive benefits in TBI [17, 135, 139, 140]. The potential psychotropic effects of these medications on agitation and aggression in TBI remain to be studied.

Hormonal Therapies

The use of estrogen therapy has demonstrated efficacy in reducing aggression in a placebo-controlled study of demented elderly men [87]. Hormonal therapies have been to treat aggression in male sex offenders as well as epileptics with aggressive syndromes [7]. The potential feminizing side effects may be problematic in male patients. This treatment may be considered as a last resort for the treatment of intractable aggression due to TBI, and requires special attention to ethical issues and informed consent prior when consider such drastic therapy.

Psychotherapeutic Interventions

Psychotherapeutic interventions require particular flexibility and resourcefulness on the part of the clinician, who must take into account the patient's cognitive capacity, pre-morbid assets and post-injury circumstances [109]. Psychoeducational interventions may help patients develop more adaptive interpersonal skills to cope with frustrating circumstances that lead to agitation and aggression [11, 39]. Anger management training, which focuses on increasing awareness of the psychophysiological symptoms of anger and symptom reduction, may be beneficial on an individual [73] or group basis [35]. More behaviorally based interventions may use point systems to reinforce desired behaviors, or differential reinforcement of other behavior (DRO) to extinguish maladaptive behaviors [73]. Patients with more severe memory deficits may require caregivers to exert a more active role in managing environmental and interpersonal stimuli that precipitate aggression [145]. Patients with less severe cognitive impairments may benefit from feedback after episodes of maladaptive behaviors may help them to better understand the relationship between stimuli, behaviors, and consequences [117]. This may lead to enhanced self-regulation, both to avoid the antecedents and to reflect prospectively on the potential consequences of aggression prior to acting. Involvement of caregivers is considered a crucial aspect of psychotherapy, since these individuals will exert a profound influence on the patient's interpersonal environment [108, 137]. Studies of elderly demented patients indicate that caregiver support that combines psychotherapeutic and educational interventions effectively delays the need for institutional placement [136]. Agitation and aggression may result from catastrophic reactions that occur when the patient becomes overwhelmed by previously manageable tasks and challenges [56, 108]. In such cases psychotherapy may focus both on management of these severe emotional reactions when they occur, but also on avoiding situations likely to precipitate such crises. This may involve addressing feelings of narcissistic vulnerability in individuals who have become painfully aware of their acquired deficits, and assisting them with the acceptance of necessary accommodations or compensatory strategies.

Suggested Guidelines for Management of Aggression

While clinical judgment and individual patient characteristics are the bedrock of all treatment, certain general guidelines may, in the author's judgment, optimize outcomes and assist patients and families in managing these troubling syndromes.

1. Engaging the patient and caregivers is of the utmost importance to reduce the likelihood of unrealistic expectations.

2. Education regarding the off-label use of medications is helpful for both ethical and risk management purposes. By explaining the risks and benefits of the proposed medication regimen, providers will help the patient and caregivers understand the variability and uncertainty associated with TBI-related behavioral disorders

3. In most cases of aggression, first line treatment will include the use of one or more mood stabilizers. The minimum effective dose is recommended, though this is highly variable and requires slow titration to minimize side effects. Despite this recommendation, clinicians should be willing, with patient and caregiver consent, to titrate to higher doses as needed if tolerated.

4. Atypical antipsychotics may be added for refractory cases, particularly when there are manic symptoms such as reduced sleep, or paranoid ideation. Bedtime dosing is recommended for sedating antipsychotics.

5. Serotonergic agents such as SSRIs and buspirone may be either added to or substituted for any of the above medications. Caution should be used if there are any vegetative signs of mania such as pressured speech or decreased need for sleep. The emergence of such symptoms may indicate a mixed bipolar syndrome and require a mood stabilizer in addition to or instead of serotonergic medications.

6. Particular attention should be paid to environmental and interpersonal factors contributing to aggression or interfering with treatment. In some cases, interventions on these fronts may reduce or, in some cases, eliminate the need for medications.

The use of structured day programs, residential, or inpatient psychiatric treatment, or in-home cognitive rehabilitation services may assist in assessment and management of these syndromes by providing additional collateral information and the ability to modify interventions much more rapidly.

LEGAL CONSIDERATIONS

Aggression and agitation are disruptive behaviors that often lead to conflict with others. This may result in a number of legal complications. In the case of a patient who becomes aggressive towards another person or causes property damage, the victim may initiate civil or criminal proceedings. Neuropsychiatric impairment, particularly frontal systems dysfunction, has been associated with criminal behavior [12, 37]. However, this association has the potential to be misapplied for the purposes of exonerating criminal behaviors, to the detriment of both the legal process as well as the field of neuropsychiatry [37, 106). Another legal complication of TBI-induced aggression may develop after aggressive and socially unacceptable behavior leads to alienation from family, loss of employment, and other adverse social outcomes. In such cases the loss of income and social standing may be considered in personal injury proceedings.

CONCLUSION

Personality changes and aggression present a major disruptive complication of TBI and a challenge to effective rehabilitation and community re-entry. The wide range of variability of TBI requires the thoughtful integration of evidence-based practices with rigorous multidisciplinary assessment. By effectively addressing the neurochemical, environmental, and psychosocial needs of these challenging patients, rehabilitation professionals may optimize treatment outcomes. The current state of the art is rich in descriptive data but quite limited in treatment data. An agenda for future research would include the following:

1. Development and validation of a consistent nosology to address various types of agitation and aggressive syndromes, as well as the underlying neurochemical and neuroanatomical substrates for individual syndromes. This nosology would be vital in designing and testing interventions across the continuum of post-TBI rehabilitation.

2. Development and validation of standardized outcome measures that may include behavioral, neurochemical, neurophysiological, and neuroimaging parameters. These measures would allow large scale aggregation of data across multiple treatment sites in order to identify promising treatments.

3. Large scale randomized controlled trials to assess the efficacy and tolerability of a wide range of medications currently believed to reduce agitation and aggression. Such studies would help clarify first line, adjunctive, and non-supported medications in patients who are highly vulnerable to medication side effects. Additionally, these trials would examine the tolerability and efficacy of medication combinations.

4. Assessment of manualized psychosocial interventions to develop evidence-based treatments for agitation and aggression throughout the post-injury recovery process. These would include individual and group psychotherapies, family interventions, and psychoeducational curricula.

As healthcare continues the sometimes painful evolution towards evidence-based practices, neuropsychiatric practitioners will be increasingly challenged to support their interventions to consumers, regulators, and payors. There are significant societal, legal, and economic reasons to prioritize the systematic study of post-TBI agitation and aggression with a view to reducing its impact on individual outcomes.

REFERENCES

[1] American Psychiatric Association, Diagnostic and Statistical Manual of Mental Disorders, 4th Edition, American Psychiatric Press, Washington, DC, 1994.

[2] Azouvi P, Jokic C, Attal N, Denys P, Markabi S, Bussel B: Carbamazepine in agitation and aggressive behaviour following severe closed-head injury: results of an open trial. *Brain Inj 1999; 13*:797-804.

[3] Barratt ES, Stanford MS, Kent TA, Felthous A: Neuropsychological and cognitive psychophysiological substrates of impulsive aggression. *Biol Psychiatry 1997;41:*1045-1061.

[4] Bellus SB, Stewart D, Vergo JG, Grace J, Barkstrom SR: The use of lithium in the treatment of aggressive behaviors with two brain-injured individuals in a state psychiatric hospital. *Brain Inj 1996; 10:*849-860.

[5] Bigler ED: Quantitative magnetic resonance imaging in traumatic brain injury. *J Head Trauma Rehabil 2001;* 16:117-134.

[6] Biton V, Mirza W, Montouris G, Vuong A, Hammer AE, Barrett PS. Weight change associated with valproate and lamotrigine monotherapy in patients with epilepsy. *Neurology 2001; 56:*172-177.

[7] Blumer D, Migeon C: Hormone and hormonal agents in the treatment of aggression. *J Nerv Ment Dis 1975;*160:127-137.

[8] Bowden CL, Calabrese JR, McElroy SL, Rhodes LJ, Keck PE Jr, Cookson J, Anderson J, Bolden-Watson C, Ascher J, Monaghan E, Zhou J: The efficacy of lamotrigine in rapid cycling and non-rapid cycling patients with bipolar disorder. *Biol Psychiatry 1999; 45:*953-958.

[9] Boyeson MG: Neurochemical alterations after brain injury. Clinical implications for pharmacologic rehabilitation. *Neurorehabil 1991;* 1:33-43.

[10] Brooke MM, Patterson DR, Questad KA, Cardenas D, Farrel-Roberts L: The treatment of agitation during initial hospitalization after traumatic brain injury. *Arch Phys Med Rehabil 1992; 73:*917-921.

[11] Brotherton FA, Thomas LL, Wisotzek IE, Milan MA: Social skills training in the rehabilitation. *Arch Phys Med Rehabil 1988;* 69:827-832.

[12] Brown GL, Ebert MH, Goyer DC, Jimerson DC, Klein WJ, Bunney WE, Goodwin FK: Aggression, suicide and serotonin: relationship to CSF amine metabolites. *Am J Psychiatry 1982; 139:*741-746.

[13] Brower MC, Price BH: Neuropsychiatry of frontal lobe dysfunction in violent and criminal behaviour: a critical review. *J Neurol Neurosurg Psychiatry 2001;* 71:720-726.

[14] Calabrese JR, Bowden CL, McElroy SL, Cookson J, Andersen J, Keck PE Jr, Rhodes L, Bolden-Watson C, Zhou J, Ascher JA: Spectrum of activity of lamotrigine in treatment-refractory bipolar disorder. *Am J Psychiatry 1999; 156:*1019-1023.

[15] Calabrese JR, Bowden CL, Sachs GS, Ascher JA, Monaghan E, Rudd GD: A double-blind placebo-controlled study of lamotrigine monotherapy in outpatients with bipolar I depression. Lamictal 602 Study Group. *J Clin Psychiatry 1999;*60:79-88.

[16] Calabrese JR, Keck PE Jr, McElroy SL, Shelton MD: A pilot study of topiramate as monotherapy in the treatment of acute mania. *J Clin Psychopharmacol 2001;* 21:340-342.

[17] Cardenas DD, McLean A, Farrell-Roberts L, Baker L, Brooke M, Haselkorn J: Oral physostigmine and impaired memory in adults with brain injury. *Brain Inj 1994; 8:*579-587.

[18] Carlsson GS, Svardsudd K, Welin L: Long-term effects of head injuries sustained during life in three male populations. *J Neurosurg 1987*; 67:197-205.

[19] Carta MG, Hardoy MC, Dessi I, Hardoy MJ, Carpiniello B: Adjunctive gabapentin in patients with intellectual disability and bipolar spectrum disorders. *J Intellect Disabil Res 2001*; 45(Pt 2):139-145.

[20] Chandler MC, Barnhill JL, Gualtieri CT: Amantadine for the agitated head-injury patient. *Brain Inj 1988;2*:309-311.

[21] Chatham-Showalter PE, Netsky-Kimmel D: Agitated symptom response to divalproex following acute brain injury. *J Neuropsychiatry Clin Neurosci 2000; 12*:395-397.

[22] Chatham-Showalter PE: Carbamazepine for combativeness in acute traumatic brain injury. *J Neuropsychiatry Clin Neurosci 1996; 8*:96-99.

[23] Cicerone KD, Tanenbaum LN: Disturbance of social cognition after traumatic orbitofrontal brain injury. *Arch Clin Neuropsychology 1997; 12:*173-188.

[24] Coccaro EF, Astoll JL, Herbert J, Schut AG: Fluoxetine treatment of impulsive aggression in DSM-III-R personality disorder patients. *J Clin Psychopharmacol* 1990; 10:373-375.

[25] Coccaro EF, Kavoussi RJ, Berman ME, Hauger RL: Relationship of prolactin response to d-fenfluramine to behavioral and questionnaire assessments of aggression in personality disordered males. *Biol Psychiatry 1996:* 40:157-164.

[26] Corrigan JD, Mysiw WJ: Agitation following head injury: equivocal evidence for a discrete stage of cognitive recovery. *Arch Phys Med Rehabil 1988; 69:*487-492.

[27] Courville, *CB: Pathology of the Central Nervous System*. Mountain View, CA: Pacific Publishers, 1937.

[28] Crescimanno G, Piazza P, Benigno A, Amato G: Effects of substantia nigra stimulation on hypothalamic rage reaction in cats. *Physiol Behav 1986; 37*:129-133.

[29] Cummings J: Cholinesterase inhibitors: a new class of psychotropic compounds *Am J Psychiatry 2000; 157:* 4-15.

[30] Cummings JL, Coffey CE: Neurobiological Basis of Behavior, in Textbook of Geriatric Neuropsychiatry, 2nd Edition. Edited by Coffey CE and Cummings JL. Washington, DC, American Psychiatric Press, 2000.

[31] Czobor P, Volvavka J, Meibach RC: The effect of risperidone on hostility in schizophrenia. *J Clin Psychopharmacol 1995;* 15:243-246.

[32] Dam H: Depression in stroke patients 7 years following stroke. *Acta Psychiatr Scand 2001; 103*:287-293.

[33] Damasio H, Grabowski T, Frank R, Galburda AM, Damasio AR: The return of Phineas Gage: Clues about the brain from the skull of a famous patient. *Science 1994; 264:*1102-1105.

[34] Delvaux V, Schoenen J: New generation anti-epileptics for facial pain and headache. *Acta Neurol Belg 2001; 101:*42-46.

[35] Delmonico RL, Hanley-Peterson P, Englander J: Group psychotherapy for persons with traumatic brain injury: management of frustration and substance abuse. *J Head Trauma Rehabil 1998; 13:*10-22.

[36] Dewar D, Graham DI: Depletion of choline acetyltransferase activity but preservation of M1 and M2 muscarinic receptor binding sites in temporal cortex following head injury: a preliminary human postmortem study. *J Neurotrauma 1996; 13:*181-187.

[37] Diaz FG: Traumatic brain injury and criminal behaviour. *Med Law 1995; 14*:131-140.

[38] Dikmen SS, Machamer JE, Winn HR, Anderson GD, Temkin NR: Neuropsychological effects of valproate in traumatic brain injury: a randomized trial. *Neurology 2000;54:*895-902.

[39] Ducharme JM: Treatment of maladaptive behavior in acquired brain injury: remedial approaches in postacute settings. *Clin Psychol Rev 2000; 20:*405-426.

[40] Dunlop TW, Udvarhelyi GB, Stedem AFA, O'Connor JMC, Isaacs ML, Puig JG, Mather JH: Comparison of patients with and without emotional/behavioral deterioration during the first year after traumatic brain injury. *J Neuropsychiatry Clin Neurosci 1991; 3:*150-156.

[41] Eichelman B: Neurochemical and psychopharmacological aspects of aggressive behavior, in *Psychopharmacology: The Third Generation of Progress.* Meltzer HY (ed). New York: Raven Press, 1987, pp. 697-704.

[42] Emrich HM, Dose M, von Zerssen D: The use of sodium valproate, carbamazepine and oxcarbazepine in patients with affective disorders. *J Affect Disord 1985; 8:*243-250.

[43] Eslinger PJ, Damasio AR: Severe disturbances of higher cognition after bilateral frontal lobe ablation: patient EVR. *Neurology 1985; 35:*1731-1741.

[44] Feeney DM, Gonzalez A, Law WA: Amphetamine, haloperidol, and experience interact to affect rate of recovery after motor cortex injury. Science 1982; 217:855-857.

[45] Ferretti L, McCurry SM, Logsdon R, Gibbons L, Teri L: Anxiety and Alzheimer's disease. *J Geriatr Psychiatry Neurol 2001; 14:*52-58.

[46] Flashman LA, Amador A, McAllister TW: Lack of awareness of deficits after traumatic brain injury. *Sem Clin Neuropsychiatry 1998;* 3:201-210.

[47] Foster HG, Hillbrand M, Chi CC: Efficacy of carbamazepine in assaultive patients with frontal lobe dysfunction. *Prog Neuropsychopharmacol Biol Psychiatry 1989;* 13:865-874.

[48] Foster HG, Hillbrand M, Silverstein M: Neuropsychological deficit and aggressive behavior: a prospective study. *Prog Neuropsychopharmacol Biol Psychiatry 1993; 17:*939-946.

[49] Galski T, Palasz J, Bruno RL, Walker JE: Predicting physical and verbal aggression on a brain trauma unit. *Arch Phys Med Rehabil 1994; 75:*380-383.

[50] Giancola PR, Martin CS, Tarter RE, Pelham WE, Moss HB: Executive cognitive functioning and aggressive behavior in preadolescent boys at high risk for substance abuse/dependence. *J Stud Alcohol 1996; 57:*352-359.

[51] Giancola PR, Mezzich AC, Tarter RE: Disruptive, delinquent and aggressive behavior in female adolescents with a psychoactive substance use disorder: relation to executive cognitive functioning. *J Stud Alcohol 1998; 59:*560-570.

[52] Giancola PR, Zeichner A: Neuropsychological performance on tests on frontal lobe functioning and aggressive behavior in men. *J Abnorm Psychol 1994; 103:*832-835.

[53] Glauser TA: Topiramate. *Epilepsia 1999;40* Suppl 5:S71-80.

[54] Gleckman AD, Brill S: The impact of brain injury on family functioning: implications for subacute rehabilitation programmes. *Brain Inj 1995; 9:*385-393.

[55] Glenn MB, Wroblewski B, Parziale J, Levine L, Whyte J, Rosenthal M: Lithium carbonate for aggressive behavior or affective instability in ten brain-injured patients. *Am J Phys Med Rehabil 1989; 68:*221-226.

[56] Goldstein K: The effect of brain damage on the personality. *Psychiatry 1952; 15:*245-260.

[57]   Goldstein LB: Basic and clinical studies of pharmacologic effects on recovery from brain injury. *J Neural Transplant Plasticity 1993; 4:*175-192.

[58]   Goyer PF, Andreason PJ, Semple WE, Clayton AH, King AC, Compton-Toth BA, Schulz SC, Cohen RM: Positron-emission tomography and personality disorders. *Neuropsychopharmacol 1994; 10:*21-28.

[59]   Grafman J, Schwab K, Warden D, Pridgen A, Brown HR, Salazar AM: Frontal lobe injuries, violence, and aggression: a report of the Vietnam Head Injury Study. *Neurology 1996;46:*1231-1238.

[60]   Grant SM, Faulds D: Oxcarbazepine. A review of its pharmacology and therapeutic potential in epilepsy, trigeminal neuralgia and affective disorders. *Drugs 1992; 43:*873-888.

[61]   Gray BG, Ichise M, Chung DG, Kirsch JC, Frank SW: Technetium-99m-HMPAO SPECT in the evaluation of patients with a remote history of traumatic brain injury: a comparison with x-ray computed tomography. *J Nuc Med 1992; 33:*52-58.

[62]   Greendyke RM, Kanter DR, Schuster DB, Verstreate S, Wootton J: Propranolol treatment of assaultive patients with organic brain disease. A double-blind crossover, placebo-controlled study. *J Nerv Ment Dis 1986; 174:*290-294.

[63]   Greve KW, Sherwin E, Stanford MW, Mathias C, Love J, Ramzinski P: Personality and neurocognitive correlates of impulsive aggression in long-term survivors of severe traumatic brain injury. Brain Inj 2001; 15:255-262.

[64]   Grunze HC, Normann C, Langosch J, Schaefer M, Amann B, Sterr A, 3: Chengappa KN, Rathore D, Levine J, Atzert R, Solai L, Parepally H, Levin H, Moffa N, Delaney J, Brar JS: Topiramate as add-on treatment for patients with bipolar mania. *Bipolar Disord 1999; 1:*42-53.

[65]   Grunze HC, Normann C, Langosch J, Schaefer M, Amann B, Sterr A, Schloesser S, Kleindienst N, Walden J: Antimanic efficacy of topiramate in 11 patients in an open trial with an on-off-on design. *J Clin Psychiatry. 2001 Jun;62(6):*464-468.

[66]   Gualtieri CT, Chandler M, Coons TB, Brown LT: Amantadine: a new clinical profile for traumatic brain injury. Clin Neuropharmacol 1989; 12:258-270.

[67]   Gualtieri CT: Buspirone for the behavior problems of patients with organic brain disorders (letter). *J Clin Psychopharmacol 1991; 11:*280-281.

[68]   GW Arana, JF Rosenbaum, Handbook of Psychiatric Drug Therapy, 4th Edition, Lippincott Williams & Wilkins, New York, 2000.

[69]   Hagen C, Malkmus D, Durham P: Levels of Cognitive Functioning. Ranchos Los Amigos Hospital, Downey, CA, 1972.

[70]   Harlow JM: Passage of an iron rod through the head. *Boston Medical and Surgical Journal 1848; 39:*389-393.

[71]   Hawkins KA, Trobst KK: Frontal lobe dysfunction and aggression: conceptual issues and research findings. *Aggression and Violent Behavior 2000; 5:*147-157.

[72]   Hawkins KA: Novel antipsychotics and the neuropsychological deficiencies of schizophrenia. *J Psychiatry Neurosci 2000; 25:*105-107.

[73]   Hegel MT, Ferguson RJ: Differential reinforcement of other behavior (DRO) to reduce aggressive behavior following traumatic brain injury. *Behav Modif 2000; 24:*94-101.

[74]   Hibbard MR, Bogdany J, Uysal Suzan, Kepler K, Silver JM, Gordon WA, Haddad L: Axis II psychopathology in individuals with traumatic brain injury. *Brain Inj 2000; 14:*45-61.

[75] Hornstein A, Seliger G: Cognitive side effects of lithium in closed head injury (letter). *J Neuropsychiatry Clin Neurosci 1989; 1:*446-447.

[76] Ichim L, Berk M, Brook S: Lamotrigine compared with lithium in mania: a double-blind randomized controlled trial. Ann Clin Psychiatry 2000; 12:5-10.

[77] JH Adams, DI Graham, TA Gennarelli, Contemporary neuropathological considerations regarding brain injury, in *Central Nervous System Trauma Status Report 1985*, National Institute of Neurological and Communicative Disorders and Stroke, Bethesda, MD, 1986, pp. 65-78.

[78] Jorge RE, Robinson RG, Starkstein SE, Arndt SV, Forrester AW, Geisler FH: Secondary mania following traumatic brain injury. *Am J Psychiatry 1993; 150:*916-921.

[79] Katz IR, Jeste DV, Mintzer JE, Clyde C, Napolitano J, Brecher M: Comparison of risperidone and placebo for psychosis and behavioral disturbances associated with dementia: a randomized, double-blind trial. Risperidone Study Group. *J Clin Psychiatry 1999 Feb;60(2):*107-115.

[80] Kelly MP, Johnson CT, Knoller N, Druback DA, Winslow MM: Substance abuse, traumatic brain injury and neuropsychological outcome. Brain Inj 1997; 11:391-402.

[81] Khan A, Faught E, Gilliam F, Kuzniecky R: Acute psychotic symptoms induced by topiramate. Seizure 1999; 8:235-237.

[82] Kim KY, Bader GM, Jones E: Citalopram for verbal agitation in patients with dementia. *J Geriatr Psychiatry Neurol 2000; 13:*53-55.

[83] Kim KY, Moles JK, Hawley JM: Selective serotonin reuptake inhibitors for aggressive behavior in patients with dementia after head injury. *Pharmacotherapy 2001; 21:*498-501.

[84] Kinsella G, Ong B, Murtagh D, et al: The role of the family for behavioral outcome in children and adolescents following traumatic brain injury. *J Consult Clin Psychol 1999; 67:*116-123.

[85] Klonoff PS, Lamb DG, Henderson SW, et al: Outcome assessment after milieu-oriented rehabilitation: new considerations. Arch Phys Med Rehabil. 1998; 79:684-690.

[86] Kreutzer JS, Marwitz JH, Witol AD: Interrelationship between crime, substance abuse, and aggressive behaviours among persons with traumatic brain injury. *Brain Inj 1995;* 9:757-768.

[87] Kyomen HH, Satlin A, Hennen J, Wei JY: Estrogen therapy and aggressive behavior in elderly patients with moderate-to-severe dementia: results from a short-term, randomized, double-blind trial. *Am J Geriatr Psychiatry 1999; 7:*339-348.

[88] Leach LR, Frank RG, Bouman DE, et al: Family functioning, social support and depression after traumatic brain injury. *Brain Inj 1994; 8:*599-606.

[89] Levin HS, Grossman RG: Behavioral sequelae of closed head injury: a quantitative study. *Arch Neurol 1978; 35:*720-727.

[90] Maeda H, Maki S: Effects of dopamine agonists on hypothalamic defensive attack in cats. *Physiol Behav 1985; 35:*89-92.

[91] Masdeu JC, Abdel-Dayem H, Van Heertum RL: Head trauma: use of SPECT. *J Neuroimag 1995; 5:*S53-S57.

[92] Maxwell WL, Polvishock JT, Graham DL: A mechanistic analysis of nondisruptive axonal injury: a review. *J Neurotrauma 1997; 14:*419-440.

[93] McAllister TW: Evaluation of brain injury related behavioral disturbances in community mental health centers. *Comm Mental Health J 1997; 33*:341-364.

[94] Messenheimer JA: Rash in adult and pediatric patients treated with lamotrigine. *Can J Neurol Sci 1998; 25:*S14-18.

[95] Mesulam MM: Principles of Behavioral and Cognitive Neurology, 2nd Edition. New York: Oxford University Press, 2000.

[96] Michals ML, Crismon ML, Roberts S, Childs A: Clozapine response and adverse effects in nine brain-injured patients. *J Clin Psychopharmacol 1993;13:*198-203.

[97] Miller L. Traumatic brain injury and aggression. In The Psychobiology of Aggression. Hillbrand M and Pallone NJ, (eds). New York: The Haworth Press, 1994:91-103.

[98] Minger SL, Esiri MM, McDonald B, Keene J, Carter J, Hope T, Francis PT: Cholinergic deficits contribute to behavioral disturbance in patients with dementia. *Neurology 2000; 55:*1460-1467.

[99] Mooney GF, Haas LJ. Effect of methylphenidate on brain injury-related anger. *Arch Phys Med Rehabil 1993; 74:*153-160.

[100] Mortimer AM: Cognitive function in schizophrenia--do neuroleptics make a difference? *Pharmacol Biochem Behav 1997: 56:*789-795.

[101] Moskowitz AS, Altshuler L: Increased sensitivity to lithium-induced neurotoxicity after stroke. *J Clin Psychopharmacol 1991; 11:*272-273.

[102] Mysiw WJ, Sandel ME: The agitated brain injured patient. Part 2: pathophysiology and treatment. *Arch Phys Med Rehabil 1997; 78:*213-220.

[103] Oder W, Goldenberg G, Spatt J, Podreka I, Binder H, Deecke L: Behavioural and psychosocial sequelae of severe closed head injury and regional cerebral blood flow: a SPECT study. *J Neurol Neurosurg Psychiatry 1992; 55:*475-480.

[104] Pande AC, Crockatt JG, Janney CA, Werth JL, Tsaroucha G: Gabapentin in bipolar disorder: a placebo-controlled trial of adjunctive therapy. Gabapentin Bipolar Disorder Study Group. *Bipolar Disord 2000; 2(3 Pt 2):*249-255.

[105] Pappius HM: Brain injury: New insights into neurotransmitter and receptor mechanisms. *Neurochem Res 1991; 16:*941-949.

[106] Perr IN: Alleged brain damage, diminished capacity, mens rea, and misuse of medical concepts. *J Forensic Sci 1991; 36:*722-727.

[107] Pietrini P, Guazzelli M, Basso G, Jaffe K, Grafman J: Neural correlates of imaginal aggressive behavior assessed by positron emission tomography in healthy subjects. *Am J Psychiatry 2000;157:*1772-1781.

[108] Pollock BG, Mulsant BH, Sweet R, Burgio LD, Kirshner MA, Shuster K, Rosen J: An open pilot study of citalopram for behavioral disturbances of dementia. Plasma levels and real-time observations. *Am J Geriatr Psychiatry 1997; 5:*70-78.

[109] Pollock IW: Individual Psychotherapy, in Neuropsychiatry of Traumatic Brain Injury. Edited by Silver JM, Yudofsky SC, Hales RE. Washington, DC, American Psychiatric Press, 1994, pp. 671-702.

[110] Prigatano GP: Personality disturbances associated with traumatic brain injury. *J Consult Clin Psychol 1992; 60:*360-368.

[111] Rao N, Jellenik HM, Woolston DC: Agitation in closed head injury: haloperidol effects on rehabilitation outcome. *Arch Phys Med Rehabil 1985; 66:*30-34.

[112] Ratey JJ, Leveroni CL, Miller AC, Komry V, Gaffar K: Low-dose buspirone to treat agitation and maladaptive behavior in brain-injured patients: two case reports (letter). *J Clin Psychopharmacol 1992; 12:*362-364.

[113] Ried LD, McFarland BH, Johnson RE, Brody KK: Beta-blockers and depression: the more the murkier? *Ann Pharmacother 1998; 32:*699-708.

[114] Rowland TR, Mysiw WJ, Bogner JA: Trazodone for post-traumatic agitation. *Arch Phys Med Rehabil 1992; 73:*963.

[115] Saija A, Hayes RL, Lyeth BG, Dixon CE, Yamamoto T, Robinson SE: The effect of concussive head injury on central cholinergic neurons. *Brain Res 1988; 452:*303.

[116] Sandel ME, Mysiw WJ: The agitated brain injured patient. Part 1: definitions, differential diagnosis, and assessment. *Arch Phys Med Rehabil 1996; 77:*617-623.

[117] Schlund MW, Pace G: Relations between traumatic brain injury and the environment: feedback reduces maladaptive behaviour exhibited by three persons with traumatic brain injury. *Brain Inj 1999; 13:*889-897.

[118] Shafer A: Complications of sedation with midazolam in the intensive care unit and a comparison with other sedative regimens. *Crit Care Med 1998; 26:*947-956.

[119] Showalter PE, Kimmel DN: Stimulating consciousness and cognition following severe brain injury: a new potential clinical use for lamotrigine. *Brain Inj 2000;14:*997-1001.

[120] Siegal A, Roeling TAP, Gregg TR, Kruk MR: Neuropharmacology of brain-stimulation-evoked aggression. *Neurosci Biobehav Rev 1999;23:*359-389.

[121] Silver JM, Yudofsky SC: Aggressive disorders, in *Neuropsychiatry of Traumatic Brain Injury*. Edited by Silver JM, Yudofsky SC, Hales RE. Washington, DC, American Psychiatric Press, 1994, pp. 313-353.

[122] Silver JM. Hales RE, Yudofsky SC: Neuropsychiatric Aspects of Traumatic Brain Injury, in *Textbook of Neuropsychiatry*, 3rd Edition, Yudofsky SC, Hales RE (Eds). Washington, DC: American Psychiatric Press, 1997, pp. 521-560.

[123] Sky AJ, Grossberg GT: The use of psychotropic medication in the management of problem behaviors in the patient with Alzheimer's disease. *Med Clin North Am 1994; 78:*811-822.

[124] Smith KR Jr, Goulding PM, Wilderman D, Goldfader PR, Holterman-Hommes, Wei F: Neurobehavioral effects of phenytoin and carbamazepine in patients recovering from brain trauma: a comparative study. *Arch Neurol 1994; 51:*635-660.

[125] Sokolski KN, Green C, Maris DE, DeMet EM: Gabapentin as an adjunct to standard mood stabilizers in outpatients with mixed bipolar symptomatology. *Ann Clin Psychiatry 1999; 11:*217-222.

[126] Soloff PH, Meltzer CC, Greer PJ, Constantine D, Kelly TM: A fenfluramine-activated FDG-PET study of borderline personality disorder. Biol Psychiatry 2000;47:540-547.

[127] Sparedo F, Gill D: Effects of prior alcohol use on head injury recovery. *J Head Trauma Rehabil 1989; 4:*75-82.

[128] Stanislav SW, Crismon ML, Childs NL: Cerebrospinal fluid monoamine metabolites and glucose metabolism in posttraumatic aggression. *Biol Psychiatry 1998; 43:* 619-621.

[129] Stanislav SW, Fabre T, Crismon ML, Childs A: Buspirone's efficacy in organic-induced aggression. *J Clin Psychopharmacol 1994; 14:*126-130.

[130] Stanislav SW: Cognitive effects of antipsychotic agents in persons with traumatic brain injury. *Brain Inj 1997; 11:*335-341.

[131] Starkstein SE, Mayberg HS, Berthier ML, Fedoroff, Price TR, Dannals RF, Wagner HN, Leiguarda R, Robinson RG: Secondary mania: neuroradiological and metabolic findings. *Ann Neurol 1990; 27:*652-659.

[132] Starkstein SE, Robinson RG: Mechanism of disinhibition after brain lesions. *J Nerv Ment Dis 1997;185:*108-114.

[133] Street JS, Clark WS, Gannon KS, Cummings JL, Bymaster FP, Tamura RN, Mitan SJ, Kadam DL, Sanger TM, Feldman PD, Tollefson GD, Breier A: Olanzapine treatment of psychotic and behavioral symptoms in patients with Alzheimer disease in nursing care facilities: a double-blind, randomized, placebo-controlled trial. The HGEU Study Group. *Arch Gen Psychiatry 2000;57:*968-976.

[134] Tatum WO 4th, French JA, Faught E, Morris GL 3rd, Liporace J, Kanner A, Goff SL, Winters L, Fix A: Postmarketing experience with topiramate and cognition. *Epilepsia 2001;42:*1134-1140.

[135] Taverni JP, Seliger G, Lichtman SW: Donepezil medicated memory improvement in traumatic brain injury during post acute rehabilitation. *Brain Inj 1998;12:*77-80.

[136] Teri L: Training families to provide care: effects on people with dementia. *Int J Geriatr Psychiatry 1999;14:*110-116.

[137] Uomoto JM, Brockway JA: Anger management training for brain injured patients and their family members. *Arch Phys Med Rehabil 1992; 73:*674-679.

[138] Van der Naalt J, Van Zomeren AH, Sluiter WJ, Minderhoud JM: Acute behavioural disturbances related to imaging studies and outcome in mild-to-moderate head injury. *Brain Inj 2999; 14:*781-788.

[139] Whelan FJ, Walker MS, Schultz SK. Donepezil in the treatment of cognitive dysfunction associated with traumatic brain injury. *Ann Clin Psychiatry 2000; 12:*131-135.

[140] Whitlock JA: Brain injury, cognitive impairment, and donepezil. *J Head Trauma Rehabil 1999; 14:*424-427.

[141] Wroblewski BA, Joseph AB, Kupfer J, Kalliel K: Effectiveness of valproic acid on destructive and aggressive behaviours in patients with acquired brain injury. *Brain Inj 1997; 11:*37-47.

[142] Yody BB, Schaub C, Conway J, Peters S, Strauss D, Helsinger S: Applied behavior management and acquired brain injury: approaches and assessment. *J Head Trauma Rehabil 2000; 15:*1041-1060.

[143] Yudofsky S, Williams D, Gorman J: Propranolol in the treatment of rage and violent behavior in patients with chronic brain syndromes. *Am J Psychiatry 1981; 138:*218-220.

[144] Yudofsky SC, Silver JM, Schneider SE: Pharmacologic treatment of aggression. *Psychiatric Annals 1987; 17:* 397-407.

[145] Zencius AH, Weslowski MD, Burke WH, McQuade P: Antecedent control in the treatment of brain-injured clients. *Brain Inj 1989; 3:*199-205.

[146] Zwil AS, McAllister TW, Raimo E: The expression of bipolar affective disorders in brain-injured patients. *Int J Psychiatry Med 1992; 22:*377-395.

In: *Focus on Aggression Research*
Editor: James P. Morgan, pp. 115-156

ISBN 1-59454-132-9
© 2004 Nova Science Publishers, Inc.

Chapter 8

ANGER, AGGRESSION, AND RISKY BEHAVIOR IN HIGH ANGER DRIVERS

Jerry L. Deffenbacher, Tracy L. Richards and Rebekah S. Lynch[*]

INTRODUCTION

In the last decade or so, the media has drawn attention to incidents involving angry, aggressive drivers and "road rage." Driver Shot after Heated Exchange, Wild Chase Results in Death of Two Angry Motorists, Motorist and Bicyclist Get into Fisticuffs… . All too often these have been the lead ins to the day's news. Newspapers, magazines, and television have been filled with examples of drivers who have engaged in aggressive, threatening, risky, dangerous, even lethal behavior. While these examples are often the most extreme, nearly every driver can identify with them. Nearly all of us have been endangered by erratic, impulsive behavior of an angry driver and have seen relatively minor incidents escalate into angry, aggressive exchanges. Most of us know otherwise reasonable individuals until they have a set of car keys in their hands. Then, like Jekyl and Hyde, the smallest of things goes wrong, and this, otherwise calm, person changes into an angry tyrant, yelling, swearing, gesturing wildly and obscenely, perhaps intimidating aggressively with his/her vehicle, becoming an embarrassment to him/herself and a menace not only to their passengers and those who share the road with them.

---

[*] This study was supported, in part, by Grant R49/CCR811509 from the Centers for Disease Control and Prevention and by 5 P50 DA07074-10 from the National Institute on Drug Abuse. Its contents are solely the responsibility of the authors and do not necessarily represent the official views of the Centers for Disease Control and Prevention.

Jerry Deffenbacher, Ph.D., and Tracy L. Richards, Ph.D., are in the Department of Psychology, Colorado State University, and Rebekah Lynch, Ph.D., is in the Nursing Program, Front Range Community College, Fort Collins, Colorado.

Correspondence should be sent to Jerry L. Deffenbacher, Department of Psychology, Colorado State University, Fort Collins, Colorado 80523-1876. E-mail: jld6871@lamar.colostate.edu.

BASIC TERMS AND CONCEPTS

Although these are unfortunately all too common experiences, terminology in the area is not precise. There are five related, somewhat overlapping concepts – road rage, angry drivers, aggression while driving, risky driving, and aggressive driving.

Although there is some dispute between the British Automobile Association and the American Automobile Association about which organization coined the term first, the American Automobile Association (1997) popularized the term "road rage" in the United States. Road rage refers to the most violent acts, acts that most likely qualify legally as at least assault or attempted assault and perhaps more serious charges, depending on the extent of the behavior and the outcomes. In a road rage incident, a driver becomes furious and engages in behavior that does or could seriously injure another driver, pedestrian, or bicyclist. A weapon may be used such as firing a gun at another driver. The vehicle may be used as a weapon such as running someone off the road, running into or over someone, or cutting in front of another driver and slamming on the brakes. The incident may involve physical assault on a person such as a fist fight, or on the vehicle such as smashing a window with a baseball bat or denting the car with a tire iron. Other road rage incidents involve a wide range of intimidating and menacing behaviors such as threatening to punch another driver, tailgating at high speeds, and the like. Road rage incidents are in many ways the most serious, often tragic, and in many cases illegal, but fortunately relatively infrequent, considering the millions of miles driven every day in the U. S. Nonetheless, and though there has been some question in the methodology of looking at published reports and police records, the rates of road rage incidents appeared to increase approximately 7% per year from 1990 through the mid-1990's (American Automobile Association, 1997).

For every incident of road rage, there are thousands, probably tens of thousands of angry drivers. Every day, there are drivers who are furious, angry, mad as hell, and the like. At the core of the angry driver's experience is a high level of angry emotionality and usually considerable physiological arousal (e.g., muscle tension, heart racing, elevated blood pressure, clenched jaws). Such angry drivers may behave aggressively. Middle fingers may be flipped; fists may be shaken; loud obscene epithets may be shouted; drivers may purposefully block another driver's path; and the like. However, the angry driver may not act out aggressively. He/she, for example, might seethe, but do nothing more than mumble and curse to him/herself, but not take it out on anyone. Another driver might become equally angry, but initiate positive coping behaviors such as backing away from the offending driver, instructing him/herself to take some deep breaths and relax, and turning on the radio to calm down and distract him/herself from the anger-arousing event. In the latter case, the driver starts out as angry as other drivers, but initiates adaptive coping behavior that reduces anger. In all three cases, drivers were very angry, but behavior was quite different. The defining characteristic of the angry driver is the high level of angry emotion and physiological arousal, not necessarily aggressive behavior. Although the frequency of angry drivers is not well documented, cases of angry drivers are much more frequent and generally much less severe than road rage incidents.

A related concept is aggression on the road. Aggression is generally considered to be behavior where the intent or goal of which is to harm, threaten, intimidate, or retaliate against a person or persons who do not seek such behavior. If this definition is expanded somewhat to fit the driving environment, aggression on the road might be defined as behavior that is intended to harm, express displeasure with, intimidate, retaliate upon or seek revenge upon, or frustrate another person and/or behavior considered to be aggressive that is done in anger (i.e., prompted and motivated by anger). Aggression might include behaviors such as giving someone the finger or making another angry gesture, shouting or swearing at the person, honking horns in anger, purposefully cutting someone off to express displeasure and retaliate, boxing someone in to teach them a lesson, tailgating another driver in anger, and trying to run someone off the road. The degree of potential harm or risk to others varies considerably with the specific aggressive act. For example, gesturing or yelling at another driver may have no consequence if the other driver does not see or hear it and still may have little consequence if the other driver ignores the behavior and does not counter-aggress. Other aggressive behaviors have greater potential for harm, because they set the stage for another person to react with aggression and escalate a cycle of reciprocal aggression. For example, one driver gives another driver the finger, and the other driver takes offense and cuts the initial driver off. An aggressive escalation may ensue, eventuating potentially in injurious, even lethal outcomes. Yet, other aggressive behavior has a significant potential for harm because of the nature of the behavior itself. For example, intentionally cutting someone off, trying to run them off the road, or purposefully bumping into their vehicle are not only acts of aggression, but also may physically harm someone as well. In summary, aggression on the road is behavior conducted in anger and/or behavior the intent of which is to harm, intimidate, communicate anger and displeasure, frustrate other drivers, and/or get back at them for perceived offenses. Aggression may or may not increase the risk of sustaining a crash, an injury, or vehicular or property damage.

Risky behavior, on the other hand, is defined exactly by the increased probability of injury, crash, property damage, and the like. Risky behavior puts the driver and/or others at risk of physical harm. As seen above, some aggressive behaviors are also risky behaviors, because they directly increase the likelihood of physical harm or injury to the driver or others (e.g., the angry driver cutting another driver off on purpose). However, there are also many risky behaviors that have little or nothing to do with anger and aggression. For example, a person may drive without his/her seatbelt fastened, drive while under the influence of alcohol or other drugs, drive a vehicle that is unsafe, drive well over the speed limit or well beyond the driving conditions, dart in and out of traffic, pass on the right, tailgate, or drift into another lane due to inattention. All of these behaviors increase physical risk to the driver and/or others, yet are not at all aggressive in terms of the prior definition. They may be momentary behaviors or persistent personal habits that are not at all done in anger or with the intent to harm. Nonetheless, they are behaviors that increase the potential for harm, but without that intent.

A final term is aggressive driving. It is often used colloquially, by the press, and by police officers to refer to a wide range of risk-enhancing behaviors or conditions (e.g., speeding, rapid lane changes, driving a vehicle with faulty equipment). This term, however, is confounded conceptually because it mixes the notions of aggressive and risky behavior under a single rubric. For the purposes of this chapter, it is suggested that the term aggressive driving be abandoned and replaced with more precise, but sometimes convergent notions of aggression and risky behavior with aggressive behavior being behavior based in anger and/or behavior the goals of which are to harm, intimidate, threaten, dominate, retaliate upon, frustrate, or otherwise express displeasure with another driver or user of the roadway, whereas risky behavior puts the individual and/or others at increased risk for injury, crash, and/or property damage. It is suggested that aggressive and risky behaviors are likely correlated, but not necessarily always mediated by the same environmental, emotional, physiological, and cognitive processes and that understanding of anger and aggression on the road would be facilitated if they are conceptually and empirically separated.

FACTORS INFLUENCING ANGER AND AGGRESSION ON THE ROAD

Anger and aggression on the road rarely occur in a vacuum or without a social or psychological context. For example, conditions in the driving environment such as congestion, impedance that slows the driver, and increased ambient temperature appear to increase anger and sometimes aggression (Deffenbacher, Deffenbacher, Lynch, & Richards, 2003; Deffenbacher, Huff, Lynch, Oetting, & Salvatore, 2000; Doob & Gross, 1968; Kenrick & MacFarlane, 1986; Shinar, 1998). At other times, a portion of the context that elicits or facilitates anger and aggression may be conditions of the vehicle such as anonymity brought on by darkened windows, apparent status of the driver, and hostile bumper stickers and other messages (Doob & Gross, 1968; Eillison, Govern, Petri, & Figler, 1995; Ellison-Potter, Bell, & Deffenbacher, 2001). The behavior of others also can elicit anger and aggression. For example, being unable to pass a slow driver who does not pull over to let others by, having another driver steal a parking place for which a person is waiting, being yelled at by another driver, or being behind inattentive an driver will increase anger and aggression (Deffenbacher, 2003; Deffenbacher, Deffenbacher, et al. 2003; Deffenbacher, Lynch, Filetti, Dahlen, & Oetting, 2003). Thus, external conditions appear to significantly influence anger and aggression while driving.

Conditions internal to the individual or person factors such as personality characteristics, emotions, and temporary states also seem to influence behavior behind the wheel. For example, drivers who experience high accident rates and engage in risky, often illegal driving also tend to be higher on general anger, aggressiveness, impulsiveness, sensation seeking, and social unconventionality and irresponsibility (e.g., Arnett, Offer, & Fine, 1997; Donovan, Queisser, Salzberg, & Umlauf, 1985; McMillen, Pan, Wells-Parker, & Anderson, 1992). General traits or characteristics of anger and aggressiveness correlate positively with and appear to carryover to anger and aggression behind the wheel (Deffenbacher, Lynch, Oetting, & Swaim, 2002; Deffenbacher, White, & Lynch, in press; Lajunen & Parker, 2001), and drivers who become involved in physical altercations with other drivers also experience more crashes and traffic tickets (Hemenway & Solnick, 1993). Moreover, self- and court-referred aggressive drivers experience greater incidences of intermittent explosive disorder and other pathology, some of which is played out on the road (Galovski, Blanchard, & Veazey, 2002). Research by Donovan, Umlauf, and Salzberg (1988) suggests that general characteristics may be associated in different ways. For example, one group of high-risk drivers exhibited the general characteristics of general anger, aggressiveness, impulsiveness, and sensation seeking, whereas a second group was characterized more by dysphoria, resentment, and covert hostile feelings and thoughts and tended to act out these aggressive feelings when driving. Thus, relatively stable person characteristics appear to correlate with and contribute to anger and aggression on the road.

More transitory psychological conditions or states appear to influence anger and aggression on the road as well. Being in an angry state is one such variable. For example, being in an angry mood was the only mood state associated with high speed and reckless driving in youth (Arnett et al., 1997). That is, adolescent drivers were more likely to drive recklessly when angry, but not when in other moods such as being anxious or depressed. Being angry, even when it has little or nothing to do with driving, facilitated reckless driving in college students (i.e., college students reported that their anger led them to engage in reckless driving) (Lynch, Morris, Deffenbacher, & Oetting, 1998; Morris, Deffenbacher, Lynch, & Oetting, 1996). Moreover, state anger, no matter its source, correlated with both aggressive and risky behavior on the road (Deffenbacher, Lynch, Oetting, & Yingling, 2001). Thus, angry mood states may show what social psychologists (e.g., Zillman, 1971) refer to as transfer effects, in which being angry seems to carry over and increase the probability of being angry and aggressive in subsequent situations, even if they are socially and psychologically very dissimilar. Other transitory conditions may contribute as well. For example, many drivers report that they are more prone to anger and aggressive behavior when they are in a hurry or pressed for time. A long line of research conducted by Berkowitz and colleagues (e.g., Berkowitz, 1990) has shown that any number of aversive physical and psychological states (e.g., being tired, hungry, hurried, sick, anxious, stressed, etc.) increase the saliency of negative imagery and associations and facilitate the experience of anger and aggression. Thus, transitory person characteristics whether an angry mood state or other conditions and experiences may influence the experience of anger and aggression while driving.

In summary, a diverse set of factors correlate with and seem to influence the probability and intensity of anger and aggression on the road. Some of these are external factors such as traffic conditions, the behavior of other drivers and users of the road such as pedestrians and bicyclists, and the nature of the social-psychological conditions such as anonymity. Others, however, are transitory and relatively stable personal characteristics. Anger and aggression while driving thus appear influenced by both situational and person characteristics.

While general person characteristics are related, are some people more vulnerable to anger behind the wheel than others? That is, is there a relatively enduring person characteristic of the tendency to become angry while driving? If so, this could be one of the primary characteristics of the angry drivers (i.e., they have a heightened vulnerability to becoming angry when driving). Anecdotal evidence noted in the opening paragraph of this chapter supports this notion (i.e., most drivers know of people who are otherwise reasonably calm, but become very angry and potentially aggressive when they encounter frustrations and hassles on the road). But, what does the literature say?

This chapter will briefly summarize the literature on driving anger as a person characteristic and articulate a series of predictions about the characteristics of high anger driver. It will then provide an empirical study, one that evaluates these predictions and assesses a number of emotional, cognitive, and behavioral characteristics of high anger drivers. Findings from this study will be integrated with the literature and extended to implications for clinical interventions and a policy consideration.

TRAIT DRIVING ANGER (A PERSON'S ANGER PRONENESS BEHIND THE WHEEL): THEORY AND FINDINGS

Trait driving anger refers to the person's general propensity to become angry encountering potential frustrations and provocations when driving. The concept of trait driving anger is derived from the state-trait model of anger (Deffenbacher et al., 1996; Spielberger, 1988), wherein a trait of anger refers to the general tendency to become angry across time and circumstances, whereas state anger refers to the momentary experience of anger arousal in a specific context or specific point in time. Adapted to anger while driving, trait driving anger would refer to the general propensity to become angry in driving-related circumstances, whereas state driving anger would refer to momentary experience of anger in a specific context.

Five specific predictions or hypotheses were derived from adapting the state-trait model to anger when driving. Specifically, if trait driving anger assesses the person's tendency to become angry when driving, then, compared to low trait driving anger individuals, high trait anger drivers should: (1) be angered by a wider range of driving-related situations (elicitation hypothesis); (2) experience more frequent anger when driving (frequency hypothesis); and (3) become more intensely angered when driving (intensity hypothesis). (4) Because increased anger may motivate and prompt aggressive behavior, high anger drivers are also expected to engage in more aggression when operating a vehicle (aggression hypothesis). (5) Moreover, because aggressive responding and positive, constructive coping with anger are minimally correlated (Deffenbacher, Lynch, Oetting, et al., 2002; Deffenbacher et al., in press), high anger drivers are also predicted to cope with or handle anger-provoking events in less constructive ways (reduced positive coping hypothesis).

Some research has supported these predictions. For example, high anger drivers appear to be angered by a wider range of potential provocations (Deffenbacher et al., 2000, Deffenbacher, Filetti, Richards, Lynch, & Oetting, 2003). Trait driving anger is associated with increased frequency and intensity of anger behind the wheel (Deffenbacher, 2003; Deffenbacher, Deffenbacher, et al., 2003; Deffenbacher et al., 2000; Deffenbacher, Lynch, Filetti, Dahlen, & Oetting, 2003; Deffenbacher, Lynch, Oetting, et al., 2001). State anger also correlates with aggressive and risky behavior (Arnett et al., 1997; Deffenbacher, Lynch, Oetting, et al., 2001). Trait driving anger correlates positively with aggressive forms of expressing anger and aggression while driving and negatively with adaptive/constructive expression of anger while driving (Deffenbacher, Lynch, Deffenbacher, & Oetting, 2001; Deffenbacher, Lynch, Oetting, et al., 2002). When driving in high impedance simulations (Deffenbacher, Deffenbacher, et al., 2003) and when visualizing an interpersonally provocative situation (Deffenbacher, 2003), trait driving anger was associated with more anger and aggression. Studies of English drivers also have shown that elements of trait driving anger are associated with traffic violations involving both aggressive and non-aggressive events (Lajunen, Parker, & Stradling, 1998; Underwood, Chapman, Wright, & Crundall, 1999). Other studies have also suggested that trait driving anger is associated with more risky, less safe driving (Deffenbacher, 2003; Deffenbacher, Deffenbacher, et al., 2003; Deffenbacher et al., 2000; Deffenbacher, Filetti, et al., 2003; Deffenbacher, Lynch, Filetti, et al., 2003; Deffenbacher, Lynch, Oetting, et al., 2001).

These studies provide initial support for the relationships of trait driving anger to other relevant constructs and for the adaptation of the state-trait model. However, there are also some problems in the extant literature. First, at least three of the studies (Deffenbacher et al., 2000; Deffenbacher, Filetti, et al., 2003; Deffenbacher, Lynch, Filetti, et al., 2003) involved clinical samples (i.e., high trait anger drivers who sought counseling for driving anger reduction). These samples are somewhat confounded. Assistance seeking confounds a clean interpretation of findings in terms of anger status. That is, a portion of the findings may be due to seeking assistance, rather than anger status per se. Second, some studies (e.g., Deffenbacher, Lynch, Oetting, et al., 2001, 2002) included full distributions of trait driving anger. While these establish general correlational relationships, they do not specifically establish characteristics of high and low anger drivers. Third, few studies provide a test of most of the state-trait hypotheses in the same study. Fourth, few studies employ a multi-method approach to hypothesis testing, thereby providing a more robust test of hypotheses. Finally, no study to date has extended a test of the state-trait model to angry/hostile thinking. That is, do high anger drivers tend to think in more hostile/aggressive and/or less constructive ways?

The present research addresses these issues. First, it partially replicates two studies (Deffenbacher, 2003; Deffenbacher, Deffenbacher, et al., 2003) that employed high and low anger, non-clinical samples and therefore have greater external validity to college student drivers in general. Second, it extends this line of research by assessing state anger, aggression, and positive coping in two different interpersonal provocations. A positive coping measure was included in these assessments, providing another evaluation of the reduced coping hypothesis. Third, it adds a measure of angry/hostile thinking, the Driver's Angry Thoughts Questionaire (Deffenbacher, Petrilli, et al., 2003), and thereby extends a test of state-trait predictions to angry/hostile thinking (i.e., high anger drivers will engage in more angry/hostile thinking and less coping thoughts). Fourth, measures of general trait anger and anger expression were included. This allowed a continued mapping of the characteristics of high anger drivers and an assessment of whether high anger drivers are more generally angry and aggressive as suggested by Lajunen and Parker (2001). Finally, this research included multiple methods (e.g., surveys and questionnaires, field diaries, and responses to visualized provocations), which provided a multi-method test of some hypothesis.

SAMPLING, INSTRUMENTATION, AND METHODOLOGY

Participants

Participants were 120 young (*M* age = 18.94, *SD* = 1.28) college students enrolled in introductory psychology at Colorado State University, a land grant university of approximately 25,000 students in a city of approximately 125,000. There were 30 male and 30 female high anger drivers and 30 male and 30 female low anger drivers. High and low anger driver status was defined, respectively, as scoring in the upper or lower quartile (scores greater than 52 or lower than 42) of the short-form of the Driving Anger Scale (Deffenbacher, Oetting, & Lynch, 1994). Of these students, 70.0% were freshmen, 16.7% sophomores, 5.8% juniors, and 7.5% seniors. They were predominantly white non-Hispanic (89.2%) with 2.5%

Native American, 1.7% African American, 0.8% Asian American, and 5.8% Latino backgrounds.

Instruments

Demographic Information

On the first page of the packet of instruments, participants reported age, gender, year in school (freshmen, sophomore, junior, senior, or other), and ethnicity (white non-Hispanic, Native American, Asian American, African American, Latino, and other).

Driving Anger Scale

This study employed both the short- (14-item) and long-forms (33-item) of the Driving Anger Scale (Deffenbacher et al., 1994). The short-form was employed to screen high and low anger drivers, and the long-form was used to address the elicitation and intensity hypotheses. In completing these scales, students rated on a 1 to 5 scale (1 = not at all, 5 = very much) the amount of anger they experience in the situation described. The short-form was developed from the most reliable cluster structure that included at least one item from each of the six subscales from the long-form. The short-form (αs = .80-.93) and long-form (α = .96) have 10-week test-retest reliabilities of .84 and .83, respectively, (Deffenbacher, 2000) and correlate .95 with each other (Deffenbacher et al., 1994). Long-form scales assess anger in six types of situations: (1) 3-item (α = .92) Hostile Gestures (e.g., others make an obscene gesture); (2) 4-item (α = .81) Illegal Driving (e.g., others going over the speed limit); (3) 4-item (α = .87) Police Presence (e.g., officer pulls you over); (4) 6-item (α = .91) Slow Driving (e.g., slow driver does not pull over to let others by); (5) 9-item (α = .92) Discourtesy (e.g., someone cuts you off); and (6) 7-item (α = .87) Traffic Obstructions (e.g., stuck in a traffic jam). Trait driving anger as measured by both forms of the Driving Anger Scale correlates positively with the frequency and intensity of anger and the frequency of aggressive and risky behavior when driving and with some crash-related outcomes (Deffenbacher, 2000; Deffenbacher, Lynch, Oetting, et al., 2001).

Personal Driving Anger Situations

The Personal Driving Anger Situations assess the individual's highest levels of anger while driving by asking the person to describe his/her two most angering situations related to driving (Deffenbacher, Lynch, Filetti, et al., 2003). After the person describes the situation, then he/she rates his/her anger on a 0-100 scale (0 = little or no anger; 100 = maximum level of anger you could ever experience). Since the Personal Driving Anger Situations are single-item measures, α reliability is not an appropriate measure of reliability, but these measures are adaptations of the Anger Situation measure (Deffenbacher, Story, Brandon, Hogg, & Hazaleus, 1988), which had 10-week test-retest reliability of .81. Trait driving anger is positively associated with anger reported on the Personal Driving Anger Situations (Deffenbacher, Lynch, Filetti, et al., 2003).

Driver's Angry Thoughts Questionnaire

The Driver's Angry Thoughts Questionnaire (Deffenbacher, Petrilli, Lynch, Oetting, & Swaim, 2003) was included to assess angry/hostile, driving-related thought processes and thereby describe angry drivers' characteristics more fully and provide a test of an extension of the aggression and reduced positive coping hypotheses to cognitive processes. Students rated on a five-point scale (1 = not at all, 5 = all the time) how often they have the thought listed or one similar to it when they are angry while driving. The Driver's Angry Thoughts Questionnaire yields five factor analytically derived scales of driving-related cognitions. (1) The 21-item Judgmental and Disbelieving Thinking scale (α = .94) includes statements of mild to moderate derogation of other drivers, statements or questions suggesting that they cannot believe others are driving the way they are, and statements that others should not be able to drive (e.g., Who do they think they are? or They are clueless.). (2) The 13-item Pejorative Labeling and Verbally Aggressive Thinking scale (α = .92) contains statements with much more negative, derogative, sometimes obscene judgments and labels and thoughts about engaging in verbally aggressive behavior (e.g., What an ass. or I am so pissed.). (3) The 14-item Revenge and Retaliatory Thinking scale (α = .93) assesses thinking about getting back at others, showing them that they cannot treat the person in the way they have, and the behaviors necessary to do so (e.g., I am not going to let them do that to me. or I am going to teach them a lesson.). (4) The 8-item Physically Aggressive Thinking scale (α = .93) contains items referring to thoughts of harming others and the behaviors necessary to do so (e.g., I want to run them off the road. or I would like to beat the hell out of them.). (5)The 9-item (α = .83) Coping Self-instruction addresses thoughts of positive, adaptive coping (e.g., Cope with it, sometimes you just have to live with bad drivers, or Just pay attention to my driving, others can be crazy if they want.). Judgmental/disbelieving thoughts correlate positively with all other scales on the Driver's Angry Thoughts Questionnaire. Pejorative labeling/verbally aggressive, physically aggressive, and revengeful/retaliatory thoughts correlate positively with each other and negatively with coping self-instruction. Thought patterns on the Driver's Angry Thoughts Questionnaire generally correlated in logical ways with trait driving anger, aggressive forms of driving anger expression, and aggressive and risky behavior on the road (Deffenbacher et al., in press; Deffenbacher, Petrilli, et al., 2003) and formed larger correlations with these than general hostile automatic thoughts (Deffenbacher, Petrilli, et al., 2003).

Driving Anger Expression Inventory

The Driving Anger Expression Inventory (Deffenbacher, Lynch, Deffenbacher, et al., 2001; Deffenbacher, Lynch, Oetting, et al., 2002) was included to map how high anger drivers express their anger when driving and to test the aggression and reduced coping hypotheses from the state-trait model. The Driving Anger Expression Inventory lists 49 different ways people can express their anger while driving. Students rated on a four-point scale (1 = almost never, 4 = almost always) how often they express their anger in this manner. The Driving Anger Expression Inventory yields two general measures, a 34-item Aggressive Expression and 15-item Adaptive/Constructive Expression. The Aggressive Expression scale breaks down into three reliable subscales such that the Driving Anger Expression Inventory yields three measures of aggressive expression and one of adaptive/constructive expression. (1) The 12-item Verbal Aggressive Expression (αs = .88 to .90) assesses the person's tendency to express anger verbally (e.g., swearing or yelling at another driver). (2) The 11-item Personal Physical Aggressive Expression scale (αs = .80 to .84) addresses the person's using his/her physical presence to express anger and intimidate (e.g., giving the other driver the finger or getting out of the car to engage in a fist fight). (3) The 11-item Use of the

Vehicle to Express Anger Scale (αs = .86 to .90) measures the driver's propensity to use the vehicle as the means of expressing anger (e.g., speeding up to frustrate another driver or driving up close to another driver's bumper). (4) The 15-item Adaptive/Constructive Expression Scale (αs = .89 to .91) assesses the driver's positive coping in the face of anger on the road (e.g., engaging in relaxation or thinking about things to distract one from provocation). Verbal, personal physical, and vehicular aggressive forms of driving anger expression correlate positively with each other, trait driving anger, risky and aggressive behavior on the road. They are not correlated with, or form small negative correlations with, the adaptive/constructive form of expression. Verbal, personal physical, and vehicular aggressive forms of anger expression also tend to correlate positively with aggressive cognitions. Adaptive/constructive expression tends to form smaller negative correlations with driving-related variables. Adaptive/constructive expression also correlated positively with coping self-instructions, but was less correlated with other cognitions behind the wheel.

Driving Log

The Driving Log (Deffenbacher et al., 2000) was included in this project to gather data in day-to-day driving conditions. It provided information not only on the number of times and miles driven, but the frequency and intensity of anger and the frequency of aggressive and risky behavior. It, therefore, provided field data from which to test the frequency, intensity, and aggression hypotheses from the state-trait model, but also information on the rates of risky behavior characteristic of high anger drivers. For three days, students recorded: (1) the number of times they drove that day; (2) the number of miles driven that day; (3) the number of times they were angry while driving that day; (4) the event eliciting the greatest amount of anger while driving that day and a rating of the intensity of that anger on a 0-100 scale (0 = no anger, 100 = maximum anger ever experienced); (5) whether they engaged in eight aggressive behaviors (e.g., making an angry gesture or cursing at another driver); and (6) whether they engaged in 12 risky behaviors (e.g., drove 10 or more miles over the speed limit or drank alcohol and drove). Trait driving anger correlates positively with the frequency and intensity of anger and the frequency of risky and aggressive behavior on the Log (Deffenbacher, Lynch, Oetting, et al., 2001).

Driving Survey

The Driving Survey (Deffenbacher et al., 2000) was included to assess four dimensions – general perceptions of self as a driver, aggression on the road, risky behavior while driving, and crash-related conditions. (1) Students provided four general ratings of self as a driver. In response to the stem, "As a driver, I am… ," they rated themselves on the following seven-point scales (1 = very calm, unaggressive, cautious, or safe, 7 = very angry, aggressive, risk taking, or unsafe). (2) On the 13-item Aggression Index (αs = .85 to .89) students reported the number of times (0 to 5+ with 5+ being treated as a 5 in analyses) they engaged in the behavior described in the last three months (e.g., having a physical fight with another driver or yelling at another driver). (3) On the 15-item Risky Behavior Index (αs = .83 to .86) students reported the number of times (0 to 5+) they had engaged in the behavior described in the last three months (e.g., drinking alcohol and driving or speeding 10-20 miles over the speed limit). (4) Students also reported (0-5+) the number of times in the last three months they had lost concentration while driving, experienced a minor loss of vehicular control, and close calls and the number of times in the last year they had received a ticket for a moving violation, had a minor accident, or had a major accident. Alpha reliabilities for the Crash-related Index have varied from .36 to .51. Since Aggression and Risky Behavior Indices formed reliable measures, their frequencies were summed into single scores of aggressive and risky behavior. Since crash-related conditions did not form a reliable index, variables were analyzed individually. Clinical and non-clinical samples of high anger drivers report more aggressive and risky behaviors and some crash-related conditions such as moving violations (Deffenbacher, 2003; Deffenbacher, Deffenbacher, et al., 2003; Deffenbacher, Filetti, et al., 2003).

Trait Anger Scale

The Trait Anger Scale (Spielberger, 1988, 1999) was included to assess the general propensity toward anger for high anger drivers. On the 10 items on the Trait Anger Scale, students rated on a four-point scale (1 = almost never, 4 = almost always) how often they generally feel or react with anger in the manner described in the item. Reported α reliabilities for the Trait Anger Scale are in the high .80 range, and two-week to two-moth test-retest reliabilities range from .70 to .77 (Jacobs, Latham, & Brown, 1988; Morris, Deffenbacher, Lynch, & Oetting, 1996). General trait anger correlates positively with other measures of anger, anger consequences, hostility, and aggression (Deffenbacher et al., 1996; Spielberger, 1988, 1999).

Anger Expression Inventory

The ways in which participants express their anger in general was assessed by the 24-item Anger Expression Inventory (Spielberger, 1988). Students rated on a four-point scale (1 = almost never, 4 = almost always) how often they express their anger in the manner described. The Anger Expression Inventory provides three eight-item measures of general anger expression (αs = .73 to .84). (1) Anger-In assesses suppressing anger, being critical, and harboring grudges (e.g., boiling on the inside but not showing it). (2) Anger-Out measures the tendency to express anger through outward, negative means involving verbal and physical aggression (e.g., striking out at whatever infuriates the individual). (3) Anger-Control addresses the person's attempts to manage their anger and calm down (e.g., calming down faster than others). Anger-In correlates minimally with Anger-Out and Anger-Control, which correlate negatively with each other. Anger-In and Anger-Out correlate positively with general trait anger, whereas Anger-Control correlates negatively. Validity for Anger-In, Anger-Out, and Anger-Control is reflected in different patterns of correlations with anger, personality, and physiological variables (Deffenbacher et al., 1996; Spielberger, 1988, 1999).

State Anger Scale

The State Anger Scale (Spielberger, 1999) was included to assess state anger and verbal and physical aggressive tendencies after visualizing two interpersonal provocations on the road. This allowed for assessment of intensity and aggression hypotheses in these two conditions. On the State Anger Scale students rated on a four-point scale (1 = not at all, 4 = very much) the degree to which they felt or experienced the condition described in the item. This scale breaks down into three, five-item measures. (1) The five-item State Anger measure (αs = .92 to .94) assesses the immediate experience of angry feelings (e.g., feeling annoyed or angry). (2) The five-item Verbal Aggression scale (αs = .93 to .94) measures immediate urges toward verbal aggression (e.g., feeling like swearing or yelling at someone). (3) The five-item index of Physical Aggression (αs = .89 to .91) assesses the momentary tendency toward physically aggressive behavior (e.g., feeling like breaking something or pounding someone). High anger drivers report more state anger and verbal and physical aggression following high impedance driving simulations or after visualizing someone stealing a parking space for which the person has been waiting (Deffenbacher, 2003; Deffenbacher, Deffenbacher, et al., 2003).

Positive Coping Scale

The two-item Positive Coping Scale (Novaco, 1975) (αs = .84 to .88) was included to assess reduced state coping following visualization of interpersonally frustrating events while driving. Students rated on a seven-point scale the likelihood for engaging in the positive behavior described. High anger drivers report reduced positive coping following impedance simulations and visualizing frustrating events on the road (Deffenbacher, 2003; Deffenbacher, Deffenbacher, et al., 2003).

Procedures

Screening

In six introductory psychology classes of 150 to 210 students, students voluntarily completed the short-form of the Driving Anger Scale and left their name and phone number if they wished to be involved in a study involving driving and emotion. Research assistants called students from the upper and low quartiles and explained that the study as a one-credit study involving questionnaires, driving diaries, and the like. Interested students were scheduled.

The Experiment

The study was conducted by undergraduate research assistants. Students completed the study in groups of 10 to 15 in a small university classroom. When they arrived, the research assistants gave students two informed consent forms and gave a brief overview of the study. Students read, signed, and returned one consent form, keeping the other for their records. Students then completed a questionnaire packet including, in order, demographic information, the long-form of the Driving Anger Scale, the Driving Anger Situations, the Driver's Angry Thoughts Questionnaire, the Driving Anger Expression Inventory, the Driving Survey, the Trait Anger Scale, and the Anger Expression Inventory. Previous research showed that this order created less confusion as measures moved from asking about anger and anger expression while driving to more general, non-driving anger and anger expression.

When all had completed the questionnaires, research assistants instructed students to listen to an audio tape. The tape asked them to close their eyes and visualize the situation described as if it were happening to them right then. The scene described the participant driving around in a parking lot for some time looking for a parking space. The participant sees another person backing out and arrives first and waits for the space to open. However, another driver coming from the other direction cuts in ahead of the participant and steals the parking spot for which the person had been waiting. Students visualized this scene for 90 seconds and then completed the State Anger Scale and the Positive Coping Scale, in that order. When all had completed these instruments, the procedure was repeated with participants visualizing a second scene. This scenario involved being the second vehicle back in a left hand turn lane. When the arrow turns green, the driver in front of the student does not move and appears to be involved in a conversation with the passenger. The other driver fails to move throughout the signal, and only moves as the arrow changes, leaving the person stuck in the left hand turn lane waiting for the next light. After 90 seconds of visualization, students again completed the State Anger Scale and Positive Coping Scale as it applied to their experience in that situation.

After students completed the second state assessment, they received three Driving Logs with instructions to complete them on three days they drove during the coming week. Participants who did not turn in Logs in 10 days were called and reminded.

FINDINGS

Data Analyses and Other Data Issues

The primary analyses in this study were 2 (Gender) x 2 (Driving Anger Level) univariate or multivariate analyses of variance. Univariate analyses of variance were employed with single variables that prior research had shown were not highly correlated, whereas multivariate analyses of variance were conducted on groups of logically related variables (e.g., measures assessed by the same methodology such as forms of expressing anger on the Driving Anger Expression Inventory), that prior research had shown were correlated with each other. Multivariate analyses employed the Wilks λ statistic and were followed up by univariate analyses of variance. Significant univariate interactions were explored by Tukey *post hoc* tests. Effect sizes are expressed in terms of eta square (η^2), and qualitative interpretation of effect sizes employed Cohen's (1988) criteria, wherein η^2 of .01 to .04 is considered a small effect size, .05 to .14 a moderate effect size, and larger than .14 is considered large.

Data are tabled by gender and driving anger level. Since analyses revealed fewer gender and interaction effects, and since anger effects are the primary focus of this chapter, univariate anger effects and effect sizes are summarized in tables, whereas gender and interaction effects are summarized in the text.

If a participant had missing or unusable data for a specific variable, the participant was dropped from analyses involving that variable, but was retained in all other analyses for which he/she had complete data. This accounts for the minor discrepancies in the degrees of freedom (*df*) in some analyses. The exception is the Driving Log. Several students lived in on-campus housing and did not have cars or drive regularly. This accounts for a larger reduction in *df* for analyses involving the Driving Log.

Exposure on the Road: Miles Driven

If high anger drivers drove more miles, then it is possible that all or a portion of their emotional and behavioral reactions could result from being exposed to more frustrations and provocations on the road. For example, if one driver logs ten times more miles than another driver, then assuming they are driving under relatively similar conditions, the first driver will be exposed to ten times as many potential provocations, to which he/she might respond with anger and/or aggression. Such differences in base rates of driving could confound an understanding of how the person's potential for anger behind the wheel (trait driving anger) may contribute to emotional and behavioral reactions while driving. To address this issue, average estimated miles driven from the demographic information, and average daily frequency of driving and miles driven from the Driven Log were analyzed (Table 1). Estimated miles driven in an average week showed no significant effects for gender, anger, or the interaction, $Fs(1, 116) = 0.58$, 2.53, and 0.05. Likewise, frequency of driving and miles driven reported on Driving Logs (Table 1) showed no significant multivariate effects for gender, anger, or the interaction, $Fs(2, 91) = 0.18$, 0.82, and 1.79. Taken together, these findings suggest that there were no meaningful or systematic differences in basic driving behavior and, therefore, potential differences in exposure to sources of frustration and provocation on the road which might account for other characteristics observed in the study and that findings are better attributed to the driver's propensity for anger while driving in interaction with the frustrations and provocations on the road.

Table 1. Frequency and Amount of Driving as a Function of Gender and Anger

Measure	Gender	Low Anger		High Anger	
		M	**SD**	**M**	**SD**
Estimated Miles Driven/wk.	M	76.76	71.36	131.40	113.14
	F	106.40	121.59	147.83	277.22
Miles Driven/day (Driving Log)	M	43.92	39.12	44.85	44.64
	F	66.77	119.83	36.60	27.20
Number of Times Driving/day	M	2.17	0.93	2.88	1.84
(Driving Log)	F	2.52	1.63	2.32	1.30

M = male.
F = female.

General Perceptions of Self as a Driver

To assess how high and low anger drivers perceived themselves as drivers, analyses began with the four ratings of self as a driver from the Driving Survey (Table 2). These measures revealed a significant multivariate effect for anger, $F(4, 113) = 41.40$, $p < .001$, $\eta^2 = 0.594$, but not for gender or the interaction, $Fs(4, 113) = 2.41$ and 0.21. Univariate analyses (Table 2) showed that high anger drivers rated themselves as significantly more angry ($M = 4.53$), aggressive ($M = 5.06$), risk-taking ($M = 4.13$) and unsafe ($M = 3.32$) drivers than did low anger drivers ($Ms = 2.58$, 3.02, 2.80, and 2.32). Anger effect sizes were quite large for these variables (Table 2).

Table 2. Ratings of Self as a Driver as a Function of Gender and Anger

| Measure | Gender | Group | | | | Univariate Anger | Anger Effect Size (η^2) |
| | | Low Anger | | High Anger | | | |
		M	SD	M	SD	$F(1, 116)$	
Calm/angry	M	2.63	0.85	4.50	0.97	128.10[*]	.525
	F	2.53	0.82	4.57	1.10		
Unaggressive/aggressive	M	3.43	1.51	5.30	1.21	75.76[*]	.395
	F	2.60	1.19	4.83	1.23		
Cautious/risky	M	3.10	1.21	4.33	1.42	33.13[*]	.222
	F	2.50	1.14	3.93	1.29		
Safe/unsafe	M	2.50	0.90	3.40	1.16	31.20[*]	.212
	F	2.13	0.68	3.23	1.10		

[*]$p < .001$.
M = male.
F = female.

The Driving Anger Scale and Responses to Most Angering Situations

The total score on the DAS and reported anger in response to the individual's two most angering situations (Table 3) revealed multivariate effects for gender and anger, $Fs(3, 112) = 4.07$ and 68.28, $ps < .01$ and $.001$, $\eta^2 s = 0.098$ and 0.646, but not for the interaction, $F(3, 112) = .075$. The most and second most angering situations demonstrated univariate gender effects, $Fs(1, 114) = 10.01$ and 4.34, $ps < .01$ and $.05$, $\eta^2 s = 0.081$ and 0.037. Men reported greater anger in both situations ($Ms = 74.58$ and 66.02) than did women ($Ms = 64.48$ and 59.31). The total score on the DAS, however, did not show a gender effect, $F(1, 114) = 0.05$. Large anger effects were found on all three measures (Table 3), due to high anger drivers reporting significantly more anger on the DAS and their two most angering situations ($Ms = 125.28$, 88.12, and 79.04) than did low anger drivers ($Ms = 80.18$, 55.95, and 46.29). While high anger drivers reported more anger on these measures, it should be noted that low anger drivers reported at least moderate anger in the two most angering situations and since the standard deviations are quite large, at least some low anger drivers reported high levels of anger in these situations.

Greater levels of anger reported by high anger drivers suggests that they experience more intense anger when driving in general and in their most anger-provoking situations. However, it is not clear if high anger drivers react with more anger to just a few situations or if they tend to react with elevated anger to a wide range of situations. If they reacted with greater anger to but a few situations, then such a finding would qualify the breadth of the tendency to react with anger behind the wheel and would require a careful mapping of which situations did and did not elicit anger. To address this issue, two additional analyses were conducted. High and low anger drivers were compared on the six subscales of the DAS and on the number of items rated 4 (much) or 5 (very much) on the DAS. It was reasoned that if high anger drivers scored higher on all DAS subscales and rated more items as eliciting much or very much anger, this would support a general tendency to react with anger across a wide range of potentially frustrating or provocative situations on the road. DAS subscales (Table 3) revealed significant multivariate effects for gender and anger, $Fs(6, 109) = 2.65$ and 38.72, $ps < .05$ and $.001$, $\eta^2 s$

= 0.127 and 0.681, but not for the interaction, $F(6, 109) = 0.70$. Although there was a significant multivariate gender effect, none of the univariate gender effects were significant. All DAS subscales revealed significant univariate anger effects (Table 3). High anger drivers reported significantly greater anger in response to hostile gestures from other drivers ($M = 11.91$), illegal driving ($M = 12.48$), the presence of police officers ($M = 13.93$), slow driving conditions ($M = 23.41$), discourteous behavior from other drivers ($M = 38.86$) and conditions that obstruct traffic or the view of the road ($M = 24.68$) than did low anger drivers ($Ms = 6.68$, 9.96, 7.81, 14.33, 26.34, and 15.07). Anger effects were consistently large, except for the moderate anger effect for anger in response to the illegal driving of others. A univariate analysis of variance on the number of situations on the DAS eliciting much or very much anger revealed a significant effect for anger, $F(1, 114) = 220.16$, $p < .001$, $\eta^2 = 0.659$, but not for gender or the interaction, $Fs(1, 114) = 0.21$ and 0.54. A large anger effect reflected that high anger drivers indicated that three times as many situations elicited much or very much anger ($M = 24.51$) compared to low anger drivers ($M = 8.32$). These findings suggest that high anger drivers, as a group, tended to experience elevated anger in response to a wide range of frustrating and potentially provocative events on the road, not just more intense anger in response to a limited number of situations. In fact, high anger drivers reported much or very much anger in response to three quarters of situations on the DAS.

Table 3. Responses to the Driving Anger Scale and Most Angering Situations as a Function of Gender and Anger

Measure	Gender	Group				Univariate Anger	Anger Effect
		Low Anger		High Anger		$F (1, 114)$	Size (η^2)
		M	SD	M	SD		
Driving Anger Scale – Total	M	79.48	20.22	126.67	14.94	194.99*	.631
	F	80.87	16.07	123.90	18.78		
Most Angering Situation	M	61.90	20.47	87.27	9.34	72.44*	.388
	F	50.00	21.66	78.97	15.11		
Second Most Angering Situation	M	49.38	19.96	82.67	11.66	103.12*	.475
	F	43.20	20.50	75.41	16.56		
Hostile Gestures	M	6.51	2.85	12.07	2.53	101.72*	.472
	F	6.83	2.94	11.76	2.95		
Illegal Driving	M	9.41	3.31	12.00	3.34	16.63*	.127
	F	10.50	3.20	12.97	3.59		
Police Presence	M	8.45	3.49	14.03	4.00	98.44*	.463
	F	7.17	2.53	13.83	3.22		
Slow Driving	M	14.55	4.23	24.00	2.80	193.63*	.629
	F	14.10	3.68	22.83	3.36		
Discourtesy	M	25.41	6.27	38.90	3.20	171.22*	.600
	F	27.27	5.79	38.83	5.04		
Traffic Obstructions	M	15.14	5.86	25.67	4.88	99.24*	.465
	F	15.00	4.37	23.69	5.74		
Number of DAS Items Rated 4 or 5	M	8.17	5.98	25.17	5.96	220.16*	.659
	F	8.47	4.70	23.86	6.90		

*$p < .001$.
M = male.
F = female.
DAS = Driving Anger Scale.

Angry/Hostile Thinking

Angry/hostile thinking patterns from the Driver's Angry Thoughts Questionnaire (Table 4) showed significant multivariate effects for gender, anger, and the interaction, $Fs(5, 112)$ = 5.11, 23.44, and 3.45, $ps < .001$, .001, and .01, $\eta^2 s$ = 0.186, 0.511, and 0.133. Judgmental/disbelieving and pejorative labeling/verbally aggressive forms of thinking demonstrated univariate interaction effects, $Fs(1, 116)$ = 4.38 and 5.86, $ps < .05$, and $\eta^2 s$ = 0.036 and 0.048. Both interactions followed the same pattern (see Table 4). Low anger male and female drivers did not differ on judgmental/disbelieving or pejorative labeling/verbally aggressive thoughts. High anger drivers were elevated on both forms of thinking, but high anger female drivers were significantly higher than high anger male drivers on these two forms of anger-related thinking. Only physically aggressive thinking revealed a significant gender effect, $F(1, 116)$ = 7.93, $p < .01$, η^2 = 0.064. Men (M = 14.73) reported more physically aggressive thoughts than women (M = 11.37). Large, significant univariate anger effects were found for all forms of angry/hostile thinking (Table 4), except for coping self-instructional thoughts for which there were no significant anger effect. High anger drivers reported more judgmental/disbelieving (M = 60.53), pejorative labeling/verbally aggressive (M = 48.77), revengeful/retaliatory (M = 37.77), and physically aggressive (M = 16.80) thinking than did low anger drivers (Ms = 43.35, 30.55, 20.10, and 9.30).

Table 4. Angry-related Thinking on the Driver's Angry Thoughts Questionnaire as a Function of Gender and Anger

| Measure | Gender | Group | | | | Univariate Anger | Anger Effect |
| | | Low Anger | | High Anger | | Anger | Size |
		M	SD	M	SD	$F(1, 116)$	(η^2)
Judgmental/Disbelieving	M	43.70	14.73	54.27	20.16	29.52[*]	.203
	F	43.00	14.61	66.80	19.07		
Pejorative Label/	M	31.83	8.61	45.33	11.94	95.33[*]	.457
Verbal Aggressive	F	29.27	10.88	52.00	9.10		
Revengeful/ Retaliatory	M	20.80	5.90	38.13	14.82	75.08[*]	.393
	F	19.40	5.79	37.40	14.51		
Physically Aggressive	M	10.13	3.92	19.33	10.66	39.34[*]	.253
	F	8.47	0.97	14.27	6.45		
Coping Self-instruction	M	20.30	6.73	18.97	6.05	0.09	.001
	F	18.03	6.14	20.03	5.59		

[*]$p < .001$.
M = male.
F = female.

Expression of Anger behind the Wheel

The aggressive and adaptive/constructive expression scales of the Driving Anger Expression Inventory demonstrated a significant multivariate effect for anger, $F(2, 115)$ = 57.56, $p < .001$, η^2 = 0.500, but not for gender or the interaction, $Fs(2, 115)$ = 0.39 and 1.50. Both aggressive and adaptive/constructive forms of expressing anger while driving revealed significant univariate anger effects (Table 5). Anger effect sizes were large and moderate, respectively. High anger drivers reported expressing their anger when driving in more aggressive and less adaptive/constructive ways (Ms = 71.72 and 27.63) than did low anger drivers (Ms = 48.22 and 33.00).

To explore the different ways in which high anger drivers may express their anger aggressively, the three subscales of the aggressive form of expressing anger (i.e., verbally aggressive, personal physical, and vehicular forms of anger expression) were subjected to a multivariate analysis (Table 5). This yielded a significant multivariate effect for anger, $F(3, 114) = 36.06$, $p < .001$, $\eta^2 = 0.487$, but not for gender or the interaction, $Fs(3, 114) = 1.86$ and 2.39. Large univariate anger effects were found for all three forms of expressing anger. High anger drivers reported employing more verbal, personal physical, and vehicular aggressive forms of expressing anger when driving (Ms = 29.40, 16.68, and 25.63) than did low anger drivers (Ms = 20.30, 12.88, and 15.03), suggesting that high anger drivers employ a variety of aggressive means of expressing their anger, rather than just one form of aggressive expression.

Table 5. Ways of Expressing Anger while Driving as a Function of Gender and Anger

Measure	Gender	Group Low Anger		Group High Anger		Univariate Anger $F(1, 116)$	Anger Effect Size (η^2)
		M	SD	M	SD		
Aggressive Expression	M	49.10	9.14	69.93	14.02	100.82*	.465
	F	47.33	9.60	73.50	16.88		
Adaptive/ Constructive	M	33.37	8.59	26.13	6.18	14.58*	.112
	F	32.63	8.99	29.13	6.65		
Verbal Aggressive	M	20.80	6.35	27.13	7.10	54.79*	.321
	F	19.80	5.80	31.67	7.55		
Personal Physical Aggressive	M	13.13	1.59	17.17	4.93	36.64*	.240
	F	12.63	1.10	16.20	4.39		
Use of the Vehicle	M	15.17	3.87	25.63	6.32	99.78*	.462
to Express Anger	F	14.90	4.66	25.63	7.65		

*$p < .001$.
M = male.
F = female.

Anger, Aggression, and Positive Coping in Response to Visualized Provocations

State measures following the visualization of being stuck behind an inattentive driver in the left hand turn lane (Table 6) revealed multivariate effects for gender, anger, and the interaction, $Fs(4, 113)$, = 2.65, 20.46, and 2.71, $ps < .05$, .001, and .05, $\eta^2 s$ = 0.086, 0.420, and 0.089. Although there was a significant multivariate interaction, none of the univariate interactions were significant. Only physical aggression demonstrated a significant univariate gender effect, $F(1, 116) = 5.23$, $p < .05$, $\eta^2 = 0.043$. Men ($M = 7.37$) experienced more urges toward physical aggression toward the offending driver than did women ($M = 6.17$). Large univariate anger effects were found on all state measures (Table 6). Men reported experiencing more anger ($M = 16.15$), verbal and physical aggression ($Ms = 14.13$ and 8.05), and less positive coping tendencies (M = 5.43) than did low anger drivers (Ms = 11.18, 8.37, 5.48, and 9.07).

Reactions to another driver stealing the parking spot for which the person had been waiting revealed a somewhat similar pattern (Table 6). State variables yielded a significant multivariate effect for gender and anger, $Fs(4, 112)$ = 3.37 and 13.39, ps < .05 and .001, $\eta^2 s$ = 0.107 and 0.323 but not for the interaction, $F(4, 112)$ = 2.01. Physical aggression demonstrated a significant univariate gender effect, $F(1, 115)$ = 9.17, p < .01, η^2 = 0.074, due to men (M = 8.21) wanting to engage in more physical aggression than women (M = 6.37). Large univariate anger effects were found for state anger and verbal and physical aggression, and a moderate anger effect for positive coping (Table 6). High anger drivers reported more anger (M = 17.60), verbal and physical aggression (Ms = 15.67 and 8.60), and less positive coping (M = 4.92) in response to another driver stealing a parking spot than did low anger drivers (Ms = 13.22, 10.39, 5.97, and 8.07).

Table 6. State Anger, Aggression and Positive Coping in Response to Visualized Provocations as a Function of Gender and Anger

| Measure | Gender | Group | | | | Univariate Anger | Anger Effect |
| | | Low Anger | | High Anger | | $F(1, 116)$ | Size (η^2) |
		M	SD	M	SD		
Other Driver Does Not Turn in Response to Left Turn Arrow							
State Anger	M	11.27	3.80	15.60	3.66	55.60*	.324
	F	11.10	3.92	16.70	3.16		
State Verbal Aggression	M	8.77	3.18	13.73	4.89	57.19*	.330
	F	7.97	3.92	14.53	4.52		
State Physical Aggression	M	5.70	1.40	9.03	4.90	23.91*	.171
	F	5.27	0.69	7.07	2.52		
State Positive Coping	M	9.10	2.70	5.07	2.89	50.47*	.303
	F	9.03	3.15	5.80	2.43		
Other Driver Steals Parking Spot							
State Anger	M	13.17	4.71	17.33	2.96	42.40*	.269
	F	13.27	3.92	17.87	2.80		
State Verbal Aggression	M	11.10	4.39	15.67	4.45	44.61*	.280
	F	9.67	4.44	15.67	3.95		
State Physical Aggression	M	6.34	2.73	10.07	5.05	18.78*	.140
	F	5.60	1.79	7.13	2.75		
State Positive Coping	M	7.93	3.23	5.40	7.46	14.62*	.113
	F	8.20	3.22	4.43	1.98		

*p < .001.
M = male.
F = female.

Day-to-day Driving Experience (Driving Log): Anger, Aggression, and Risky Behavior

Driving Log measures were averaged across the three days of driving and subjected to multivariate analyses. Measures from the Driving Log (Table 7) revealed a significant multivariate effect for anger, $F(4, 87)$ = 18.84, p < .001, η^2 = 0.464, but not for gender or the interaction, $Fs(4, 87)$ = 1.58 and 0.23. Anger intensity and the frequency of anger, aggression and risky behavior (Table 7) all demonstrated large, significant univariate anger effects. High anger drivers reported more frequent and intense anger in their daily driving (*Ms* = 2.01 and 58.66) than did low anger drivers (*Ms* = 0.88 and 22.74). High anger drivers also engaged in more aggressive and risky behavior in their day-to-day driving (*Ms* = 2.24 and 3.36) than did low anger drivers (*Ms* = 0.57 and 1.58). In fact, high anger drivers were angered 2.3 times more frequently and engaged in 3.9 times more aggressive behavior and 2.1 times more risky behavior while driving than low anger drivers. These findings are not only statistically significant, but the numbers take on added meaning when it is remembered that they are daily averages. Over time, they take on added significance not only for the high anger driver, but also for those with whom they share the road. Suppose, for example, that students drive 300 days per year, and data are extrapolated over a driving year. Low anger drivers would become angry 263 times and engage in 171 aggressive and 474 risky behaviors in a year, whereas high anger drivers would have been angry 592 times and would have engaged in 673 and 1009 risky behaviors in the same period of time.

Table 7. Anger, Aggression, and Risky Behavior in
Daily Driving (Driving Log) as a Function of Gender and Anger

Measure	Gender	Group				Univariate Anger	Anger Effect
		Low Anger		High Anger		$F(1, 90)$	Size (η^2)
		M	*SD*	*M*	*SD*		
Anger Frequency	M	0.70	0.45	1.97	1.38	29.45*	.247
	F	1.06	0.83	2.05	1.09		
Anger Intensity	M	22.78	17.12	61.25	24.78	62.85*	.411
	F	22.71	19.20	56.07	24.80		
Aggression Frequency	M	0.44	0.61	2.10	1.51	42.05*	.318
	F	0.69	0.77	2.39	1.66		
Risky Behavior Frequency	M	1.53	1.09	3.51	2.16	32.91*	.268
	F	1.67	1.27	3.21	1.36		

*$p < .001$.
M = male
F = female.

Aggression and Risky Behavior on the Road: Driving Survey Results

Reports of aggressive and risky behavior in the last three months from the Driving Survey (Tables 8 and 9) yielded a significant multivariate effect for anger, $F(2, 115) = 43.38$, $p < .001$, $\eta^2 = 0.430$, but not for gender or the interaction, $Fs(2, 115) = 1.11$ and 0.03. Both variables demonstrated large univariate anger effects (Tables 8 and 9). High anger drivers engaged in significantly more aggressive and risky behavior while driving (*Ms* = 22.73 and 31.83) than did low anger drivers (*Ms* = 6.95 and 16.32). Relative rates of aggression and risky behavior on the Driving Survey were very similar to those found on the Driving Log. High anger drivers reported 3.3 times more aggression and 2.0 times more risky behavior over the last three months than did low anger drivers.

From the total of aggressive behaviors, it is clear that high anger drivers were more aggressive, but it is not clear if high anger drivers engaged in a variety of aggressive behaviors or if they tended to favor a few aggressive behaviors that were repeated more often. To address this issue and to assess the relative rates of different types of aggressive behavior, the thirteen aggressive behaviors (Table 8) were subjected to a multivariate analysis. Aggressive behaviors showed a significant multivariate effect for anger, $F(13, 104) = 6.77$, $p < .001$, $\eta^2 = 0.459$, but not for gender or the interaction, $Fs(13, 104) = 1.70$ and 0.38. Moderate to large univariate anger effects were found for all aggressive behaviors (Tale 8), except for physical fights with other drivers which was done infrequently, but which approached significance ($p < .09$) and was only committed by high anger drivers. High anger drivers drove in a high state anger more often ($M = 3.02$) and reported losing control of their anger more often ($M = 0.77$) than did low anger drivers ($Ms = 1.12$ and 0.07). High anger drivers engaged in significantly more verbally aggressive behavior than low anger drivers. They swore at or yelled at other drivers and pedestrians more often ($Ms = 3.02$ and 2.25) and were more likely to engage in arguments with other drivers and passengers ($Ms = 0.88$ and 1.67) than were low anger drivers ($Ms = 1.38, 0.58, 0.05,$ and 0.58). High anger drivers also engaged in more physically aggressive behavior. They made more angry gestures at other drivers and pedestrians ($M = 2.52$) and were more likely to have broken or damaged a part of their vehicle in anger ($M = 0.57$) than low anger drivers ($Ms = 0.92$ and 0.12). High anger drivers were also more likely to use their vehicle as an instrument of aggression. They were more likely to have flashed their lights or honked their horns in anger ($Ms = 1.45$ and 2.52) and to have tailgated or cut another driver off in anger ($Ms = 2.22$ and 1.82) than low anger drivers ($Ms = 0.40, 0.82, 0.60,$ and 0.32). Thus, as a group, high anger drivers did not employ a small number of forms of aggression frequently, but engaged in a wide range of aggressive behavior on the road.

The relative rates of behavior were also quite different in many cases. For example, compared to low anger drivers, high anger drivers drove in a very angry state 2.7 times more often, but were 11.4 times more likely to have lost control of their anger. They swore or yelled at other drivers and pedestrians 2.2 and 3.9 times more often, but were 17.7 times more likely to have engaged in a verbal argument with another driver and were 2.9 times more likely to have argued with a passenger in their vehicle. They were 2.7 times more likely to have made an angry gesture at another driver or pedestrian and 4.8 times more likely to have physically damaged or broken something on their vehicle in anger. They were 3.6 and 3.1 times more likely to have flashed their lights and honked their horn in anger and 3.7 and 5.7 times more likely to have tailgated another vehicle or cut another driver off in anger.

Table 8. Three-month Rates of Aggressive Behavior as a Function of Gender and Anger

Measure	Gender	Group Low Anger		High Anger		Univariate Anger $F(1, 116)$	Anger Effect Size (η^2)
		M	SD	M	SD		
Total Aggressive Behavior	M	7.57	5.77	23.77	13.72	79.10*	.407
	F	6.33	5.92	21.70	11.02		
Drove Very Angry	M	1.30	1.32	3.17	1.53	51.11*	.306
	F	0.93	1.08	2.87	1.80		
Lost Control of Anger	M	0.10	0.32	0.87	1.63	14.00*	.108
	F	0.03	0.18	0.67	1.18		
Swore at Other	M	1.50	1.64	2.83	1.91	28.80*	.199
Driver/Pedestrian	F	1.27	1.39	3.20	1.69		
Yelled at Other	M	0.43	0.90	2.23	1.83	33.51*	.224
Driver/Pedestrian	F	0.73	1.29	2.27	2.03		
Argument with Other	M	0.03	0.18	1.00	1.39	22.76*	.164
Driver							
	F	0.07	0.25	0.77	1.29		
Angry Gesture	M	1.13	1.14	2.77	1.74	38.24*	.248
	F	0.70	0.99	2.27	1.66		
Physical Fight with	M	0.00	0.00	0.07	0.25	3.07	.026
Other Driver	F	0.00	0.00	0.03	0.18		
Flashed Lights in Anger	M	0.57	1.22	1.90	2.01	16.44*	.124
	F	0.23	0.77	1.00	1.39		
Honked Horn in Anger	M	0.73	1.11	2.53	1.83	38.75*	.250
	F	0.90	1.16	2.50	1.74		
Tailgated in Anger	M	0.60	1.16	2.13	2.10	29.51*	.203
	F	0.60	1.19	2.30	1.86		
Cut Other Driver	M	0.43	1.17	1.97	2.06	30.37*	.208
off in Anger	F	0.20	0.48	1.67	1.75		
Argument with Passenger	M	0.53	0.82	1.57	1.29	22.80*	.164
	F	0.63	1.13	1.77	1.61		
Damaged Vehicle in	M	0.20	0.55	0.73	1.41	8.51†	.068
Anger							
	F	0.03	0.18	0.40	0.73		

†$p < .01$.
*$p < .001$.
M = male.
F = female.

As with aggressive behavior, the total risky behavior index showed that high anger drivers engaged in more risky driving behavior on the road. However, it does not reveal whether high anger drivers engage in a few risky behaviors repeatedly or a wide range of risky behaviors, nor does it address the relative rates of specific risky behaviors. To explore these issues, the risky behavior index was broken down into its fifteen individual items (Table 9). Risky behaviors revealed multivariate effects for gender and anger, $Fs(15, 102) = 2.01$ and 4.30, $ps < .05$ and .001, $\eta^2 s = 0.228$ and 0.387, but not for the interaction, $F(15, 102) = 0.92$. Drinking and being drunk and driving and rapidly switching lanes to speed through slower traffic demonstrated significant univariate gender effects, $Fs(1, 116) = 4.11, 9.08$, and 5.92, $ps < .05$, $\eta^2 s = 0.034, 0.073$, and 0.049. Men were more likely to consume alcohol and drive, to drive while intoxicated, and to change lanes to speed through traffic (Ms = 1.23, 0.73, and 3.68) than women (Ms = 0.68, 0.13, and 3.02). Significant univariate anger effects were found on all risky driving-related behaviors, except for drinking and being drunk while driving (Table 9). High anger drivers were more likely to drive without their seatbelts (M = 2.43) and to speed 10-20 mph or more than 20 mph over the limit (Ms = 4.28 and 2.77) than were low anger drivers (Ms = 1.27, 3.03, and 1.37). High anger drivers were also more likely to have drifted into another lane of traffic (M = 1.48), to have changed lanes or passed in an unsafe manner (Ms = 1.83 and 2.08), and to have made an illegal turn (M = 1.75) than were low anger drivers (Ms = 0.75, 0.62, 0.77, and 0.65). High and low anger drivers also approached stoplights and intersections differently. High anger drivers were more likely to have gone out of turn at a red light or stop sign (M = 1.37), to have run a red light or stop sign (M = 1.22), and to have entered an intersections when the light was turning red (M = 2.78) than were their low anger peers (Ms = 0.50, 0.55, and 1.70). Other risky behaviors also showed anger effects. High anger drivers were more likely to have tailgated or followed another driver too closely (M = 2.62), to have switched lanes rapidly to speed through traffic (M = 3.92), and to have driven recklessly (M = 1.52) than were low anger drivers (Ms = 0.92, 2.78, and 0.42). In summary, high anger drivers engaged in significantly more risk-enhancing behavior than did low anger drivers. This was not because low anger drivers simply did not drive in unsafe, risky ways, because they did. For example, low anger drivers averaged three incidences of speeding in the 10-20 mph range and over one time of speeding more than 20 mph over the limit. They also engaged in nearly three incidences of rapid lane changes in order to speed through traffic and nearly two incidents of entering an intersection when the light was turning red. However, high anger drivers engaged in more of nearly all risky behaviors.

As with aggressive behavior, relative rates of risky behavior differed for high and low anger drivers. Compared to low anger drivers, they engaged in one and a half to two times more speeding 10-20 mph over the limit, rapid lane switching to speed through traffic, entering an intersection when the light was turning red, and driving without their seatbelt fastened. They engaged in two to two and a half times more speeding 20 mph over the limit, drifting into another lane, and running a red light or stop sign. They were two and a half to three times more likely to pass unsafely, tailgate, change lanes in an unsafe manner, go out of turn at a red light or stop sign, or make an illegal turn. Finally, they were 3.6 times more likely to report reckless driving. So, once again, the relative rates of risky behaviors for high and low anger drivers were not only statistically significant, but practically meaningful as well.

Table 9. Three-month Rates of Risky Behavior as a Function of Gender and Anger

Measure	Gender	Low Anger		High Anger		Univariate Anger $F(1, 116)$	Anger Effect Size (η^2)
		M	**SD**	**M**	**SD**		
Total Risky Behavior	M	17.87	8.53	33.50	15.49	51.29[*]	.307
	F	14.77	8.63	30.17	13.27		
Drove without Seatbelt	M	1.60	1.98	2.57	2.37	9.85[†]	.078
	F	0.93	1.60	2.30	2.12		
Drank and Drove	M	0.83	1.34	1.63	2.11	2.36	.020
	F	0.67	1.09	0.70	1.18		
Drunk and Drove	M	0.40	0.89	1.07	1.89	3.39	.028
	F	0.10	0.43	0.17	0.46		
10-20 mph over Speed Limit	M	3.20	1.32	4.43	1.14	29.06[*]	.200
	F	2.87	1.41	4.13	1.20		
20+ mph over Speed Limit	M	1.60	1.73	3.00	2.05	18.23[*]	.136
	F	1.13	1.50	2.53	1.85		
Passed Unsafely	M	0.93	1.29	2.10	1.92	21.89[*]	.159
	F	0.60	1.07	2.07	1.74		
Followed too Closely	M	0.80	1.06	2.50	1.82	33.85[*]	.226
	F	1.03	1.47	2.73	1.91		
Changed Lanes Unsafely	M	0.60	0.81	1.87	1.59	24.95[*]	.177
	F	0.63	0.96	1.80	1.73		
Drifted into Another Lane	M	0.73	0.79	1.53	1.61	10.28[†]	.081
	F	0.77	1.14	1.43	1.33		
Rapid Lane Changes	M	3.10	1.58	4.27	1.34	17.10[*]	.128
	F	2.47	1.31	3.57	1.74		
Out of Turn at Stop Sign/light	M	0.47	0.68	1.63	1.63	16.41[*]	.124
	F	0.53	1.04	1.10	1.13		
Made an Illegal Turn	M	0.77	0.94	1.38	1.84	19.71[*]	.145
	F	0.53	0.94	1.67	1.49		
Reckless Driving	M	0.70	0.95	1.60	1.79	22.60[*]	.163
	F	0.13	0.35	1.43	1.48		
Ran Red Light/ Stop Sign	M	0.47	0.68	0.93	1.57	8.32[†]	.067
	F	0.63	1.00	1.50	1.57		
Entered Intersection Light	M	1.67	1.32	2.53	1.87	14.85[*]	.114
Turning Red	F	1.73	1.29	3.03	1.61		

[†] $p < .01$.
[*] $p < .001$.
M = male.
F = female.

Crash-related Conditions: Results of the Driving Survey

Losses of concentration on the road, minor losses of vehicular control, and close calls in the last three months and moving violations and minor and major accidents in the last year are summarized in Table 10. Because these variables are not highly correlated, they were analyzed by 2 (Gender) x 2 (Driving Anger Level) univariate analyses of variance. Analyses showed that gender was not related to loss of concentration, minor losses of vehicular control, or close calls, $Fs(1, 116) = 0.21, 1.01,$ and 1.41. Anger (Table 10) and interaction effects were also not significant for minor loss of vehicular control, $F(1, 116) = 0.68$. Loss of concentration and close calls (Table 10) revealed significant anger effects. High anger drivers reported more losses of concentration ($M = 3.35$) and close calls ($M = 1.63$) than low anger drivers ($Ms = 2.77$ and 0.78). Anger effect sizes were small and moderate, respectively. However, significant interaction effects qualify these anger effects. Interaction effects were significant for losing concentration while driving and close calls in the last three months, $Fs(1, 116) = 4.10$ and 4.56, $ps < .05$, $\eta^2 s = 0.034$ and 0.038. Female drivers accounted for both interactions. High and low anger male drivers did not differ on frequency of losing concentration or close calls (Table 10). Low anger female drivers were, however, somewhat lower than male drivers on both variables, whereas high anger female drivers were significantly higher than low anger female drivers and tended to be higher than male drivers on these variables.

Table 10. Crash-related Conditions as a Function of Gender and Anger

Measure	Gender	Group Low Anger		High Anger		Univariate Anger $F(1, 116)$	Anger Effect Size (η^2)
		M	SD	M	SD		
Lost Concentration	M	3.00	1.29	3.03	1.85	4.61[†]	.038
while Driving	F	2.53	1.43	3.67	1.32		
Minor Loss of	M	0.97	1.22	1.27	1.39	3.45	.029
Vehicular Control	F	1.00	1.15	1.60	1.52		
Close Call	M	0.90	1.03	1.30	1.34	16.26[*]	.123
	F	0.67	0.80	1.97	1.35		
Moving Violations	M	0.47	0.51	0.90	1.27	6.64[†]	.054
	F	0.40	0.77	0.90	1.21		
Minor Accidents	M	0.20	0.41	0.43	1.01	1.51	.013
	F	0.33	0.71	0.43	0.73		
Major Accidents	M	0.03	0.18	0.17	0.38	1.43	.012
	F	0.03	0.18	0.00	0.00		

[†] $p < .05$.
[*] $p < .001$.
M = male
F = female.

Moving violations in the last year showed a significant effect for anger (Table 10), but not for gender or the interaction, $Fs(1, 116) = 0.03$ and 0.03. High anger drivers experienced slightly more than twice as many moving violations ($M = 0.90$) than low anger drivers ($M = 0.43$), and the effect size was moderate. Minor accidents showed no significant effects for gender, anger, or the interaction, $Fs(1, 116) = 0.24$, 1.51, and 0.24. Major accidents, however, showed significant gender and interaction effects, $Fs(1, 116) = 3.96$ and 3.96, $ps < .05$, $\eta^2 s = 0.033$ and 0.033, but no effect for anger (Table 10). Gender effects were really accounted for by the interaction. High anger male drivers had more major accidents than low anger male or than low or high anger female drivers; the latter three groups did not differ significantly from one another (see Table 10).

General Anger and General Anger Expression

Trait anger and forms of general anger expression (Table 11) revealed a significant multivariate effect for anger, $F(4, 113) = 23.06$, $p < .001$, $\eta^2 = 0.449$, but not for gender or the interaction, $Fs(4, 113) = 0.62$ and 1.77. No anger effect was found for Anger-In, but large univariate anger effects were found for the Trait Anger Scale, Anger-Out and Anger-Control (Table 11). High anger drivers reported significantly more trait anger ($M = 23.32$) and Anger-Out ($M = 18.72$) and significantly less Anger-Control ($M = 20.57$) than did low anger drivers ($Ms = 15.72$, 14.58, and 25.87).

Table 11. General Anger and Anger Expression while
Driving as a Function of Gender and Anger

| Measure | Gender | Group | | | | Univariate Anger | Anger Effect |
| | | Low Anger | | High Anger | | | |
		M	*SD*	*M*	*SD*	$F(1, 116)$	Size (η^2)
Trait Anger Scale	M	16.23	4.86	22.80	5.37	79.48[*]	.407
	F	15.20	2.75	23.83	5.21		
Anger-In	M	16.40	4.87	16.13	4.78	2.51	.021
	F	15.03	3.27	17.80	4.17		
Anger-Out	M	15.40	2.81	18.20	4.60	37.38[*]	.244
	F	13.77	2.86	19.23	4.19		
Anger-Control	M	26.07	4.51	21.27	4.10	41.74[*]	.265
	F	25.67	4.82	19.87	4.52		

[*]$p < .001$.
M = male.
F = female.

DISCUSSION AND CONCLUSIONS

Findings will be discussed in terms of defining and describing the characteristics of high anger drivers. Findings will be related to the literature and to predictions derived from the state-trait model of anger as applied to anger while driving. Then, findings will be related to interventions for driving anger reduction and to public policy issues, specifically issues about how such information might be used in making judgments about auto insurance rates.

Differences in Driving Behavior: A Possible Explanation of Findings?

Findings do not appear to be a result of differences in basic driving behavior. High and low anger drivers drove equivalent miles (estimates from demographic data and the Driving Log) and equally often (Driving Log). Given equivalent amounts and frequencies· of driving, high and low anger drivers likely drive under similar circumstances and are not exposed to different amounts of frustration and provocation on the road. That is, differences observed between high and low anger drivers do not appear attributable to differential exposure to provocation and frustration, but to be better accounted for by the interaction of driver characteristics (trait driving anger) with relatively similar driving conditions.

Range of Events Triggering Anger

Assessing the range of events triggering anger for participants was somewhat compromised in the current study, because indices employed were not independent from the participant selection process and the operational definition of high and low anger drivers. With this caveat in mind, two sources of data suggest that high anger drivers are angered by a wider range of situations than low anger drivers. Specifically, high anger drivers scored higher on all six subscales of the long version of the Driving Anger Scale and rated three times as many situations as eliciting "much" or "very much" anger. In fact, they rated items as triggering much or very much anger on approximately three fourths of the items on the long-form of the Driving Anger Scale. Similar differences in elicitation of anger were noted in clinical samples (Deffenbacher et al., 2000; Deffenbacher, Filetti, et al., 2003; Deffenbacher, Lynch, Filetti, et al., 2003), but the current study extends findings to high anger drivers in general, not just high anger drivers admitting a problem with driving anger. Findings also support the elicitation hypothesis (i.e., high anger drivers will have anger more easily triggered than low anger drivers) of the state-trait theory adapted to driving anger.

Frequency of Anger Experienced

Driving Logs showed that high anger drivers became angry twice as often as low anger drivers, a difference similar to that reported in other studies (Deffenbacher, 2003; Deffenbacher, Deffenbacher, et al., 2003). Statistical effect size was large, and differences in the number of times high and low anger drivers would become angry over a year's time were quite large. These findings suggest quite meaningful differences in how often high and low anger drivers become angry and support the frequency hypothesis (i.e., that high anger drivers will be angered more frequently than low anger drivers) from the state-trait model.

Intensity of Anger Experienced

High anger drivers rated themselves as angrier drivers (Driving Survey) and reported more intense anger across a wide range of potential provocations (Driving Anger Scale) and in response to their personally most anger-provoking events (Anger Situations). High anger drivers reported more intense anger (State Anger Scale) in response to visualizing both an inattentive driver who impedes their driving and another driver stealing a parking spot for which the person had been waiting. The intensity of anger in day-to-day driving (Driving Log) was also significantly higher for high anger drivers. Anecdotal evidence regarding anger intensity on the Driving Log also supports differences in anger intensity. High anger drivers report that they feel they begin to lose control of their anger when the anger level reaches approximately 40 on the 100-point intensity scale. Table 7 shows that, on average, anger intensity for high anger drivers was well above this level, averaging greater than 60, whereas low anger drivers were well below this point, averaging in the low 20's. Thus, it appears that high anger drivers not only experience more frequent anger, but also are more intensely angered when they are angered behind the wheel. These findings replicate other studies, which also report greater anger intensity for high anger individuals (Deffenbacher, 2003;

Deffenbacher, Deffenbacher, et al., 2003). The present study not only replicates this general finding, but also extends it to an additional visualized provocation. This conclusion is strengthened by the fact that evidence came from several different methodologies (i.e., general self-report, idiographic self-report, ratings in response to visualized provocations, and field diaries). In summary, findings from this study strongly support the intensity hypothesis (i.e., that high anger drivers will experience more intense anger in the face of frustration and provocation than low anger drivers) from the state-trait model. Moreover, multiple converging sources of data supported this hypothesis.

Angry/Hostile Thinking

Emotional reactions were not the only differences between high and low anger drivers. High anger drivers think in more hostile and aggressive ways as well. For example, high anger drivers are more prone to think in negative, judgmental, exaggerated, name calling types of ways as reflected in elevated levels of judgmental/disbelieving and pejorative labeling/verbally aggressive thinking on the Driver's Angry Thoughts Questionnaire. Implications for anger arousal and aggression for these two types of thinking, however, may be quite different. Although the two scales correlate positively (Deffenbacher et al., in press; Deffenbacher, Petrilli, et al., 2003), they differ in content. Judgmental/disbelieving thoughts certainly involve attention to other drivers, their behavior, and road conditions. However, judgments are less harsh and often involve thoughts that the person cannot believe others are driving the ways they are or that the other driver does not understand the potential consequences of their behavior. These thoughts do not, however, typically include highly negative labels or thoughts of revenge, retaliation, great displeasure, and bringing harm to others. Other research (Deffenbacher et al., in press; Deffenbacher, Petrilli, et al., 2002) has shown that this type of thinking correlates positively with coping self-instruction as well as more aggressive forms of thinking. That is, judgmental/disbelieving thinking is positively related to both aggressive and positive coping thoughts. Judgmental/disbelieving thoughts may alert and focus attention and lead to some angry arousal, but it may not directly channel that arousal toward aggression. It may take other aggressive thoughts such as the highly negative labeling (e.g., "asshole") and prompts for verbal aggression involved in pejorative labeling/verbally aggressive thinking (e.g., "I'm going tell that idiot off"), for physical aggression involved in physically aggressive thinking (e.g., "I'd like to punch his lights out") and/or for revenge and counter-attack on the perceived source of provocation involved in revengeful/retaliatory thinking (e.g., "I show that son of a bitch. I'll box him in and see how he likes it.") to channel arousal toward aggressive urges and behavior. High anger drivers were also higher on all three of these forms of hostile/aggressive thinking which may predispose them toward greater aggressive expression of anger and aggressive behavior on the road. Interestingly, high and low anger drivers did not differ on the level of coping self-instruction, which is consistent with the very low negative correlations of coping self-instruction with driving anger (Deffenbacher, Petrilli, et al., 2003). That is, a lowered tendency to think of constructive, adaptive ways of handling anger did not discriminate high from low anger drivers. Only the more aggressive forms thinking did. They reported engaging in much more hostile, antagonistic, labeling, verbally and physically aggressive thoughts, and thoughts of seeking revenge and retaliation upon others.

Differences in thinking patterns extend predictions of state-trait theory to the realm of cognition. Theoretical predictions were previously made for emotions and behavior, but current findings also suggest that high anger drivers are also characterized by more hostile/aggressive thinking. Given that this is the first study exploring potential cognitive differences in high and low anger drivers, these findings await replication, but they suggest that differences previously reported for emotion and behavior are, to a significant degree, mirrored in thought as well. Findings also support one of two extensions of the state-trait model. Elevations on the three aggressive forms of thinking (i.e., pejorative labeling/verbally aggressive, physically aggressive, and revenge/retaliatory thinking) support the extension of the aggression hypothesis to aggressive cognition. Absences of differences on coping self-instruction suggest that the reduced positive coping hypothesis did not extend to cognitive processes, at least as represented by the coping self-instruction scale of the Driver's Angry Thoughts Questionnaire.

Anger Expression

High anger drivers reported that they generally tended to express their anger behind the wheel in more aggressive ways and that they were less likely to cope constructively or adaptively when angry, as reported by others (Deffenbacher, 2003; Deffenbacher, Deffenbacher, et al., 2003). The form of their aggressive anger expression was not limited. High anger drivers reported they were more likely to express their anger via verbal aggression through things such as yelling or swearing another driver. They were also more likely to aggress physically wherein their person was the instrument of aggression through things such as giving another driver the finger or attempting to get out of the vehicle and have a physical altercation with another driver. They were also more likely to use their vehicle as an instrument of aggression through things such as cutting another driver off or tailgating as means of expressing their anger and frustration. Moreover, they were significantly less likely to try to handle their anger in positive, constructive ways. Thus, high anger drivers appear more likely to deal with their anger in aggressive ways and less likely to check or counter those aggressive tendencies.

Prior research suggests that thought and behavioral patterns may be linked (Deffenbacher et al., in press; Deffenbacher, Petrilli, et al., 2003). Although there was a general pattern of positive correlations among aggressive thoughts and aggressive forms of anger expression, some thought patterns were more highly related to specific forms of anger expression. For example, pejorative labeling/verbally aggressive thinking was more strongly associated with verbally aggressive expression, revengeful/retaliatory thinking with using the vehicle to express anger, and coping self-instruction more with adaptive/constructive anger expression. Physically aggressive thought patterns were highly correlated with both physically aggressive expression and with using the vehicle as the instrument of aggression. Such findings not only provide evidence of discriminant validity for the two measures involved, but also suggest that looking at specific thought-action patterns may provide a more precise understanding of high anger drivers.

Aggression on the Road

High anger drivers rated themselves as more aggressive drivers. However, as noted in the introduction, this may or may not always refer aggression as defined in the psychological literature and, thus, may not be a strong support of greater aggression in high anger drivers. However, other data suggest that high anger drivers do engage in more driving-related aggression. For example, in response to visualizing an inattentive driver whose carelessness prevents the person from making a left hand turn and another driver who steals the parking spot for which the person had been waiting, high anger drivers reported greater urges to engage in both verbal and physical aggression. In both situations, high anger drivers also were less likely to cope in positive, constructive ways. High anger drivers engaged in roughly four times more aggression in day-to-day driving (Driving Log) than low anger drivers. Relative rates in aggression were not only statistically significant, but also very meaningful when extrapolated over time. Similar findings were found for reports of aggression on the road over the last three months (Driving Survey). High anger drivers reported 3.3 times more aggression.

A breakdown of the type of aggressive behavior showed that high anger drivers engaged in greater amounts of all types of aggressive behavior. They reported more verbal (e.g., cursing and yelling at other drivers and arguments with other drivers and passengers), physical (e.g., gestures towards other drivers and physical assault on their vehicle), and vehicular (e.g., horns honked, lights flashed, tailgating, and cutting off other drivers in anger) aggression. Relative differences were also quite different in many cases. For example, high anger drivers were 18 times more likely to have an argument with another driver and, respectively, six and four times more likely to cut someone off or tailgate them in anger. Thus, high anger drivers were not only engaging in some behaviors that may have little consequence (e.g., swearing at another driver), but also some behaviors that by their very nature have a much greater probability of escalating aggression (e.g., an argument with another driver) and/or physical harm (e.g., cutting others off or tailgating in anger). Thus, the type of aggressive behavior was important as well as the frequency. High anger drivers also reported that they were more likely to lose control of their anger while driving. Although they were over 10 times more likely to lose control of their anger than low anger drivers, the mean was less than one time in the last three months. Given that the means for many of the forms of aggression were significantly more frequent than this, it suggests that high anger drivers did not consider engaging in many of these behaviors, which constituted losing control of their anger. This finding suggests that a significant number of aggressive behaviors may be done in anger, but not to the point of losing control of anger, at least from the driver's perspective. This also supports the importance of researchers asking about specific type of aggressive behavior and not assuming that these can be fully captured by inquiring about the most "angry" incidents (i.e., situations in which a perception of the loss of control may be needed).

Findings on aggressive forms of expression and aggression (i.e., elevations on the three aggressive forms of anger expression, state verbal and physical aggression in response to the visualized scenarios, and reported aggression on driving diaries and on the three-month survey) strongly supported the aggression and reduced positive coping (i.e., lower levels of adaptive/constructive anger expression and lower positive coping in response to the visualized scenarios) hypotheses from the state-trait model. Confidence in these findings is strengthened by three things. First, findings were replicated across methodologies (e.g., visualized scenarios, driving diaries, and general surveys). Second, statistical effect sizes were generally large across measures and methodologies, and the relative rates and absolute differences between high and low anger drivers were quite large. Third, findings replicate and extend those reported in earlier studies (Deffenbacher, 2003; Deffenbacher, Deffenbacher, et al., 2003). In summary, high anger drivers are not only angrier, but also engage in more aggression on the road.

Risky and Unsafe Driving

High anger drivers rated themselves as riskier and less safe drivers than low anger drivers. Other data support these global perceptions. High anger drivers reported twice as much risky behavior on both the driving diaries and three-month survey. Similar findings have been found in other studies of college student drivers (Deffenbacher, 2003; Deffenbacher, Deffenbacher, et al., 2003). A breakdown of the survey results showed that high anger drivers engaged more frequently in nearly all types of risky behaviors (e.g., speeding, passing and changing lanes in an unsafe manner, running red lights or stop signs, rapid lane switching to speed through traffic, and tailgating). Reckless driving was the largest difference with high anger drivers engaging in over three and a half times more reckless driving. The one exception to group differences was drinking or being intoxicated and driving. However, given the importance of this behavior and how the relatively low frequency of the behavior may have interacted with the size of the sample to produce non-significant findings, this behavior should continued to be studied in future research.

Unsafe driving was reflected in other reports as well. High anger drivers experienced more losses of concentration while driving and close calls in the last three months and approximately twice as many moving violations in the last year, as reported in other studies (Deffenbacher, 2003; Deffenbacher, Deffenbacher, et al., 2003). Although there were no differences in minor accident rates, high anger male drivers experienced more major accidents in the past year, a finding not replicated in other studies, but worthy of continued examination.

In general, high anger drivers engaged in significantly more unsafe and risky behavior while driving. Some of these behaviors carry a significant degree of potential harm to the driver and/or others. While findings are generally consistent with other studies, it should not be concluded that these behaviors are necessarily mediated or prompted by anger. In some instances they may be, as in the case of the angry, distracted driver who tailgates or runs a red light. However, a direct anger-related link is often not present. For example, when driving in low impedance, minimal frustration simulations, high anger drivers were four times more likely to speed 10-20 mph over the limit (40% vs. 10%), and all (12%) individuals speeding 20 mph over the limit were high anger drivers. However, anger and aggression levels were uniformly low for both groups and thus could not have been a factor in accounting for speeding. The tendency to become angry behind the wheel (trait driving anger) is associated with other characteristics such as impulsiveness, which may partially account for increased risk-taking behind the wheel (e.g., Deffenbacher, Filetti, et al., 2003). Thus, although aggression and risky behavior behind the wheel are highly correlated (*rs* in .50 to .60 range), they are not necessarily mediated by the same situational, emotional, or psychological conditions.

General Anger Constructs: A More Parsimonious Explanation of Findings?

High anger drivers reported greater trait anger and greater general outward, negative expression of anger (Anger-Out) and less controlled forms of anger expression (Anger-Control), a finding also reported in other studies (Deffenbacher, 2003). Driving-related thoughts in the Driver's Angry Thoughts Questionnaire also correlate with general hostile automatic thoughts (Deffenbacher, Petrilli, et al., 2003). Such results might suggest that findings in the current study might just as easily accounted for by more general characteristics (Lajunen & Parker, 2001). If this were the case, it would lessen the value of and weaken construct validity of driving-related measures of anger, angry cognitions, and anger expression. It could be argued that driving-specific measures are not needed and that findings could be explained by the more general constructs.

Four lines of evidence weaken this argument. First, although measures of driving anger, anger expression, and angry cognitions correlate with parallel general measures, the degree of correlation tends to be only moderate. For example, trait driving anger on the Driving Anger Scale and general trait anger on the Trait Anger Scale correlate in the .25 to .40 range (Deffenbacher, 2000). This suggests a significant correlation, but a significant degree of non-overlap as well. Constructs are correlated, but appear moderately independent. Second, regression models show that both general and driving-related measures account for significant amounts of variance in important driving-related behaviors such as aggressive and risky behavior. However, regression models including driving-related measures account for more variance than do general measures, often upwards to double the amount of variance accounted for (Deffenbacher et al., in press; Deffenbacher, Petrilli, et al., 2003; Deffenbacher, Lynch, Oetting, et al., 2003). This suggests that driving-related measures and constructs account for more of the phenomena than general constructs. Third, there is evidence of incremental validity for many of the driving-related measures. For example, measures of driving anger expression add significant variance to the prediction of aggressive and risky behavior above and beyond that provided by the Anger Expression Inventory (Deffenbacher et al., in press; Deffenbacher, Lynch, Oetting, et al., 2003). Likewise, angry driving-related cognitions, as measured by the Driver's Angry Thoughts Questionnaire, add incrementally to the prediction of aggression and risky behavior beyond that provided by a general measure of hostile thoughts. Fourth, there are significant content differences in the nature of the measures. For example, verbal and personal physical forms of aggression on the Driving Anger Expression Inventory might be subsumed under Anger-Out, but there is simply no parallel to using the vehicle to express anger. This form of anger expression is unique to the driving environment and expressing anger therein. It, and other driving-specific measures, therefore, add measurement of unique properties that are not available in more general measures. In summary, the evidence suggests that driving-specific and general measures and their underlying constructs are correlated, but somewhat independent phenomena.

Driving-related anger and anger expression likely interact and reciprocally influence each other, sometimes contributing to negative spirals of anger and aversive experience. If an individual is high on both trait driving anger and general trait anger and associated negative forms of anger expression, then those characteristics may influence each other by excitation transfer effects (Zillman, 1971). For example, let's suppose that late in the afternoon this individual experiences frustration at work and reacts with an increase in anger and handles it badly by arguing with and yelling at a co-worker. He/she then leaves work and gets into his/her car in an angry, irritable, frustrated state and begins the commute home. He/she is now entering an environment to which he/she is already vulnerable to anger arousal and dysfunctional anger expression. Sure enough, he/she encounters heavy traffic and is cut off by another driver. The anger from the work environment carries over like a cup of emotional gasoline and temper flares even more than it would normally. The driver shouts obscenities, gives the other driver the finger, and races ahead, only to hit his/her brakes to avoid hitting another car. More anger is added to the seething cauldron of experience as the driver utters obscenities between clenched teeth. The driver arrives home in an angry, bitter state, only to encounter a difficult interaction with a roommate or spouse. Anger and elevated aggressive tendencies carryover again to this next interaction, which is more angry and frustrating than it need be. Thus, rather than needing driving-related and general constructs to be independent, they can be seen as correlated characteristics which may cross influence each other and together may provide improved understanding of driving and commuter stress phenomena.

Intervention for the Reduction of Driving Anger

High trait driving anger is a risk factor for more frequent and intense anger when driving and for more aggression and risky behavior. However, can anything be done to reduce this anger behind the wheel? Recent studies from our research group have shown promise for reducing that anger and some of the associated problems.

In these studies high anger introductory psychology students became eligible for intervention programs if they: (a) scored in the upper quartile on the Driving Anger Scale; (b) identified their anger behind the wheel as a personal problem for which they wanted help; and (c) accepted conditions of the study, which included random assignment to a no treatment control. Participants were assessed on a pretreatment, one-week posttreatment, one-month posttreatment, and, in most cases, one-year posttreatment basis. Instruments have been added to the assessment battery as they have been developed, but typically included at least the Driving Anger Scale, the Driving Survey, the Driving Log, and the Trait Anger Scale. Interventions have been delivered in one-hour, weekly small groups of five to 10 participants. Interventions were compared to the no treatment control to assess absolute effectiveness and to each other to assess relative effectiveness.

In the first study (Deffenbacher et al., 2000), clients receiving counseling received either an applied relaxation coping skills intervention or a cognitive-relaxation coping skills intervention. In the first two sessions of the applied relaxation coping skills condition, clients were trained in progressive relaxation and in four relaxation coping skills with which to lower anger arousal quickly: (a) relaxation imagery (i.e., visualizing a situation that triggered relaxation); (b) breathing-cued relaxation (i.e., taking three to five deep breaths and relaxing with each breath out); (c) cue-controlled relaxation (i.e., slowly saying a word or phrase that had been paired with and triggers relaxation); and (d) relaxation without tension (i.e., focusing upon and letting areas of tension relax). Clients also tracked and logged their emotional, physiological, cognitive and behavioral reactions to driving-related, anger-provoking situations while driving. This was done to increase the client's awareness of his/her anger experience and the situations in which it was experienced. This increased awareness was to serve as a cue for applying relaxation skills in the future. Beginning with the third session, clients employed relaxation coping skills to lower anger. In the session, clients visualized situations that elicited anger, experienced anger arousal, and then employed relaxation coping skills to lower anger arousal. Over the next five sessions, the degree of anger arousal elicited by the anger imagery was increased, and the degree of therapist assistance in retrieval of relaxation was decreased. This was done to foster the development of client self-control over anger arousal. Outside of sessions, clients employed relaxation coping skills to lower anger while driving. These experiences were discussed and refined for the development of increased self-management of anger in vivo.

The cognitive-relaxation condition added cognitive restructuring to the self-managed relaxation coping skills. Starting with the third session a specific anger-engendering cognitive pattern was introduced. Clients identified examples of their thinking that revealed this type of cognitive error (e.g., overgeneralized thinking in which broad generalizations and misattributions are made or catastrophic thinking in which highly negative, exaggerated labels are put on events such as "horrible," "awful," or "I can't stand it."). Twenty to thirty minutes were spent identifying alternative, less angering thoughts with which to counter and replace the highly angering thoughts. These alternative thoughts were rehearsed along with relaxation coping skills to lower anger aroused by the anger scenes. The remainder of the protocol followed the general steps outlined above for the relaxation coping skills program.

Compared to the no treatment control, both interventions reduced levels of reported anger while driving. On some measures, the relaxation intervention was superior to the cognitive-relaxation condition. The cognitive-relaxation condition, however, lowered risky behavior, whereas the relaxation condition did not. Aggression while driving, trait anger, and general anger expression were not changed.

This study was a promising clinical trial. However, it revealed several weaknesses. First, the cognitive portion of the cognitive-relaxation condition introduced a general type of dysfunctional cognition each session, whether it was centrally related to the anger scenes of the day. An alternative would have been to identify cognitive problems and constructive cognitive counters for each scene and rehearse those. That way cognitive change would be more logically linked to cognitive processes involved in the specific situations dealt with in that session, rather than being an arbitrary class of cognitive distortions. Over sessions, general cognitive themes and their counters could be identified. This change seemed a more appropriate, flexible way of attending to the cognitive portion of the intervention. Second, application of skills to address aggressive urges had not been targeted specifically in the original protocol, because it was thought that lowering anger would automatically address this issue. However, given that aggression was not lowered, it appeared that this issue should be targeted directly. Third, application to non-driving situations and other emotions such as anxiety had not been targeted effectively either. This too seemed an oversight that should be incorporated in protocol redesign.

In the next study (Deffenbacher, Filetti, Lynch, Dahlen, & Oetting, 2002), the cognitive-relaxation condition was revised to include the change in cognitive restructuring and use of coping skills to address the link between anger and aggression and for reducing other types of anger and negative feelings. Both relaxation and cognitive-relaxation interventions lowered driving anger, aggressive driving anger expression, aggression while driving, and trait anger. The cognitive-relaxation condition reduced risky behavior, whereas the relaxation condition did not. With this exception, there was no evidence of differential treatment effects. Additionally, effects were maintained at year follow-up. Thus, it appeared that the revised approaches were achieving some of the desired effects in broadened effects.

A third, larger study compared these two revised interventions again (Richards, Deffenbacher, Filetti, Lynch, & Kogan, 2001), but this time in a design with a larger sample size which had greater power to detect potential differences between active treatment conditions. Both interventions effectively reduced driving anger, aggressive expression of driving anger, aggression, and trait anger. However, at some points in time, the relaxation condition reduced risky behavior compared to the control, suggesting that findings for risky behavior in prior studies were somewhat unstable. Effects were again maintained at year follow-up, supporting long-term driving anger reduction effects for relaxation and cognitive-relaxation coping skills approaches.

A fourth study (Kogan, Richards, & Deffenbacher, 2001) adapted Beck's cognitive therapy to driving anger reduction. This intervention addresses both cognitive restructuring and the identification of alternative, more adaptive behaviors with which to handle anger-provoking situations. Appropriate cognitive and behavioral coping skills were identified in the first portion of the session and then were rehearsed to lower anger aroused by the driving-related scenes in the second half of the session. Application of cognitive and behavioral coping skills were encouraged through homework assignments parallel to those in the relaxation and cognitive-relaxation protocols, but emphasized the application of cognitive and behavioral coping skills. Cognitive therapy was compared to the relaxation coping skills condition and a no treatment control. Compared to the control group through the one-month follow-up, both interventions lowered driving anger, angry/hostile cognitions, aggressive anger expression, aggression, and trait anger. Both also increased adaptive/constructive forms of anger expression. There was no evidence of differential treatment effects, and neither intervention reduced reported risky behavior. A year follow-up (Deffenbacher, Richards, & Kogan, 2002) showed that effects maintained. Cognitive therapy and relaxation coping skills did not differ from one another, but compared to the control, revealed lower driving anger, angry cognitions, aggressive anger expression, aggression, trait anger, and anger-out. The relaxation coping skills condition reported lower risky behavior than the control, whereas cognitive therapy did not differ from either group on risky behavior. Cognitive therapy increased adaptive/constructive anger expression, whereas the relaxation condition did not differ from either cognitive therapy or the control on this measure. Neither condition altered either anger-in or anger-control.

Taken together, these studies suggest that relaxation, cognitive-relaxation, and cognitive-behavioral interventions can lower anger behind the wheel, aggressive anger expression, and aggression. Generally, treatment effect sizes were large. Sometimes, adaptive/constructive anger expression was improved and risky behavior was reduced, but these were not consistent findings. When protocols address application to other sources of anger, trait anger was reduced and in some studies outward, negative expression of general anger as well. Effects are maintained at short- (one-month) and long- (one-year) term follow-ups, suggesting maintenance of anger reduction effects. Thus, at this point there appear some promising, cost-effective, short-term treatment approaches for reducing driving anger.

Implications of Current Findings for Intervention

These studies provide a promise of helping angry drivers, but what are the implications of the findings of this study for such interventions? Treatment implications are outlined below.

1. High anger individuals are angered by many different sources of frustrations and provocation. Interventions should assist them in identifying the situations to which they respond with greatest anger and to link treatment strategies to those situations. The situations to which the individual is most vulnerable to anger arousal can become cues for the application of the skills and strategies learned in counseling.

2. High anger drivers are more intensely angered behind the wheel. In addition to identifying the situations to which they are most vulnerable, interventions should assist them in identifying the patterns of emotional, physiological, cognitive, and behavioral responding when angry and to employ intervention strategies when anger arousal increases. These experiences and internal processes can also become cues for the application of skills learned in therapy.

3. High anger drivers engage in more negative/verbally aggressive, physically aggressive, and revengeful/retaliatory thought processes. These appear not only to be part of an aversive experience for the angry driver, but also to be correlated with differential forms of anger expression. If interventions do not target these hostile/aggressive thought processes directly as in cognitive-relaxation coping skills training or cognitive therapy, then cognitive measures should be included to make sure that other interventions such as relaxation interventions lead to reductions in angry/hostile cognitions.

4. High anger drivers engage in more aggressive anger expression and aggressive behavior behind the wheel. Interventions should make sure that intervention strategies are targeted to and rehearsed for the urge to aggress. Otherwise, anger may be lowered, but the prompting of aggression may not be reliably reduced. Interventions should be developed and evaluated which address aggressive behavior directly (e.g., identification and rehearsal of aggression-incompatible and safe driving behaviors with which to handle anger-provoking events on the road).

5. Given that some thought processes are more highly correlate with certain anger expression styles, if an intervention targets both cognitive and behavioral processes as Beck's cognitive therapy does, then therapists may wish to target these cognition-behavior links as a unit.

6. High anger drivers engage in more risky behavior, and interventions have not consistently altered this behavior. It is suggested that interventions identify conditions associated with risky behavior and train the application of intervention skills for the urge to engage in risky behavior. If risky behavior is related to being in an angry state, then rehearsal should focus on identifying those conditions and explicitly training application of skills to the anger-risky behavior link. However, many risky behaviors are not related to anger. If interventions are going to try to alter risky behavior, then they must also assist clients in identifying the internal and external conditions which prompt risky behavior and then rehearse strategies for those conditions, because they may be quite different from those involved in anger.

7. The correlation of and potential interaction of driving-related anger and anger expression and general anger and general anger expression also have implications for treatment as well. Specifically, time and attention should be directed to identifying

potential reciprocal influences of one domain on the other. Clients should be trained to identify and apply intervention strategies to break up these connections and abort cycles of anger and stress from driving and non-driving circumstances. For example, the driver who is getting into his/her car in an angry, agitated state from work might apply relaxation coping skills for three to five minutes before leaving the parking lot. Alternatively, when arriving home from an angry, frustrating commute, he/she might take a time out from a potential argument at home, go to another room, and apply cognitive and relaxation coping skills to lower anger, change anger-engendering thinking, and return to the discussion with a plan for problem resolution, rather than a engaging in a bitter argument. Thus, treatment programs can use the correlation of anger-related phenomena and adapt intervention strategies in a least two ways. First, as in the example above, intervention strategies can be applied to reduce the reciprocal influence of one aspect of anger and anger expression on another and decrease transfer effects. Second, intervention strategies (e.g., relaxation coping skills, cognitive restructuring, deployment of aggression incompatible behavior, use of time outs, etc., which were developed for application to anger behind the wheel) can be trained for application to other sources of anger (e.g., anger in the work place having nothing to do with driving) and even other arousal states (e.g., anxiety, stress and embarrassment). This can lead to more global change for the client and not necessarily take a great deal more therapeutic time and resources.

These are suggestions for using the nature of high anger driver's experience to improve interventions for driving anger reduction. The driving anger reduction studies serendipitously identified another group with potential implications for intervention and prevention. The first study (Deffenbacher et al., 2000) sought to identify relative risk factors of the high anger client group. To achieve this, a group of low anger drivers were defined and selected as they were in the current study. That is, the low anger group was in the lower quartile on trait driving anger and indicated that they did not have a problem with anger, but wished to participate in study on driving anger. The latter condition was constructed in order to garner names and phone numbers of potentially interested low anger participants. However, we noticed another group. These were students who were psychometrically in the upper quartile on driving anger, but who checked the box indicating that they did not have a personal problem with driving anger (i.e., a high anger, non-problem admitting group). This group was interesting. Perhaps, this group was angry, but not an aggressive, risk-taking, ticket-receiving group who experiences very many negative consequences. That is, they might be angry, but not engage in other behaviors that would lead their anger to become problematic. If so, then they should be studied so that their protective factors and natural coping processes could be identified and inform intervention efforts. That is, interventions might benefit from knowing what high anger/no problem individuals were doing naturally that their high anger/problem admitting peers were not doing. On the other hand, perhaps these high anger/no problem individuals were just as aggressive and risk-taking as the high anger/problem admitting individuals, but deny, ignore, minimize or simply accept as normal problems and issues. If this were the case, then counseling and anger reduction interventions are of little relevance, because they had been offered free, readily accessible, short-term counseling and turned it down. If they were at significant risk, then other prevention interventions would need to be designed and tested, because this high anger/no problem group did not see counseling as relevant to them.

Two studies (Deffenbacher, Filetti, et al., 2003, Deffenbacher, Lynch, Filetti, et al., 2003) compared these high anger/no problem drivers to high anger/problem admitting and low anger/no problem individuals. Deffenbacher, Lynch, Filetti, et al. (2003) found few differences between the two high anger groups. Both high anger groups were at elevated risk for anger, aggressive anger expression, aggression and risky behavior on the road, and experienced more of some crash-related outcomes. They reported less adaptive/constructive expression of driving-related anger. They also did not differ from each other, but reported more trait anxiety and general trait anger and more outward negative and less controlled general anger expression than the low anger group. The second study (Deffenbacher, Filetti, Richards, et al., 2003) doubled the sample size and thereby its statistical power to identify differences between the two high anger groups. Both groups were again at elevated risk compared to low anger drivers. The two groups of high anger drivers did not differ on reported anger, risky behavior, or impulsiveness. High anger/problem admitting drivers, however, reported greater aggression on one measure of driving-related aggression, greater aggressiveness on verbal, physical and vehicular forms of expressing anger, greater general trait anger, and more aggressive, less controlled forms of expressing general anger than the high anger/no problem group. The latter findings suggest that high anger/problem admitting individuals may. be somewhat more aggressive and may experience more negative consequences from that aggressiveness and thereby be at a higher stage of readiness for counseling or therapy when it was offered. On the other hand, as noted in both studies, the high anger/no problem drivers are still at considerable risk, compared to low anger drivers, and yet require a different kind of intervention design, because they were offered and did not take advantage of counseling. Readiness, denial, and minimization processes of this group need to be studied, and interventions that target such processes such as motivational interviewing (Miller & Rollick, 1991) need to be adapted to this population and evaluated.

Policy Implications: What about Insurance Rates?

This and other studies have shown that high anger drivers are at elevated risk for more frequent and intense anger, more aggressive and risky behavior, more moving violations, losses of concentration and close calls, and the like. If high anger drivers are at higher risk and low anger drivers at lower risk, should not these characteristics influence the auto insurance rates? For example, in this same population, auto insurance companies often offer good student discounts, because good students are demonstrably at lower risk. Therefore, if high anger drivers are at elevated risk, should this not be used actuarially to adjust their premiums and potentially influence policy issuance at all?

This question is more than a question of social policy. It is also a question of valid science. The risk factor relationships established in this study and others were established under a specific set of conditions. Data are collected under anonymous, no contingency conditions. That is, students do not put their name or other personally identifying information on the data, and there are no consequences for their data, other than perhaps research credit for participation. This raises a significant question of valid scientific generalization of findings to the auto insurance situation. In the insurance situation, data would not be collected anonymously. The person's uniquely identifying information is directly connected so that it could be used for premium adjusting purposes. Moreover, there is a very clear contingency related to responding. The person knows that the data reported may and likely will influence insurance rates. Knowledge of this contingency may influence information reported and potentially the relationships among variables. Finally, data collected for insurance purposes are not publicly verifiable. Most of the data being reported deal with internal states like anger and angry cognitions and behavioral tendencies like anger expression. Unlike grades used for the good student discount where a publicly verifiable document can and must be produced, the risk factors in the current study are much more open to conscious and unconscious bias. Thus, it is far from clear, at a scientific level, whether findings from studies such as this one can be generalized validly to situation of insurance rate adjustment, where the conditions are very different than those under which risk factor relationships were initially established.

This, however, is partially an empirical question. Data can be collected under conditions that are not anonymous and where very clear financial contingencies are present. If the levels of reported anger, angry cognitions, anger expression, etc. do not change in their levels and/or their correlations with insurance-related outcomes (e.g., aggressive and risky behavior), then findings could be validly generalized. However, if insurance uses of the data dramatically changes the data and relationships among them, and there are certainly reasonable incentives for inaccurate reporting, then empirical basis for extrapolating findings would be seriously called into question.

The scientific question of valid generalization of findings can be asked and hopefully answered. Two studies in our research program are currently under way which address this issue. Introductory psychology and upper division students have been randomly asked to complete questionnaires like the ones employed in this study under one of two conditions. In one case, they completed them under the typical anonymous, non-contingent conditions. In the other, students were asked to imagine that they have been asked to complete these questionnaires by their insurance agent and to assume that their responses will influence their auto insurance rates, potentially even issuance of a policy. Studies such as this can assist in establishing whether risk factor relationships from anonymous, non-contingent responding can be generalized validly to the insurance environment.

SUMMARY

High anger drivers differed significantly from low anger drivers in many ways. They were angered by more things, and responded with anger more frequently and intensely. They engage in more aggressive thinking about other drivers (e.g., highly negative labeling, thoughts of verbal and physical aggression, thoughts of revenge and retaliation, etc.) and report more use of verbal, physical, and vehicular ways of expressing their anger. They also engage in less adaptive/constructive expression of anger and positive coping when faced with anger-provoking conditions. They engage in more aggressive and risky behavior behind the wheel and experience more of some crash-related outcomes (e.g., moving violations and close calls). They reported more general trait anger and more outward negative, less controlled forms of general anger expression. Greater general anger and poorer ways of handling that anger, along with other characteristics such as greater impulsiveness and greater trait anger, likely make them more vulnerable to getting into their vehicles in an angry or distressed state, to react poorer to frustrating events on the road, and to experience carryover of anger and stress effects into and out of the driving environment. Moreover, these findings did not appear to be moderated by gender, as there were very few gender by anger level interactions, and there were relatively few gender main effects as well.

Theory testing also fared well, as most theoretical predictions derived from the state-trait model of anger received support. High anger drivers reacted with anger to more driving situations (elicitation hypothesis), with more frequent and intense anger (frequency and intensity hypotheses), reported more aggression and aggressive forms of anger expression (aggression hypothesis), and lower adaptive/constructive anger expression and positive coping (reduced coping hypothesis). Hypothesis testing was successfully extended to angry/hostile thinking. High anger drivers reported more judgmental/disbelieving, pejorative labeling/verbally aggressive, physically aggressive, and revengeful/retaliatory thinking, supporting the extension of the aggression hypothesis to cognitive processes. Only coping self-instruction failed to show a difference between high and low anger drivers, which did not support the extension of the reduced coping hypothesis to thought processes.

REFERENCES

American Automobile Association (1997). *Aggressive driving: Three studies*. Washington, D. C.: American Automobile Association Foundation for Traffic Safety.

Arnett, J. J., Offer, D., & Fine, M. A. (1997). Reckless driving in adolescence: 'State' and 'trait' factors. *Accident Analysis and Prevention, 29*, 57-63.

Berkowitz, L. (1990). On the formulation and regulation of anger and aggression: A cognitive-neoassociationist view. American Psychologist, *45*, 494-503.

Cohen, J. (1988). *Statistical power analysis for the behavioral sciences (2nd ed.)*. Hillsdale, NJ: Erlbaum.

Deffenbacher, J. L. (2003). Angry college student drivers and a test of state-trait theory. *Psicologia Conductual, 11*, 163-177.

_____ . (2000). The Driving Anger Scale (DAS). In J. Maltby, C. A. Lewis, & A. Hill (Eds.), *Commissioned reviews of 250 psychological tests* (pp. 287-292). Lampeter, Wales, United Kingdom: Edwin Mellen Press.

Deffenbacher, J. L., Deffenbacher, D. M., Lynch, R. S., & Richards, T. L. (2003). Anger, aggression, and risky behavior: A comparison of high and low anger drivers. *Behaviour Research and Therapy, 41*, 701-718.

Deffenbacher, J. L., Filetti, L. B., Lynch, R. S., Dahlen, E. R., & Oetting, E. R. (2002). Cognitive-behavioral treatment of high anger drivers. *Behaviour Research and Therapy*, 40, 717-737.

Deffenbacher, J. L., Filetti, L. B., Richards, T. L., Lynch, R. S., & Oetting, E. R. (2003). Characteristics of two groups of angry drivers. *Journal of Counseling Psychology, 50*, 123-132.

Deffenbacher, J. L., Huff, M E., Lynch, R. S., Oetting, E. R., & Salvatore, N. F. (2000). Characteristics and treatment of high anger drivers. *Journal of Counseling Psychology, 47*, 5-17.

Deffenbacher, J. L., Lynch, R. S., Deffenbacher, D. M., & Oetting, E. R. (2001). Further evidence of reliability and validity for the Driving Anger Expression Inventory. *Psychological Reports*, *89*, 535-540.

Deffenbacher, J. L., Lynch, R. S., Filetti, L. B., Dahlen, E. R., & Oetting, E. R. (2003). Anger, aggression, risky behavior, and crash-related outcomes in three groups of drivers. *Behaviour Research and Therapy*, *41*, 333-349.

Deffenbacher, J. L., Lynch, R. S., Oetting, E. R., & Swaim, R. C. (2002). The Driving Anger Expression Inventory: A measure of how people express their anger on the road. Behaviour Research and Therapy, *40*, 717-737.

Deffenbacher, J. L., Lynch, R. S., Oetting, E. R., & Yingling, D. A. (2001). Driving anger: correlates and a test of state-trait theory. *Personality and Individual Differences*, *31*, 1321-1331.

Deffenbacher, J. L., Oetting, E. R., & Lynch, R. S. (1994). Development of a driving anger scale. *Psychological Reports*, *74*, 83-91.

Deffenbacher, J. L., Oetting, E. R., Thwaites, G. A., Lynch, R. S., Baker, D. A., Stark, R. S., Thacker, S., & Eiswerth-Cox, L. (1996). State-trait anger theory and the utility of the Trait Anger Scale. *Journal of Counseling Psychology*, *43*, 131-148.

Deffenbacher, J. L., Petrilli, R. T., Lynch, R. S., Oetting, E. R., & Swaim, R. C. (2003). The Driver's Angry Thoughts Questionnaire: A measure of angry cognitions when driving. *Cognitive Therapy and Research*, *27*, 383-402.

Deffenbacher, J. L., Richards, T., & Kogan, L. (2002, August). *Long-term effects of relaxation and cognitive therapies for driving anger*. Paper presented at 110th Annual Convention of the American Psychological Association, Chicago, Illinois.

Deffenbacher, J. L., Story, D. A., Brandon, A. D., Hogg, J. A., & Hazaleus, S. L. (1988). Cognitive and cognitive-relaxation treatments of anger. *Cognitive Therapy and Research*, *12*, 167-184.

Deffenbacher, J. L., White, G. S., & Lynch, R. S. (in press). Evaluation of two new scales assessing driving anger: The Driving Anger Expression Inventory and the Driver's Angry Thoughts Questionnaire. *Journal of Psychopathology and Behavioral Assessment*.

Donovan, D. M., Queisser, H. R., Salzberg, P. M., & Umlauf, R. L. (1985). Intoxicated and bad drivers: Subgroups within the same population of high-risk drivers. *Journal of Studies on Alcohol*, *46*, 375-382.

Donovan, D. M., Umlauf, R. L., & Salzberg, P. M. (1988). Derivation of personality subtypes among high-risk drivers. *Alcohol, Drugs, and Driving*, *4*, 233-244.

Doob, A. N., & Gross, A. E. (1968). Status of frustrator as an inhibitor of horn-honking responses. Journal of Social Psychology, 76, 213-218.

Ellison-Potter, P. A., Bell, P. A., & Deffenbacher, J. (2001). The effects of trait driving anger, anonymity, aggressive stimuli on aggressive driving behavior. *Journal of Applied Social Psychology*, *31*, 431-443.

Galovski, T., Blanchard, E. B., & Veazey, C. (2002). Intermittent explosive disorder and other psychiatric comorbidity among court-referred and self-referred aggressive drivers. *Behaviour Research and Therapy*, *40*, 641-651.

Hemenway, D., & Solnick, S. (1993). Fuzzy dice, dream cars and indecent gestures: Correlates of driving behaviour? *Accident Analysis and Prevention*, *25*, 161-170.

Jacobs, G. A., Latham, L. E., & Brown, M. S. (1988). Test-retest reliability of the State-Trait Personality Inventory and the Anger Expression Scale. *Anxiety Research*, *1*, 363-365.

Kenrick, D. T., & MacFarlane, S. W. (1986). Ambient temperature and horn honking: A field study of the heat/aggression relationship. *Environment and Behavior, 18*, 179-181.

Kogan, L. R., Richards, T. L., & Deffenbacher, J. L. (2001, August). *Effects of relaxation and cognitive therapy for driving anger reduction.* Paper presented at the 109th Annual Convention of the American Psychological Association, San Francisco, California.

Lajunen, T., & Parker, D. (2001). Are aggressive people aggressive drivers? A study of the relationship between self-reported general aggressiveness, driver anger and aggressive driving. *Accident Analysis and Prevention, 33*, 243-255.

Lajunen, T., Parker, D., & Stradling, S. G. (1998). Dimensions of driver anger, aggressive and highway code violations and their mediation by safety orientation in UK drivers. *Transportation Research, Part F, 1*, 107-121.

Lynch, R. S., Morris, C. D., Deffenbacher, J. L., & Oetting, E. R. (1998, August). *Prospective study of anger consequences.* Paper presented at the 106th Annual Convention of the American Psychological Association, San Francisco, California.

McMillen, D. L., Pang, M. G. Wells-Parker, E., & Anderson, B. J. (1992). Alcohol, personality traits, and high risk driving: A comparison of young, drinking driver groups. *Addictive Behaviors, 17*, 525-532.

Morris, C. D., Deffenbacher, J. L., Lynch, R. S., & Oetting, E. R. (1996, August). *Anger expression and its consequences.* Paper presented at the 104th Annual Convention of the American Psychological Association, Toronto, Ontario, Canada.

Miller, W. R., & Rollnick, S. (1991). *Motivational interviewing: Preparing people to change addictive behavior.* New York: Guilford.

Novaco, R. W. (1975). *Anger control.* Lexington, Massachusetts: Heath.

Potter, P. A., Govern, J. M., Petri, H. L., & Figler, M. H. (1995). Anonymity and aggressive driving behavior: A field study. *Journal of Social Behavior and Personality, 10*, 265-272.

Richards, T. L., Deffenbacher, J. L., Filetti, L. B., Lynch, R. S., & Kogan, L. R. (2001, August). *Short- and long-term effects of interventions for driving anger reduction.* Paper presented at the 109 th Annual Convention of the American Psychological Association, San Francisco, California.

Shinar, D. (1998). Aggressive driving: The contribution of the drivers and the situation. *Transportation Research Part F: Traffic Psychology and Behaviour, 1F2*, 137-159.

Spielberger, C.D. (1988). *State-Trait Anger Expression Inventory (1st ed.).* Odessa, Florida: Psychological Assessment Resources.

_____ . (1999). *State-Trait Anger Expression Inventory (2nd ed.).* Odessa, Florida: Psychological Assessment Resources.

Underwood, G., Chapman, P., Wright, S., & Crundall, D. (1999). Anger while driving. *Transportation Research, Part F 2*, 55-68.

Zillman, D. (1971). Excitation transfer in communication-mediated aggressive behavior. *Journal of Experimental Social Psychology, 7*, 419-434.

In: *Focus on Aggression Research*
Editor: James P. Morgan, pp. 157-174

ISBN 1-59454-132-9
© 2004 Nova Science Publishers, Inc.

Chapter 9

THE IMPACT OF GENDER AND STRESS ON TRAFFIC AGGRESSION: ARE WE REALLY THAT DIFFERENT?

Dwight A. Hennessy,
Department of Psychology, Buffalo State College
David L. Wiesenthal, Christine Wickens and Michele Lustman
Department of Psychology, York University

ABSTRACT

Drivers completed a questionnaire assessing their driver stress, likelihood of engaging in mild forms of driver aggression, and the frequency of past driver violence. Male and female drivers reported similar levels of mild driver aggression, but driver violence was more frequent among male drivers. Finally, driver stress susceptibility was linked to both mild driver aggression and driver violence. The findings suggest that context, personal dispositions, and behavioral form are important in understanding gender differences in aggression.

Road rage, aggressive driving, and anger while driving have recently received a great deal of public attention. The rising number of vehicles and commuters has made aggressive driving both a more pertinent and pressing issue. Although driving may appear to be an independent and isolating activity, it is in fact an interactive endeavor. On the roadway, drivers must focus on the behavior of strangers, where the behavior of one individual has a direct and immediate impact on all other motorists present. Motorists can cause frustration, inconvenience, and physical harm to other road users. As a result, the roadways are fertile grounds for both provocatively aggressive behaviors and subsequent retaliatory actions, making highways an optimal setting to witness and to study violence and aggression.

Driving, for most, is a daily activity, engaged in as a means to an end. It allows individuals to get to and from work and to perform their daily errands. But, because time appears to be such a limited commodity, and driving is most often a goal directed behavior, obstacles that may impede the attainment of these goals can become a source of great stress and anxiety. As a result, drivers are more likely to engage in mild forms of driver aggression, including horn honking, swearing, and yelling at other drivers (Gulian, Matthews, Glendon, Davies, & Debney, 1989a; Hennessy & Wiesenthal, 1997, 1999a; Wiesenthal, Hennessy, & Gibson, 2000). Because of its relationship with traffic violations (Novaco, 1991) and traffic collisions

(Matthews, Dorn, & Glendon, 1991), driver aggression poses a potential danger, directly or indirectly to all road users.

A Canadian survey done by the Maritz Automotive Research Group, revealed that 38% of Ontario drivers reported experiencing some sort of abuse while driving in the past year and furthermore, two out of three respondents admitted to having driven aggressively in the last year (Toljagic, 2000). Similarly, in a survey of its Washington, D.C. area members, the American Automobile Association (AAA) reported that 90% of drivers had witnessed aggressive driving behavior in the last month (National Conference of State Legislatures, 2000). The impact of aggressive driving has also been a reason for concern. According to the congressional testimony of Dr. Ricardo Martinez, head of the National Highway Traffic Safety Administration (NHTSA), abusive and aggressive driving is involved in two thirds of fatal highway crashes and in one third of injury highway crashes. Driver aggression is a contributing factor in nearly 28,000 highway deaths and 1 million injuries per year in the United States ("Road Rage", 1997).

Key Words: gender; socialization; aggression; violence; automobile.

DEFINING AGGRESSIVE DRIVING

One of the more controversial issues in the study of aggressive driving has been the difficulty surrounding the way to operationally define the behavior. Definitions that encompass a full spectrum of behaviors ranging from minor traffic violations, such as speeding or passing on the right, to more dangerous and extreme incidents of violence, such as shootings, have been considered too broad and too general. In order to make any meaningful progress in the area it is necessary to clearly identify what constitutes aggressive driving. According to Tasca (2000), it is essential that the specific driving behaviors that constitute aggressive driving be included in the definition, particularly if road safety programs are to be evaluated. It is also important that a distinction be made between aggressive driving and the more extreme behavior commonly referred to as "road rage". Tasca argued that including the rare and criminal behavior of road rage in a general definition of aggressive driving would shift the focus away from more prevalent and more modifiable driving behaviors. Tasca also emphasized the importance of examining the driving behavior in terms of its motivation or intent. His definition focused on deliberate and willful driving behaviors, where behaviors that are a result of error or inattention, would not be included. Specifically, Tasca argued that "a driving behavior is aggressive if it is deliberate, likely to increase the risk of collision and is motivated by impatience, annoyance, hostility and/or an attempt to save time" (p.8). This definition emphasized that these behaviors are not deliberate attempts to injure or collide with other road users, but that these behaviors are likely to increase the likelihood of the occurrence of such events.

Other researchers have also emphasized the distinction between aggressive driving and road rage. Ellison-Potter, Bell, and Deffenbacher (2001) referred to aggressive driving as "any driving behavior that intentionally…endangers others psychologically, physically, or both" (p.432). They defined road rage as a more extreme form of aggressive driving that involves "assaultive behavior with the intent of bodily harm and possible homicide" (p.432). Moreover, they likened the distinction between aggressive driving and road rage to the difference between traffic offenses and criminal offenses, respectively.

Hennessy (2000a) also focused on the issue of intent, specifying three types of driving actions. The first two, violent driving and aggressive driving were very similar to the definitions of road rage and aggressive driving provided by Ellison-Potter et al. However, Hennessy (2000a) also identified a third type of driving behavior, which he referred to as assertive driving. These behaviors (e.g. weaving in and out of lanes, speeding, etc.) are motivated by time urgency or self-oriented concerns rather than by a motivation to harm others.

The addition of this third classification serves to emphasize the role of intent in aggression studies and corresponds to an important distinction in aggression made by Goranson (1970). According to Goranson, there are two types of behavioral definitions of aggression: the harm intent definition and the response form definition. The harm intent definition consists of the measurement of the intentional infliction of pain or injury upon another individual. In typical social psychological experiments, this would be measured by the number, intensity, or duration of electric shocks that participants would be willing to administer to another individual. The response form definition focuses on the physical characteristics of the aggressive acts. Examples of these features could include hitting, kicking, or punching. Most driving research to date has focused on the aggressive act rather than on the intent behind the act.

FRUSTRATION-AGGRESSION HYPOTHESIS

Research focusing on identifying predictors of driving anger and aggression have looked at the role that both situational and personality factors may play. One of the explanations for aggressive driving has been linked to the frustration-aggression hypothesis (Dollard, Doob, Miller, Mowrer, & Sears, 1939). According to this theory, frustration, which is defined as anything which interferes with goal-directed behavior, gives rise to a desire to harm another person or object perceived to be the source of frustration. In driving situations, environmental factors such as congestion, bad weather, or road construction can lead to frustration. These factors may impede the driver's ability to reach his/her goal and reduce the amount of perceived control over the situation. Another source of frustration may come from the behavior of other drivers. Driving too fast, too slowly, or in a seemingly inconsiderate fashion may produce a sense of frustration for other drivers. The driving environment is a social setting with rules and norms that define appropriate and inappropriate behaviors (Rothe, 1994). When these rules are violated, other drivers become angry and want the transgressors punished (Wiesenthal et al., 2000).

GENDER DIFFERENCES IN AGGRESSION

One predictor of aggressive driving behavior that has received significant attention is a driver's gender. Generally speaking, males are more likely to be the source and the target of aggressive acts, and to hold more favorable attitudes toward aggression (Harris, 1996; Harris & Knight-Bohnhoff, 1996; Lindeman, Harakka, & Keltikangas-Jarvinen, 1997; Tomada & Schneider, 1997). When examining crime statistics, males are approximately seven times more likely than females to be accused of homicide and twice as likely to be the victim of this crime (Statistics Canada, 2003). When examining overall differences in aggressive behavior between men and women, meta-analytical reviews have shown that males are more aggressive than females, although the difference is not always extreme (Bettencourt & Miller, 1996; Eagly & Steffen, 1986; Hyde, 1984; Maccoby and Jacklin, 1974). Despite this evidence of male aggression, however, the commonly held perception of women as "nonaggressive" is not entirely accurate. Until recently, most research has focused on physical forms of aggression, which constitute a more male-typical hostility (Fry & Gabriel, 1994). This has resulted in an underestimation of the female propensity for aggressive acts. Female aggression often takes the form of indirect or relational hostility such as rumor-mongering, ignoring someone in a social setting, or secretly destroying their personal property. When this form of aggression is assessed, studies have shown that females are more hostile than males (Björkqvist, Österman, & Lagerspetz, 1994; Österman et al., 1998).

Different situational factors have also been found to influence the existence of gender differences in aggression. Graham and Wells (2001) found that males are more likely to report physical aggression with a stranger, whereas females are more likely to report physical aggression with an intimate. Male aggression is more likely in a bar or public place, whereas female aggression is more likely at home or at work (Graham & Wells, 2001). Furthermore, Harris (1996) found that evaluations of the justifiability of aggressive behaviors varied according to the gender of the aggressor and of the target. In a meta-analysis, Bettencourt and Miller (1996) determined that, although men are generally more aggressive than women, the reverse pattern emerged when the aggressor had been provoked. In a second meta-analysis examining the role of provocation in cases where violent cues were present, Bettencourt and Kernahan (1997) found that provocation eliminated these gender differences in aggression.

In addition, the laboratory setting itself may be a causal factor contributing to the empirical findings of greater male aggression. Social desirability may pressure research participants, particularly female participants, to follow traditional gender roles. In support of this contention, Frodi, Macaulay, and Thome (1977) compared laboratory and field or questionnaire studies, and found that smaller differences in aggression were reported using the latter research method.

When explaining the greater tendency for male aggression and the pattern of circumstances surrounding female aggression, three theories have been postulated. Krahé (2001) has labeled these theories as (a) the hormonal explanation, (b) the sociobiological model, and (c) the social role model. The hormonal explanation suggests that the male sex hormone testosterone is responsible for increased aggressive tendencies, possibly through androgen-organized neural networks. Empirical studies of this theory have been highly discrepant, some providing strong evidence for the hormonal explanation, others finding a negative relationship between testosterone and aggression, and still others finding no relationship at all (Archer, 1991). Some studies have even found evidence of a testosterone-aggression correlation in human females (e.g., Cashdan, 2003; von der Pahlen, Lindman, Sarkola, Mäkisalo, & Eriksson, 2002). Although several meta-analyses have found a weak, but positive, relationship between testosterone and human aggression, and have identified several variables that modify this relationship (Archer, 1991; Archer, Birring, & Wu, 1998; Book, Starzyk, & Quinsey, 2001; Knight, Guthrie, Page, & Fabes, 2002), there is still no consensus on the validity of this theoretical explanation of gender differences in aggression (Archer, 1999; Krahé, 2001).

The sociobiological model, also known as the evolutionary approach, suggests that male aggression is an adaptive strategy to maximize access to attractive, reproductive females. By demonstrating their status and power, males can outperform their male competitors, attract available females, and be more likely to reproduce (Krahé, 2001; Wilson & Daly, 1985). Furthermore, Campbell (1999) argued that reduced aggressive tendencies in females are due to the mother's presence being more critical for her offspring's survival and thus to endanger herself also jeopardizes her offspring's chances of survival. Mothers, therefore, should be more concerned with their own survival, and should be less likely to become involved in life-threatening acts of aggression and more likely to resolve disputes using indirect strategies. Although many crime statistics, anthropological studies, and research into the developmental differences between boys and girls (see Campbell, 1999) may be used to confirm the potential veracity of evolutionary claims, it is impossible for the sociobiological model to ever be supported by cause-effect experimental research. As a completely unfalsifiable claim, the best that proponents of the evolutionary approach can do is to provide explanations of existing data, rather than testing experimental hypotheses. For this reason, the sociobiological model can never be accepted with absolute certainty.

Finally, the social role model, also known as the social structural theory, cites contrasting social positions of men and women as the origin of gender differences in aggression (Eagly & Wood, 1999). Rather than blaming differences in evolved psychological dispositions or neurological pathways, proponents of the social role model claim that physical sex differences, in interaction with social and ecological conditions, determine which social roles are held by men and which are held by women. The nature of the activities associated with these roles then determine the placement of these positions in the social structure. Since men normally fall into roles associated with greater power and status, they engage in more dominant behavior, that is more assertive and overtly aggressive than is the subordinate behavior produced by low power and low status female roles. Furthermore, members of society communicate gender-stereotypic expectations in their interactions and can cause targets of these expectations to engage in gender-stereotypic behavior (Eagly, 1997; Eagly & Wood, 1999). The fact that levels of both male and female aggression differ across cultures (e.g., Ramirez, Andreu, & Fujihara, 2001) provides support for the influence of society and environment on gender differences in social behavior.

Some researchers have attempted to make the evolutionary and social role models compatible with each other (e.g., Krahé, 2001; Schaller, 1997). This mixed approach postulates that the two theories differ in terms of the distal versus proximal nature of their respective causal influences of gender differences in aggression. Specifically, the sociobiological model focuses on distal factors that explain the long-term emergence of gender differences in social behavior, whereas the social role model focuses on the proximal factors that influence an individual in his or her own lifetime. Eagly and Wood (1999), however, have dismissed this mixed approach and argue that both theories "identify psychological causes (i.e., evolved dispositions, role expectations) that operate in the present and that exert their impact through more proximal processes (e.g., emotions, perceptions)" (p. 409). As with the hormonal explanation of gender differences, it is clear that controversy surrounds both the evolutionary and social role theories as well.

THE ROLE OF GENDER IN AGGRESSIVE DRIVING BEHAVIOR

One of the recommended approaches (Björkqvist, Österman, & Kaukiainen, 1992) for more accurately assessing the role of gender in human aggression has been the adoption of more naturalistic studies. One setting that is highly conducive to such naturalistic research is the driving environment, including roads and highways. This is a setting with which virtually all members of society are well acquainted, and it is a common place for individuals to unabatedly express raw aggression or to retaliate against it.

As with general aggression research, the findings concerning gender differences in roadway hostility have been mixed. For the most part, transportation statistics indicate that male drivers are more likely to be involved in vehicle collisions (Evans, 1991; Ontario Ministry of Transportation, 2001), and a long line of research has found that male drivers are more aggressive in their driving attitudes and behaviors than are females. For instance, Yagil (1998) examined gender differences in the propensity to commit traffic violations. Females expressed a stronger sense of obligation to obey traffic laws, even in situations where violations were not perceived as risky. Males were more likely to underestimate the risk of various traffic violations, to overestimate their driving ability, and hence to feel more confident in complying selectively with traffic laws. In a survey of Swedish car owners, Åberg and Rimmö (1998) found that males actually did report committing more driving violations than females. Similarly, Miller, Azrael, Hemenway, and Solop (2002) telephoned a random sample of licensed drivers in Arizona, and asked them for self-reports of various rude or aggressive roadway behaviors such as obscene gestures, tailgating, and using one's vehicle to impede another's progress. These behaviors were found to be more common among male drivers than among female drivers.

As roadway hostility is a direct form of aggression, it should not be surprising that there is an extensive literature citing heightened roadway aggression among males. This gender difference, however, may not always be obtained, as in Hauber's study (1980) where drivers were observed as they approached a pedestrian crossing and encountered a confederate crossing without traffic lights. Male and female drivers were equally likely to respond aggressively: failing to stop, forcing the pedestrian to increase his or her walking speed, gesturing or shouting at the pedestrian, or honking their horn at the pedestrian. McGarva and Steiner (2000) had participants drive their own vehicles along a predetermined route. At a particular intersection, participants were honked and gestured at by a male confederate in another vehicle. Similar to Hauber's findings, no gender differences in aggressive responses to this provocation were found. Hennessy and Wiesenthal (1997, 1999a) interviewed participants on cellular telephones while they were commuting along urban highways. Males and females were equally likely to report experiencing driver stress and exhibiting mild aggressive behaviors such as horn honking, purposely tailgating other drivers, flashing high-beams, gesturing, or swearing at other drivers.

Questionnaire studies that have examined driver aggression have also produced results suggesting a lack of gender differences. For instance, Matthews, Dorn, and Glendon (1991) failed to find any differences between men and women when they administered the Driving Behavior Inventory, a measure of trait susceptibility to driving stress. Similarly, although Deffenbacher, Oetting, and Lynch (1994) found differences in what angered males and females, the overall levels of anger exhibited by young men and women were equal. Researchers have also found no gender differences in self-reported highway violations

(Parker, Lajunen, & Stradling, 1998) or in self-reported driving anger, suggesting that female drivers become irritated for the same reasons and to the same extent while driving as do males (Lajunen, Parker, & Stradling, 1998). Likewise, Hennessy and Wiesenthal (2002a, 2002b) found that gender failed to predict self-reported mild aggressive roadway behavior. They did find that males reported greater roadway violence than females, but only in association with a strongly vengeful attitude.

The anonymity provided by an automobile is a likely explanation for the absence of gender differences in driver aggression. When in the confines of one's vehicle, a driver becomes anonymous; unidentifiable by others and hence not subject to evaluation, criticism, judgment, or punishment (Ellison, Govern, Petri, & Figler, 1995; Ellison-Potter, Bell, & Deffenbacher, 2001; Zimbardo, 1969). Anecdotal reports of socially inappropriate acts occurring in vehicles (e.g., talking to oneself, picking one's nose, sexual acts) attest to this fact (Ellison-Potter et al., 2001). Empirical studies have also supported the role of anonymity in unsafe or aggressive driving behavior. Greater degrees of anonymity (e.g., convertible versus hard-top vehicle, vanity license plate, tinted windows, night-time versus day-time) have been associated with greater traffic law infractions and acts of aggressive driving and with less proper driving behavior (Ellison et al., 1995; Ellison-Potter et al., 2001; Wiesenthal & Janovjak, 1992). This sense of anonymity may reduce the perceived risk of detection and punishment for unsafe driving behavior (Freedman, 1982; Zimbardo, 1969). Proponents of the social structural theory (Eagly & Wood, 1999) might argue that anonymity reduces the pressure to conform to the female gender role. Socialization to this gender role normally restrains aggressive tendencies in women (Anderson & Bushman, 2002; Eagly & Steffen, 1986; Greenglass & Noguchi, 1996); however, anonymity may provide a rare opportunity for women to disregard this prescribed code of conduct. Moreover, in large urban areas, the lack of repeated interactions with another driver reduces the threat of retaliation against an aggressive female driver (Hennessy & Wiesenthal, 1999b). The vehicle itself represents an equalizing force or weapon (Marsh & Collett, 1987), providing both men and women equal power to aggress against those who provoke them on roadways, while offering a means of escape from such encounters (Marsh & Collett, 1987). As well, the fact that much roadway aggression is a retaliation against perceived provocation on the part of another driver may also explain why gender differences do not emerge in all studies. As indicated in the meta-analyses by Bettencourt and Miller (1996) and by Bettencourt and Kernahan (1997), provocation often results in an equal tendency among the genders to aggress.

HYPOTHESES

The current study examined gender differences in mild driver aggression and past violent driving behavior. The following hypotheses were postulated:

1. There will be no gender differences in ratings of mild aggressive behaviors.
2. High stress drivers will report greater mild driver aggression than low stress drivers.
3. Males will demonstrate greater frequency of past violent driving behavior than females.
4. Driver violence will be greater among high stress drivers than low stress drivers.

METHOD

Participants

The present study included 122 female and 70 male participants from the student and employee populations of York University, as well as from the general Metropolitan Toronto population. Fifty-one participants were recruited from the undergraduate research participant pool at York University and received one experimental credit for their involvement ($n = 34$ females and $n = 17$ males). All others were obtained as voluntary participants through posted signs, personal contact, and word of mouth.

All participants commuted on a daily basis and a minimum of three years driving experience was required. The average was 8.75 years experience ($M = 7.02$ years for female and $M = 11.77$ years for male drivers) and their ages ranged from 19-68 years, with an average of 26.22 years ($M = 25.83$ years for female and $M = 28.60$ years for male drivers). The average driving time ranged from 15 minutes to 270 minutes per day, with an average of 93.96 minutes per day ($M = 94.19$ minutes for female and $M = 93.57$ minutes for male drivers).

Measures

Driving Behavior Inventory--General (DBI-Gen)

Driver stress was measured using the Driving Behavior Inventory-General Driver Stress scale (DBI-Gen) (Gulian et al., 1989a). The DBI-Gen consists of 16 items that tap a general disposition, or "trait" susceptibility, to driver stress. Previous research has established the DBI-Gen as a valid and reliable measure of trait driver stress across cultures (Glendon, Dorn, Matthews, Gulian, Davies, & Debney, 1993; Hennessy & Wiesenthal, 1999a; Lajunen, Corry, Summala, & Hartley, 1998; Matthews et al., 1991; Matthews, Tsuda, Xin, & Ozeki, 1999). Hennessy and Wiesenthal (1997) have found the DBI-Gen to accurately predict actual stress levels measured in both low and high traffic congestion. In the present study, responses were made on a Likert scale ranging from 0 to 100, indicating the level of agreement with each statement, rather than on the original 0 to 4 Likert scale. Previous research has shown this revision to maintain high reliability ($\alpha = 0.90$) (Hennessy & Wiesenthal, 1997). Scoring consisted of the mean response to the 16 items, with higher scores indicating greater trait driver stress susceptibility.

Self Report Driver Aggression

The Self Report Driver Aggression questionnaire was designed to tap general self report driving behavior patterns (Hennessy & Wiesenthal, 1999a, 2001). Items were based on behaviors identified by Gulian, Debney, Glendon, Davies, and Matthews (1989b) as common coping responses to driving demands, while other items were generated from interviews with highway commuters (Hennessy, 2000b). Participants were asked to rate the likelihood of generally engaging in five mild aggressive behaviors (i.e. horn honking out of frustration, swearing/yelling, purposeful tailgating, flashing high beams, and hand gestures). Responses were placed on a Likert scale ranging from 0 = "not at all" to 5 = "nearly all the time". An aggregate driver aggression score was calculated as the mean response to the five items.

Hennessy (2000b) has found that self reported driver aggression scores correlated highly with actual acts of aggression occurring in high congestion conditions ($r = .643$).

Self Report Driver Violence

The Self Report Driver Violence questionnaire was designed in order to evaluate the frequency of personally initiated violent driving behaviors. Six items were introduced by Novaco (1991), while one item was identified through interviews with commuters (Hennessy, 2000b). Participants were asked to indicate the frequency of previously initiating each of the violent driving behaviors (i.e. verbal confrontations, physical confrontations, chasing other vehicles, drive-by shootings, throwing objects, purposeful contact, and vandalizing vehicles). An aggregate violence score was calculated as the cumulative frequency of the individual violence items.

Procedure

Participants completed the DBI-Gen, the Self Report Driver Aggression questionnaire, and the Self Report Driver Violence questionnaire anonymously. Due to the sensitive nature of the present driving measures, instructions stressed the confidentiality of all responses.

RESULTS

Intercorrelations, means, standard deviations, and alpha reliabilities for the DBI-Gen, Self Report Driver Aggression, and Self Report Driver Violence questionnaires appear in Table 1. The DBI-Gen demonstrated the greatest internal consistency ($\alpha = .83$), while the Self Report Driver Aggression and Self Report Driver Violence questionnaires demonstrated moderate reliability ($\alpha = .75$ and .69 respectively). Separate hierarchical entry stepwise regressions were used to determine predictors of mild driver aggression and driver violence. The procedure for each was to enter gender, age, and driver stress forcibly and add all cross product interactions stepwise on the first run. If any interactions were significant, they would be entered forcibly on the second run along with the implicated main effects. All other significant main effects would be added stepwise on the second run. However, in the event that no interactions proved significant on the first run, the main effects would be entered stepwise on the second run. This strategy has been reported elsewhere (e.g. Kohn, Gurevich, Pickering, & Macdonald, 1994; Kohn & Macdonald, 1992; Hennessy & Wiesenthal, 2001). Table 2 contains the final regression models for mild driver aggression and driver violence.

Table 1. Intercorrelations, Means, Standard Deviations and
Alpha Reliabilities for the Driving Behaviour Inventory (DBI-Gen),
Self Report Driver Aggression, Self Report Driver Violence, Age, and Gender

	1	2	3	4	5
1. Driving Behaviour Inventory–Gen	–	–	–	–	–
2. Self Report Driver Aggression	.57*	–	–	–	–
3. Self Report Driver Violence	.27	.39*	–	–	–
4. Driver Age	-.40*	-.24	-.12	–	–
5. Driver Gender	-.00	.09	.23	.17	–
Mean	37.22	1.43	1.84	26.22	–
SD	17.23	0.85	4.50	10.39	–
Minimum	.63	0	0	19	–
Maximum	83.13	4.40	41.0	68	–
A	.83	.75	.69	–	–

$n = 192$.
*$p < .01$.

Table 2. Significant Predictors of Mild Driver Aggression and Driver Violence

Criterion	Predictor	b	t
Mild Aggression	Driver Stress	0.281	9.66*
	Intercept	0.381	3.19
$R^2 = 0.33, F(1,191) = 93.65, p<.01$			
Driver Violence	Driver Stress	2.193	3.45*
	Driver Gender	0.710	4.00*
	Intercept	-3.786	-3.34
$R^2 = 0.13, F(2,189) = 13.93, p<.01$			

$n = 192$.
*$p < .01$.

Mild Driver Aggression

A mild driver aggression score was calculated as the mean response to individual aggression items. Higher scores represented a greater likelihood of exhibiting mild driver aggression. Mild aggression was predicted by the main effect of driver stress (see Table 2). Hypothesis 1 was confirmed in that the likelihood of exhibiting mild aggression was similar for male and female drivers. Also, consistent with hypothesis 2, mild driver aggression increased with driver stress susceptibility, where high trait stress drivers reported greater mild driver aggression than low stress drivers.

Driver Violence

An aggregate driver violence score was calculated as the total frequency of the individual violence items. Higher scores represented a greater frequency of initiating past violent driving behaviors. Driver violence was predicted by the main effects of driver gender and driver stress (see Table 2). Consistent with hypothesis 3, male drivers reported greater frequency of past violent driving behaviors than female drivers. Hypothesis 4 was also confirmed in that high stress drivers reported greater violence than low stress drivers.

It should be noted that due to the low base rate of driver violence, the distribution of violence scores was positively skewed. Despite this fact, the present study demonstrated a link between violence, stress, and gender at the higher limits of violence scores, where relationships are underestimated by multiple regression analysis, and no link at the lower limits of violence scores, where relationships are overestimated (see Tabachnik & Fidell, 1989).

DISCUSSION

Driver Gender, Aggression, and Violence

Consistent with previous research (Hennessy & Wiesenthal, 1997, 1999a), the present study failed to demonstrate a general gender difference in the likelihood of mild driver aggression. Female drivers reported equivalent tendencies toward mild aggression as male drivers. Despite the prevailing notion that men are generally more aggressive than females, the present study highlights the importance of contextual information in evaluating the prevalence of female aggression (see Bjorkqvist et al., 1992; Deaux & Major, 1987; Eagly, 1987). The driving environment represents a unique setting that is equally conducive to aggression among male and female drivers. Considering that the vehicle itself represents a very powerful and dangerous weapon possessed by all drivers (Marsh & Collett, 1987), the means to engage in aggression is equalized across gender. In situations where drivers perceive that they have been placed at risk in some way by another driver, fear, anger, and perceptions of provocation may result (Wiesenthal et al., 2000), which have previously been found to heighten the potential for female aggression (Bettencourt & Miller, 1996; Blanchard & Blanchard, 1992; Fraczek, 1992; Frodi et al., 1977).

Anonymity and deindividuation within the driving environment may also contribute to the escalation of female aggression. It can be very difficult to identify the gender of another motorist in any given situation, due to the low probability of repeated interactions or extended contact with those motorists. As a result, anonymous drivers are more prone to defy restraints against harming others (Novaco, 1991). Considering that females have traditionally been socialized to refrain from aggressive behavior (Eagly & Steffen, 1986), the anonymity of the driving environment and perceptions of deindividuation represent a unique opportunity for liberation from gender roles, thus facilitating the expression of aggressive tendencies. Further, the potential for personal repercussions as a result of aggressive behaviors are minimized with anonymity, leading to a heightened sense of control over victims. This inability to identify a driver as female may contribute to feelings of power and control over other drivers, increasing the potential for antinormative behaviors (i.e., mild aggression) among female drivers (Lightdale & Prentice, 1994).

The present findings have also demonstrated the importance of the form of aggressive behavior in evaluating gender differences. As has been found in previous research (Hennessy & Wiesenthal, 2002a), violent driving behavior was more pronounced among males. According to Meerloo (1968), violence can be defined as a more extreme manifestation of aggressive behavior. Similarly, Hennessy (1999, 2000a) has classified driver violence as a distinct category of driving behaviors that are more severe and potentially dangerous than milder aggression.

One possible explanation for this gender difference may be that violent driving behaviors involve a predominance of physical actions directed toward other drivers. According to Buss and Perry (1992), males are more prone to exhibit physical or overt aggression than females. Violent driving behaviors also require prolonged contact with a victim, which likely minimizes perceptions of anonymity and heightens the potential for reciprocal acts of aggression and violence.

Another potential reason for the gender difference in driver violence may be that female drivers are more restrained in situations representing personal risk or danger. According to Berkowitz (1988), the fear that aggressive behavior could lead to retaliation may reduce aggressive tendencies. Compared to males, females are generally more accurate at predicting the potential for harm and future repercussions within dangerous or risky situations (Eagly & Steffen, 1986). Within the driving environment, this tendency may lead females to avoid violent actions due to the elevated risk of personal injury.

The Impact of Stress on Aggression and Violence

Previous research has found that psychological stress can heighten the potential for general aggressive behavior (Cohen, 1980; Hennessy & Wiesenthal, 1997; Wiesenthal et al., 2000). The present study found that both males and females who perceived the driving environment as stressful reported a greater likelihood of engaging in mild forms of driver aggression. Driver stress has been described as a consequence of negative evaluations of driving stimuli, leading to irritation, frustration, and negative affect (Gulian et al., 1989a; Hartley & El Hassani, 1994; Hennessy & Wiesenthal, 1997). Under such conditions, highly stressed drivers are more likely to perceive other drivers as the source of frustration (Hennessy, 2000b; Gulian et al., 1989b) and to interpret undesirable actions from other drivers as personal and purposeful behaviors, leading to increased aggression (Wiesenthal et al., 2000). The link between traffic stress and aggression may not stop in the traffic environment, as current research has found that a stressful commute can carry over to the workplace environment and increase the likelihood of some forms of workplace aggression (Hennessy, 2003) which highlights the potential destructiveness of roadway stress.

High stress drivers were also found to report elevated incidents of past driving violence compared to low stress drivers. Despite the fact that driver violence has been considered in the present study as a more extreme and potentially dangerous form of driver aggression, little research has been conducted regarding the antecedents of violence compared to aggression. It is possible that among a small segment of drivers, the irritation and frustration experienced in stressful conditions contribute to violent behavior. However, previous evidence of this process is unclear. It is also probable that consideration of other personal and situational factors is necessary to more fully understand the link between stress and violence. For example, driving vengeance, which is the desire to harm other drivers in response to a perceived injustice, is more common among male drivers and among those under the influence of driver stress (Hennessy, 2000b; Wiesenthal et al., 2000). Considering that violent drivers in the present study were predominantly male, it is possible that a vengeful attitude contributed to the association between stress and violence. Further research is needed to more clearly understand the antecedents and consequences of driver violence.

Future Directions

One limitation of the present study was the fact that self report measures of behavior and stress were used, which lack contextual information present in actual driving situations. According to Hennessy (2000b), aggressive behavior does not occur in isolation, but is partially determined by aspects within the instigating environment, such as traffic congestion and provocation from other drivers. According to Rotton, Gregory, and Van Rooy (in press), situational factors are often overlooked in traffic research and need to be investigated further. In a similar respect, driver stress has also been found to be highly dependent on the interaction of situational and individual factors (Hennessy & Wiesenthal, 1997). As a result, responses in the present study may not have accurately reflected true behavioral tendencies or stress reactions that occur in actual traffic situations. Another limitation was that the female sample was slightly younger and less experienced than the male sample. Previous research has found that age is negatively related to both driver stress and aggression (Hauber, 1980; Gibson & Wiesenthal, 1996). Although small, the age difference may account for elevated aggression among the female sample. Future research should employ a more diverse age sample in order to present a clearer analysis of driver stress, aggression, and violence.

Further, the fact that all measures were based on self reports raises the issue of common method variance. Due to the fact that all individual responses come from the same source, any reporting bias in one questionnaires may be present in all, which may ultimately serve to inflate relationships between factors (Podsakoff & Organ, 1986). However, Harman's one factor test was conducted to determine the impact of common variance in the present study (Podsakoff & Organ, 1986). The fact that more than one factor emerged, and that the strongest factor accounted for no more than 15% of variance, suggests that common method variance was unlikely an issue. Despite this fact, subsequent research may be strengthened by the inclusion of more objective measures of dangerous and destructive driving behavior, such as verbal aggression, tailgating, and speeding, from archival, natural and simulated sources.

Finally, the chosen behavior measures used a forced choice response method. It is possible that the limited options provided were those that masked potential gender differences in aggression, while highlighting gender differences in driver violence. The use of open-ended behavior responses in future research could provide a wider variety of possible behavior outcomes.

REFERENCES

Åberg, L., & Rimmö, P. (1998). Dimensions of aberrant driver behaviour. *Ergonomics, 41,* 39-56.

Anderson, C. A., & Bushman, B. J. (2002). Human aggression. *Annual Review of Psychology, 53,* 27-51

Archer, J. (1991). The influence of testosterone on human aggression. *British Journal of Psychology, 82,* 1-28.

_____ . (1999). Risk-taking, fear, dominance, and testosterone. *Behavioral and Brain Sciences, 22,* 214-215.

Archer, J., Birring, S. S., & Wu, C. W. (1998). The association between testosterone and aggression among young men: Empirical findings and a meta-analysis. *Aggressive Behavior, 24,* 411-420.

Berkowitz, L. (1988). Frustrations, appraisals, and aversively stimulated aggression. *Aggressive Behavior, 10,* 59-73.

Bettencourt, B. A., & Miller, N. (1996). Gender differences in aggression as a function of provocation: A meta-analysis. *Psychological Bulletin, 119,* 422-447.

Bettencourt, B. A., & Kernahan, C. (1997). A meta-analysis of aggression in the presence of violent cues: Effects of gender differences and aversive provocation. *Aggressive Behavior, 23,* 447-456.

Björkqvist, K., Österman, K., & Kaukiainen, A. (1992). The development of direct and indirect aggressive strategies in males and females. In K. Björkqvist & P. Niemelä (Eds.), *Of mice and women: Aspects of female aggression* (pp. 51-64). New York: Academic Press.

Björkqvist, K., Österman, K., & Lagerspetz, K. (1994). Sex differences in covert aggression among adults. *Aggressive Behavior, 20,* 27-33.

Blanchard, D. C., & Blanchard, R. J. (1992). Sex, drugs, and defensive behavior: Implications for animal models of defense. In K. Bjorkqvist & P. Niemela (Eds.), *Of mice and women: Aspects of female aggression,* (pp. 318-329). New York: Academic Press.

Book, A. S., Starzyk, K. B., & Quinsey, V. L. (2001). The relationship between testosterone and aggression: A meta-analysis. *Aggression and Violent Behavior, 6,* 579-599.

Buss, A. H., & Perry, M. (1992). The Aggression Questionnaire. *Journal of Personality and Social Psychology, 63,* 452-459.

Campbell, A. (1999). Staying alive: Evolution, culture, and women's intrasexual aggression. *Behavioral and Brain Sciences, 22,* 203-214.

Cashdan, E. (2003). Hormones and competitive aggression in women. *Aggressive Behavior, 29,* 107-115.

Cohen, S. (1980). Aftereffects of stress on human performance and social behavior: A review of research and theory. *Psychological Bulletin, 88,* 82-108.

Deaux, K. K., & Major, B. (1987). Putting gender into context: An interactive model of gender related behavior. *Psychological Review, 94,* 369-389.

Deffenbacher, J. L., Oetting, E. R., & Lynch, R. S. (1994). Development of a driving anger scale. *Psychological Reports, 74,* 83-91.

Dollard, J., Doob, L., Miller, N., Mowever, O. H., & Sears, R. R. (1939). *Frustration and aggression.* New Haven, CT: Yale University Press.

Eagly, A. H. (1987). *Gender differences in social behavior: A social-role interpretation.* Hillsdale, NJ: Erlbaum.

_____ . (1997). Sex differences in social behavior: Comparing social role theory and evolutionary psychology. *American Psychologist, 52,* 1380-1383.

Eagly, A. H., & Steffen, V. J. (1986). Gender and aggressive behavior: A meta-analytic review of the social psychological literature. *Psychological Bulletin, 100,* 309-330.

Eagly, A. H., &Wood, W. (1999). The origins of sex differences in human behavior. *American Psychologist, 54,* 408-423.

Ellison, . A., Govern, J. M., Petri, H. L., & Figler, M. H. (1995). Anonymity and aggressive driving behavior: A field study. *Journal of Social Behavior and Personality, 10,* 265-272.

Ellison-Potter, ., Bell, P., & Deffenbacher, J. (2001). The effects of trait driving anger, anonymity, and aggressive stimuli on aggressive driving behavior. *Journal of Applied Social Psychology, 31,* 431-443.

Evans, L. (1991). *Traffic safety and the driver.* New York: Van Nostrand Reinhold.

Fraczek, A. (1992). Patterns of aggressive-hostile behavior orientation among adolescent boys and girls. In K. Bjorkqvist & P. Niemela (Eds.), *Of mice and women: Aspects of female aggression,* (pp. 107-112). New York: Academic Press.

Freedman, J. L. (1982). Theories of contagion as they relate to mass psychogenic illness. In M. J. Colligan, J. W. Pennebaker, & L. R. Murphy (Eds.), *Mass psychogenic illness* (pp. 171-182). Hillsdale, NJ: Erlbaum.

Frodi, A., Macaulay, J., & Thome, P. R. (1977). Are women always less aggressive than men? A review of the experimental literature. *Psychological Bulletin, 84,* 634-660.

Fry, D. P., & Gabriel, A. H. (1994). The cultural construction of gender and aggression. *Sex Roles, 30,* 165-167.

Gibson, P. M., & Wiesenthal, D. L. (1996). The Driving Vengeance Questionnaire: The development of a scale to measure deviant drivers' attitudes. *LaMarsh Research Programme Report Series, 54,* LaMarsh Research Programme on Violence and Conflict Resolution. York University: Toronto, Canada.

Glendon, A. I., Dorn, L., Matthews, G., Gulian, E., Davies, D. R., & Debney, L. M. (1993). Reliability of the Driving Behaviour Inventory. *Ergonomics, 36,* 719-726.

Goranson, R.E. (1970). Media violence and aggressive behavior: A review of experimental research. In L. Berkowitz (Ed.), *Advances in experimental social psychology: Vol. 5* (pp.2-31). New York: Academic Press.

Graham, K., & Wells, S. (2001). The two worlds of aggression for men and women. *Sex Roles, 45,* 595-622.

Greenglass, E. R., & Noguchi, K. (1996). *Longevity, gender, and health: A psychocultural perspective.* Position paper presented at the first meeting of the International Society of Health Psychology, Montreal, Canada.

Gulian, E., Matthews, G., Glendon, A.I., Davies, D.R., & Debney, L.M. (1989a). Dimensions of driver stress. *Ergonomics, 32,* 585-602.

Gulian, E., Debney, L. M., Glendon, A. I., Davies, D. R., & Matthews,G. (1989b). Coping with driver stress. In F. McGuigan,W. E. Sime, & J. M. Wallace (Eds.), *Stress and tension control* (Vol 3, pp. 1732-186). New York: Plenum Press.

Harris, M. B. (1996). Aggression, gender, and ethnicity. *Aggression and Violent Behavior, 1,* 123-146.

Harris, M. B., & Knight-Bohnhoff, K. (1996). Gender and aggression: II. Personal aggressiveness. *Sex Roles, 35,* 27-42

Hartley, L. R., & El Hassani, J. (1994). Stress, violations, and accidents. *Applied Ergonomics, 25,* 221-230.

Hauber, A. R. (1980). The social psychology of driving behavior ad the traffic environment: Research on aggressive behavior in traffic. *International Review of Applied Psychology, 29,* 461-474.

Hennessy, D. A. (1999). Evaluating driver aggression. *Unpublished Major Area Paper.* York University: Toronto, Canada.

_____ . (2000a, November 9). A review of the literature on aggressive driving research [Msg 2]. Message posted to http://www.aggressive.drivers.com/board/messages/25/49.html

Hennessy, D. A. (2000b). The interaction of person and situation within the driving environment: Daily hassles, traffic congestion, driver stress, aggression, vengeance and past performance. *Dissertation Abstracts International: Section B: The Sciences and Engineering. Vol. 60 (8-B)*, 4301.

Hennessy, D. A. (2003*). From driver stress to workplace aggression.* Symposium presented at Annual American Psychological Association Convention. Toronto ON, Canada: August 7 – 10.

Hennessy, D. A., & Wiesenthal, D. L. (1997). The relationship between traffic congestion, driver stress, and direct versus indirect coping behaviors. *Ergonomics, 40,* 348-361.

_____ . (1999a). Traffic congestion, driver stress, and driver aggression. *Aggressive Behavior, 25,* 409-423.

_____ . (1999b, December). *Roadway aggression and female drivers: An applied evaluation* (Report No. 58). North York, Ontario, Canada: York University, LaMarsh Centre for Research on Violence and Conflict Resolution.

_____ . (2001). Further validation of the Driving Vengeance Questionnaire (DVQ). *Violence and Victims, 16,* 565-573

_____ . (2002a). Aggression, violence, and vengeance among male and female drivers. *Transportation Quarterly, 56,* 65-75.

_____ . (2002b). The relationship between driver aggression, violence, and vengeance. *Violence and Victims, 17,* 707-718.

Hyde, J. S. (1984). How large are gender differences in aggression? A developmental meta-analysis. *Developmental Psychology, 20,* 722-736.

Kohn, P. M., Gurevich, M., Pickering, D. I., & Macdonald, J. E. (1994). Alexithymia, reactivity, and the adverse impact of hassles based stress. *Personality and Individual Differences, 16,* 805-812.

Kohn, P. M., & Macdonald, J. E. (1992). Hassles, anxiety, and negative well-being. *Anxiety, Stress, and Coping, 5,* 151-163.

Knight, G. P, Guthrie, I. K., Page, M. C., & Fabes, R. A. (2002). Emotional arousal and gender differences in aggression: A meta-analysis. *Aggressive Behavior, 28,* 366-393.

Krahé, B. (2001). *The social psychology of aggression* (2nd ed.). Philadelphia, PA: Taylor & Francis Inc.

Lajunen, T., Corry, A., Summala, H., & Hartley, L. (1998). Cross cultural differences in driver' self assessments of their perceptual motor and safety skills: Australian and Finns. *Personality and Individual Differences, 24,* 539-550.

Lajunen, T., Parker, D., & Stradling, S. G. (1998). Dimensions of driver anger, aggressive and highway code violations and their mediation by safety orientation in UK drivers. *Transportation Research Part F, 1,* 107-121.

Lightdale, J. R., & Prentice, T. A. (1994). Rethinking sex differences in aggression: Aggressive behavior in the absence of social roles. *Personality and Social Psychology Bulletin, 20,* 34-44.

Lindeman, M., Harakka, T., & Keltikangas-Jarvinen, L. (1997). Age and gender differences in adolescent reactions to conflict situations: Aggression, prosociality, and withdrawal. *Journal of Youth and Adolescence, 26,* 339-351.

Maccoby, E. E., & Jacklin, C. N. (1974). *The psychology of sex differences*. Stanford, CA: Stanford University Press.

Marsh, P., & Collett, P. (1987). The car as a weapon. *Et Cetera, 44,* 146-151.

Matthews, G., Dorn, L., Glendon, A.I. (1991). Personality correlates of driver stress. *Personality and Individual Differences, 12,* 535-549.

Matthews, G., Tsuda, A., Xin, C., & Ozeki, Y. (1999). Individual differences in driver stress vulnerability in a Japanese sample. *Ergonomics, 42,* 401-415.

McGarva, A. R., & Steiner, M. (2000). Provoked driver aggression and status: A field study. *Transportation Research Part F, 3,* 167-179.

Meerloo, J. A. M. (1968). Human violence versus animal aggression. *Psychoanalytic Review, 55,* 37-56.

Miller, M., Azrael, D., Hemenway, D., & Solop, F. I. (2002). 'Road rage' in Arizona: Armed and dangerous. *Accident Analysis and Prevention, 34,* 807-814.

National Conference of State Legislatures (NCSL), Environment, Energy and Transportation Program (2000, January). *Aggressive driving: Background and overview report*. Retrieved April 14, 2003, from http://www.ncsl.org/programs/esnr/aggrdriv.htm.

Novaco, R.W. (1991). Aggression on Roadways. In R. Baenninger (Ed.), Targets of violence and aggression (pp.253-326). North-Holland: Elsevier Science Publisher.

Ontario Ministry of Transportation. (2001). *Ontario Road Safety Annual Report.* Ontario: Ministry of Transportation.

Österman, K., Björkqvist, K., Lagerspetz, K. M. J., Kaukiainen, A., Landau, S. F., Frączek, A., & Caprara, V. (1998). Cross-cultural evidence of female indirect aggression. *Aggressive Behavior, 24,* 1-8.

Parker, D., Lajunen, T., & Stradling, S. (1998). Attitudinal predictors of interpersonally aggressive violations on the road. *Transportation Research Part F, 1,* 11-24.

Podsakoff, P. M., & Organ D. W. (1986). Self reports in organizational research: Problems and prospects. *Journal of Management, 12,* 531-544.

Ramirez, J. M., Andreu, J. M., & Fujihara, T. (2001). Cultural and sex differences in aggression: A comparison between Japanese and Spanish students using two different inventories. *Aggressive Behavior, 27,* 313-322.

Road Rage: Causes and dangers of aggressive driving: Hearing before the Subcommittee on Surface Transportation of the Committee on Transportation and Infrastructure, House of Representatives, 105th Cong., 1 (1997).

Rothe, J.P. (1994) *Beyond Traffic Safety*. New Brunswick, NJ: Transaction Publishers

Rotton, J., Gregory, P. J., & Van Rooy, D. L. (in press). Behind the wheel: Construct validity of aggressive driving scales. In D. A. Hennessy & D. L. Wiesenthal (Eds.), Contemporary issues in traffic research and road user safety. New York: Nova Science.

Schaller, M. (1997). Beyond "competing," beyond "compatible". *American Psychologist, 52,* 1379-1380.

Statistics Canada. (2003). Justice and crime. Retrieved May 5, 2003 from http://www.statcan.ca.

Tabachnik, B. G., & Fidell, L. S. (1989). *Using multivariate statistics* (2nd ed.). New York: Harper & Row.

Tasca, L. (2000). *A review of the literature on aggressive driving research*. Paper presented at the Aggressive Driving Issues Virtual Conference. Retrieved April 1, 2003 from http://www.aggressive.drivers.com/board/messages/25/49.html.

Toljagic, M. (2000, October 28). Motorists tuning in to road rage. *The Toronto Star*, pp.G1-G2.

Tomada, G., & Schneider, B. H. (1997). Relational aggression, gender, and peer acceptance: Invariance across culture, stability over time, and concordance among informants. *Developmental Psychology, 33,*601-609.

von der Pahlen, B., Lindman, R., Sarkola, T., Mäkisalo, H., & Eriksson, C. J. P. (2002). An exploratory study on self-evaluated aggression and androgens in women. *Aggressive Behavior, 28,* 273-280.

Wiesenthal, D. L., Hennessy, D. A. (1999). Driver stress, vengeance and aggression. What is "road rage." *Proceedings of the Canadian Multidisciplinary Road Safety Conference XI*, Halifax, Nova Scotial, Canada.

Wiesenthal, D. L., Hennessy, D. A., & Gibson, P. (2000). The Driving Vengeance Questionnaire (DVQ): The development of a scale to measure deviant drivers' attitudes. *Violence and Victims, 15,* 115-136.

Wiesenthal, D. L., Hennessy, D. A. (2001). *Gender, driver aggression and driver violence: An applied evaluation. Sex Roles, 44,* 661-677.

Wiesenthal, D. L., & Janovjak, D. P. (1992, May). *Deindividuation and automobile driving behaviour* (Report No. 46). North York, Ontario, Canada: York University, LaMarsh Centre for Research on Violence and Conflict Resolution.

Wilson, M., & Daly, M. (1985). Competitiveness, risk-taking and violence: The young male syndrome. *Ethology and Sociobiology, 6,* 59-73.

Yagil, D. (1998). Gender and age-related differences in attitudes toward traffic laws and traffic violations. *Transportation Research Part F, 1,* 123-135.

Zimbardo, P. G. (1969). The human choice: Individuation, reason, and order versus deindividuation, impulse, and chaos. In W. J. Arnold & D. LeVine (Eds.), *Nebraska Symposium on Motivation: Current Theory and Research in Motivation, Volume 17* (pp. 237-307). Lincoln, NE: University of Nebraska Press.

In: *Focus on Aggression Research*
Editor: James P. Morgan, pp. 175-187

ISBN 1-59454-132-9

Chapter 10

WHEN MUSIC HEALS

Darren Savarimuthu
North London Forensic Service

ABSTRACT

The aim of this chapter is to promote the use of musical interventions with clients who have learning disabilities and mental illness. Musical interventions with these groups of patients/clients were found to be effective in reducing self-injurious behaviour, aggression and other behaviour, which challenge the service providers, carers and health professionals. Music is also found to have the potential to improve the communication skills of clients and useful in maintaining their psychological well-being. Music has also been regarded as beneficial to people with mental illness and emotional deficits that can be aggressive and challenging. Due to its abilities, music activity is wisely been coined as 'musical intelligence' to show the potential of the intervention in healthcare settings. This chapter therefore shows that music, though not widely used in the field of nursing, can be an effective medium through which the quality of life of clients can be enhanced whilst reducing behaviours such as self-harm, aggression and agitation.

INTRODUCTION

Challenging behaviour such as aggression and self-injurious behaviour (SIB) are very common in people with severe and profound learning disabilities and also with people who suffers mental health problems (Bowles 1998). Over the past few years researchers have studied these behaviours so that valuable information could be gathered to design interventions with the ultimate goal of reducing or eliminating them (Durand & Mapstone 1998, withers 1995, Emberson 1990, Ferry 1992, Carson & Clare 1998, Morgan & Mackay 1998) People with mental illness and learning disabilities are often viewed as devalued individuals and may be subject to bad treatment by the society. Their physical, functional and mental impairments might be partly responsible for them being perceived by some as 'deviant'. This can result in them being rejected by their community, society as a whole, and even relatives and health services (Osburn 1998). Being labelled and stereotyped as deviant or 'abnormal' can cause frustration and there can be reluctance to seek treatment or help from health professionals. However, when these people are successfully identified for care they often fail to comply with their treatment on a long-term basis.

People with mental health problems often show aggression and poor coping skills, which can be described as challenging. The prevalence of agitated behaviour within the psychiatric field according to Goddaer and Abraham (1994) is around 42.8 to 86.3 %. This clearly suggests a high level of violence in mental health settings.

The concept of social role valorisation (SRV) is mainly aimed at providing support for people with learning disabilities. On the other hand the National Service Framework (NSF) came in force to help, support and protects people with psychiatric illnesses. Both the SRV and the NSF have common objective in providing the best available treatment and support to the highest standard possible. Both government documents tend to empower people so that despite having a mental illness and/or learning disability their integration into society as valued individuals can be as smooth as possible and respected by others. Paramount in this chapter is the desire to demonstrate that musical activities can be one of the interventions, which can enhance the quality of life of people with mental illness and learning disabilities (Trevarthan 1999, Nordoff & Robins 1992, Alvin & Warwick 1994).

The main aims of this chapter are firstly, to demonstrate that interventions using music can positively influence challenging behaviour (Gagner- Tjellesen et al. 2001) and secondly, to promote the implementation of musical activities with clients/patients as part of a treatment package to improve their health. This chapter also intends to show the therapeutic value of music in both psychiatric and learning disabilities facilities.

MUSIC THERAPY

Saroyan (1990) claims that since the 1950's music intervention has been a recognised and appreciated means to treat the physically and mentally impaired patients. Music was incorporated with the most traditional therapies in hospitals, institutions and schools. Podalsky (1954) argues that many centuries ago music was used to treat mental health problems. People treated included famous names such as King Philip V of Spain, King Ludwig II of Bovaria and King George of Great Britain. During the 18the century Partiger published the first experiments involving music as a therapeutic intervention (Buckwalter et al. 1985). Following further research it was later recognised that music improves health by focusing on the different physical, psychological and emotional aspects of individuals. On the other hand, at the University of Michigan music is used as a medium whereby patients can calm their nerves and ease their pain by being creative and properly expressing their feelings (Ann 1995). Music intervention at the University takes different forms such as singing, hand bell ringing, drumming and listening to music, which help patients to learn to communicate and interact through the language of music. Music as a therapeutic intervention is also found to be very effective in the critical care environment, surgical settings, dental surgeries and mental health issues, as a control for pain, anxiety and promotion of relaxation (McClellan 1991, Biley 2000, Covington 2001). Stevens (1990), on the other hand, suggests that music has the power to drive away the feelings of fear and anxiety when facing the unknown alone.

Nordoff and Robins (1975) are regarded as the pioneers of music therapy. They used music interventions to treat children with developmental delay (Gilroy & Lee 1995). From a child developmental point of view it is understood and appreciated that from birth music has a great influence on the way babies communicate. Babies tend to make a variety of sounds in order to communicate with their mothers (Hughes 2003). This shows the importance of sound as a form of communication where verbal expression is minimal. In the past, music therapy was considered to be an inspiration to evoke God, and to hold and express the greatness of the human spirit (Pavlicevic 1995). However, it was in the 1950s when music was seriously used as a therapeutic intervention and was characterised by the emphasis of 'music as healing' (Gilroy & Lee 1995). Layman (1999) states that music therapy is the controlled use of music with the objective of helping people to overcome their problems. Whereas Bruscia (1987), suggests that music therapy involves the use of organised music in the development of the client-therapist relationship to promote the physical, mental, social and emotional well being of the client.

Today music has gained significant recognition in many different clinical settings and is playing an important part in the field of learning disabilities (Dimond 1998), especially with people with who have severe and profound disabilities, in people who suffer emotional and behavioural problems, mental health, neurology, forensic psychiatry and palliative care (Hughes 2003). However, the first group of clients treated with music therapy were children with autism or cerebral palsy. It is strongly believed that music facilitates language development, play, physical development and relationships with children with special needs (Streeter 1993). A wider range of conditions has been treated since music was first used as a therapeutic intervention (Gilroy & Lee 1995, Wigram & Skille 2000).

In the past, ancestors used to strike sticks and rocks against the ground in the hope to create some sort of music and it have since associated with drumming. Since then music has gone a long way with its healing effects and as such it has been used as a therapeutic tool to help patients with Alzheimer's disease. It is said that drumming significantly reduced stress amongst Vietnam veterans and other sufferers of trauma by changing the brain waves patterns. With people who suffer from psychiatric illnesses there is the argument that music helps them express their emotions verbally, physically or mentally. Music also teaches patients to develop appropriate social skills, which in turn can foster appropriate and meaningful interaction with others. Anxiety can be reduced and self-esteem can be enhanced by music interventions, where subsequently there is freedom of expression in a safe and therapeutic environment (Saroyan 1995). Lund (2003) suggests that music produces its medicating effects by stimulating animal spirits, which reside within the human brain. These stimuli flow through the nerves to create the desired effects.

It can be argued that, despite the powerful influence of the medical world, where the care of clients is pivoted around their physical needs, music therapy is gradually becoming and important alternative in meeting the emotional, mental and psychological needs of patients (Trevarthen 1999, Hughes 2000). Based on the Streeter's (1993) argument, the author believe that since people with learning disabilities may be functioning at a mental age similar to that of a child, the use of music can be very useful in promoting the communication skills of the clients whilst focusing on their different developmental stages.

It is argued that in mental health settings, music can provide a process whereby patients can express their feelings appropriately without recourse to aggression or agitation. In forensic psychiatry, for example, where violent and aggressive behaviour are quite common, music intervention can become an important source from which patients can learn to control there anger, express their dissatisfaction appropriately and become aware of their feelings by interacting more easily. The author, having experience in forensic psychiatry, believes that patients who are detained under sections for treatment learn that they are hopeless and that support is minimal, other than being medicated. These patients respond by being aggressive and tend to disengage from any form of rapport. However, there is a degree of hope that music intervention on its own or associated with other forms of interventions such as gentle teaching can help build an honest and truthful relationship between patients and professionals.

The essence of SRV is to allow people with learning disabilities to undergo life experiences that increase their personal fulfilment and self-determination without feeling stereotyped (Wolfensberger 1998, MacDonald et al. 1999). One of the difficulties in successfully implementing SRV is finding ways of facilitating the integration of clients into the community and to combat social isolation (Osburn 1998, Wolfensberger 1998). This integration can be a very slow and difficult process, which can be delayed further due to a lack of availability of appropriate services within the community.

Clients with SIB and other challenging behaviour will need extra support if the principles of SRV and NSF are to be implemented. People who display challenging behaviour limit their chances of being accepted in community settings (Thompson & Gray 1994). The author believe that by designing effective interventions to reduce their inappropriate behaviours, these individuals will have a better chance of being viewed positively within society

Musical intervention is not guaranteed to always achieve SRV and NSF. However, based on the benefits it offers music therapy can be very useful in facilitating and improving social integration. It can offer people with learning disabilities and mental health problems an environment in which they cab develop and expand their social, mental cognitive and physical skills and improve their life (MacDonald et al 1999) and in which they can learn to build a sound rapport with others and enjoy healthy behaviour (Alvin & Warwick 1994)

LEARNING DISABILITIES, MUSIC AND AGGRESSION

Lawes and Woodcock (2000) believe that music therapy is very effective in managing aggressive and self-injurious behaviour. Evidence suggests that music brings about a mental, emotional and physical calmness (Nordoff & Robins 1992, Biley 1992) with aggressive clients (Barber 1999, Gagner-Tjellesen et al 2001). Aggressive and SIB can be very challenging and carers sometimes fail to deal with it in the correct manner such as failing to provide adequate stimulation (Morgan & Mackay 1998). Ritchie (1993) suggests that musical activities are an effective approach in any attempt use to try to reduce aggressive behaviour.

Experiments carried out in the past (Durand & Mapstone 1998) suggest that fast-beat music is useful in controlling challenging behaviour with aggressive clients. Slow- beat music, on the other hand, was associated with a higher rate of inappropriate behaviour in some clients. These results suggest that, depending on the conditions and behaviours, different types of music may be used with individuals with learning disabilities. Biley (1992) commented on the choice of music and suggested the following pieces of music:

1.   Love Themes volumes 1 and 2 by Mantovani
2.   Reflections by the Moonlight Moods orshectra
3.   In the mood for love by Geoff and his orchestra

Mozart is another name, which is well recommended, especially the trumpet and the horn concerts (Alvin & Warmick 1994). Biley (2001) mentioned classical music such as Pachilbel's 'Canon in D', 'Vaughan Williams' 'Lark Ascending' and Handel's 'Water Music' for helping people to relax. These suggestions were however, believed to be based on the choice and preferences of the general population. For clients with learning disabilities the choice of music can be a very different and difficult issue since there can be misinterpretations regarding their expressed choice. The authors therefore believe that the right or most appropriate type of music can only be selected after identifying the preference of the clients. This can be determined by observing their behaviour and response to different types of music. Providing them with the right type of music to express themselves and improve their communication can be crucial when attempting to reduce SIB. Layman (1999) suggests that music therapy improves the communication skills of clients while focusing on their emotions and feelings.

All people, including those with learning disabilities need defences to manage their anxiety and anger (Corrigan 1991, Lawrenson & Lindsay 1998). Clients need the skill and support to be able to mange anger and anxiety effectively and music can help them achieve this. Music interventions work as a non-invasive and non-threatening treatment and reduce anxiety by promoting the psychological, emotional and physiological well-being of the clients (Barber 1999, Covington 2001). Brewer (1998) argues that music therapy decreases aggressive behaviour by, managing psycho-physiological stress, pain and anxiety. The beneficial effects are caused by the significant physiological and biochemical effects of sounds (particularly their pitch), volume and timbre on the body (Wigram & Skille 2000)

Musical activities can be implemented in three different ways namely, through records or cassettes, live music or vibrational sensations. Irrespective of the method used, music helps to reinforce appropriate behaviour. Background music is another form of musical intervention and is found to be very useful in creating an environment where clients can relax and fell better.

Savarimuthu (unpublished data) has been working with a person who was diagnosed with mental health problems in addition to other medical conditions. When the person's favourite CD's, specially ' Pan Pipe Moods' and 'Gentle Moods' Volumes 3 and 4 by ' The intimate Orchestra', were played in the background, she acknowledge feeling very relaxed and happy.

Covington (2001) stated that when the ear perceives sound, sensory stimulation is produced which can physiologically produce mental images that promote relaxation. Our body is very sensitive to the action of music on the ears. Waves are produced by air molecules, which reach the porous skin on a molecular, atomic and subatomic level (McClellan 1988). Therefore, different music resonates differently with the physical body depending on the type of music.

Similarly, perhaps, Barber (1999) described a study conducted on a client who exhibited challenging behaviour and became agitated if his needs were not met. Every time these behaviours were displayed, the client was encouraged to go into a room where taped relaxation music was played. This intervention was carried out for about 2 months and an evaluation at the end showed that the behaviour of the client improved considerably.

Holford (1999) presents a different point of view suggesting that health professionals usually impose music therapy on clients when tackling specific problems. She further argues that this sort of practice does not provide long-term solutions and believe that participatory music making involve clients without forcing them. Music making, she argues, helps clients to express their needs in a more appropriate way. This argument is supported by Bunnel (1997), who encourages participatory music believing it allows clients communicate their emotions and feelings. Both the involvement of Bunnel (1997) and Holford (1999) with clients with learning disabilities suggests that active participation can make music therapy more interesting and successful. They believe that clients should be encouraged to participate in music making, as it promotes self-esteem and confidence.

However, participation should not be restricted only to those with the ability to play a musical instrument (Gillam 1996). The safety of clients is very important during musical activities, because music is a powerful tool and responses from clients can be very strong and difficult to control (Bracefield et al 2000)

Some health professionals do still not view intervention-using music as a beneficial tool. This is due to misunderstanding and misconceptions especially regarding hearing impaired individuals and people who have problems with verbal communication (Bracefield et al 2000). Fortunately, the literature suggests that clients, irrespective of their level of disability, can benefit from interventions using music (Gagner-Tjellesen et al 2001). Clients with hearing impairment should not be assumed to be incapable of appreciating music stimuli.

Music being extremely flexible, can, nevertheless, be altered to suit the hearing level, language level and music preference of individual clients. Sight, smell and touch are the other senses, which allow sound to be perceived.

People with learning disabilities may be functioning at a very low level of intellectual ability and may therefore experience little, if any, music input. For this reason some issues should be considered prior to any musical intervention (Table 1).

Table 1. Issues to Consider Prior to Musical Intervention

Assessment
Means of gaining and maintaining attention and concentration
Patients/clients past history
Choice of music, age and culture
Measurable aims and goals
Gains may be very small
Any negative response to music

To better appreciate the effects of music on people with learning disabilities, it is essential to devise a method whereby it is possible to measure small changed which can be tailored to each individual (Oldfild & Adams 1995). This would help to detect very small changes in behaviour. It is also important to bear in mind that changed may take a long time to occur so that facilitator must not lose hope and discontinue the intervention. Difficulty can also arise when observing and interpreting the response of clients to sound or music (Alvin & Warwick 1994). This exercise may become easier after a few sessions with the clients where the responses are identified and understood.

In 2001 the report 'Valuing People: A New Strategy For Learning Disabilities For the 21st Century' (DOH 2001) was published. This referred to people with learning disabilities and claimed that they were more susceptible to mental health problems than the general population. The government policy is that this group of people should be able to access services and be treated in the same way as anybody else. The causative factors of metal health problems have been studies in the past (Casey 1993, Vernon 1997, Smith 2000). In the field of learning disabilities, it has been found that frustration with communication is one of the main contributing factors for the prevalence of mental health problems (Moss 1995).

Music is recognised as a form of universal communication and helps to create an environment where clients can have meaningful interaction with their facilitator and other people (Schalkwijk 1994). By improving the communication skills of clients using music, there is the possibility of preventing and controlling mental health problems in some cases. Biley (2000) referred to studies, which claimed that music has the potential to treat long-term mental health problems by decreasing psychotic symptoms (Hamer 1991). Optimising the mental health of clients sometimes allow them to reduce their intake of psychotic drugs

MENTAL HEALTH, MUSIC AND VIOLENCE

Violence is common in mental health setting (Doyle and Dolan 2002). There is a link established between mental health and violence and as such this issue is always high on the political and mental health agenda (Doyle and Dolan 2002).

People who suffer from mental illness do not need any expertise in the field of music therapy to be able to enjoy its therapeutic effects. The fundamental ingredient of music forms the basis of social communication. Hughes (2003) explained a study involving an individual who was diagnosed with paranoid schizophrenia in a mental health unit. The patient was violent and spent some time in prison but he always claimed to be well. On admission to the unit the patient was playing piano to himself in an obsessive way. The way he played piano was described as confused and lacking organisation. After three years the music therapist managed to build a working relationship with the patient and the patient could express himself through music and his piano playing changed to become more communicative and responsive (Hughes 2003). As a result the patient managed to gain insight into his illness and the way he interacted with others had changed as well. He was able to build up his confidence and he could also discuss his paranoid ideas in a more open way.

Another interesting study (Glater 1999) showed that music could help people with paranoia. The study was about a man who was admitted to a psychiatric health facility. He was risk assessed as having increased paranoia and strange behaviour. The patient displayed aggressive behaviour by threatening his children and wife. The latter did not feel safe as her husband threatened to hit her. The patient also developed the habit to defecate in his clothes and in the house. However, the violent behaviour displayed by that individual was of one of the major concerns together with the delusional beliefs manifested. However, the patient had some musical skills such as singing, dancing and good participation in musical improvisations (Glater 1999). Another good element worth noting was that he was keen to see the music therapist on a daily basis. The patient responded very well to music intervention, as he could better express his emotions, had a better self-image and was able to form trusting relationship with others. His psychotic delusions remained present but his verbalisation increased and his violent behaviour was somehow reduced. Many people hear voices although not suffering from mental illness. There are many reasons for why people hear voices such as bereavement, trauma, depression and sexual abuse (Place 2003). When executing and responding to these voices, people can become violent and aggression. All the above can be controlled by music interventions.

The author can reflect on one of his personal experience working with a patient in a medium secure psychiatric forensic unit. At some stage during the patient's detention the he started to respond to voices and pacing up and down the ward. The patient started to display inappropriate facial expression and became physically and verbally aggressive. At that time he was offered the best possible intervention before eventually medicated by applying physical restraint. However, reflecting on the incident the author believes that there were alternative simple interventions, which could have been used to treat, control and even prevent the patient from displaying hostile and aggressive behaviour. During a risk assessment it was suggested that the patient was responding to some sort of internal stimuli, which could have well been dealt in a more sensitive way. Place (2003) suggests that listening to music on personal stereos can reduce the frequency of auditory hallucinations. There is evidence to explain that music becomes the main focus rather than the voices the patient hears; and it also reduces stress (Place 2003). However, some types of music can trigger aggression. Fast beat music and violent lyrics can increase the level of agitation in some patients. On the other hand Lai (1999) suggests that music be played in the dining environment to reduce psychiatric patients' aggressive behaviour.

MUSIC, MENTAL ILLNESS AND SEXUALITY

In the UK many patients are detained under the Mental Health Act 1983 after having come in contact with the legal justice system. Most of the offences involve a degree of violence. These patients are cared and treated in a way for them to gain some insight into their offences and their health conditions. One of the goals of their treatment is that thereafter they can be integrated into the society as valued individuals. People end up in prison for a number of reasons. One of these reasons is related to inappropriate sexual behaviour. Sexual disinhibition from some of the patients has resulted in cases of rape and sexual assaults, which are amongst the most common offences. A treatment package is usually set up involving the multi disciplinary team to address the many issues manifested within these patients. Music is one of the practices, which offer a very useful help towards controlling that behaviour. Music is found to lower testosterone in men and increase the same hormone in females (Glausiusz 2001), which as a result can control their sex drive. It is argued that in the early civilisation humans used to form communities to control sexual frustration. This was achieved by implementing music interventions. On the other hand it is found that drummers had an increased level of white blood cells commonly known as natural killer cells, which tend to destroy cancer cells (Glausiusz 2001).

Patients who show aggressive and challenging behaviour towards others often end up being secluded. Seclusion is a therapeutic intervention where patients are given the opportunity to be medicated, counselled, advised and allowed time to reflect on their actions for the purpose of finding ways to express their feelings without causing any harm. Based on the known benefits of music intervention one can suggest that during the time patients remain in seclusion, music can be played in the room so that there can be easy de-escalation of any aggressive behaviour. The environment in the seclusion becomes calming with a therapeutic effect to control anger.

CONTRA-INDICATIONS

On the other hand, musical intervention may have a negative impact on clients. One example is when client is attached to a particular piece of music and rejects what the facilitator offers. Another example is when a client displays inappropriate behaviour, which does not allow the aims and objectives of the musical intervention to be met, and which hinders therapeutic contact with the facilitator (Schalkwijk 1994). In these cases, interventions using music should be discontinued but reintroduced at a later stage when the client is more willing to concentrate and cooperate with the facilitator. The age and culture of clients are important issues, which need careful consideration since their choice of music may be different. Past experience can also be triggered by specific music where clients may feel upset and/or vulnerable. Evidence also suggests that music associated with violent lyrics such as 'heavy metal' can have a negative impact on clients (McCraty et al 1998). Clients who have criminal history need to be thoroughly assessed for any inappropriate response to music. Some types of music can have adverse effect of clients' health and this knock off effect can disrupt their treatment.

EXPERTISE

It is open to speculation whether or not activities involving music become therapeutic when facilitated by a professional music therapist. Hooper (1991) argues that if there is a significant and positive impact on the quality of life of a client, then musical activities are therapeutic regardless of who is facilitating the musical activities. Certain aspects of music do not need the hands of the expert but can be facilitated by anyone who enjoys music (Covington 2001). Gillam (1996) suggests that therapists do not necessarily need to be experts as long as they are keen to experiment using musical interventions. Bunnell (1997) explains how music intervention can be organised and delivered in a systematic way to achieve specific objectives not necessitating the presence of a trained music therapist.

In the past, many people who have been professional therapist have successfully implemented interventions using music with clients. The success of music interventions depends partly upon the approach and attitude taken towards the activity and on the aim and objectives set. It is however, not in the interests of the client if the activity is not meaningful and does not have specified objectives. To successfully implement musical activities with clients with mental health and learning disabilities, Wood (1993) believes that there is the need for the facilitator to be able to relate with the clients. She also suggest that neither great expertise in the field of music therapy nor the availability of the best equipment for the intervention would be of use if the facilitator cannot relate to the clients at a therapeutic level.

CONCLUSION

This chapter has explored the benefits of music for people with learning disabilities and who display challenging behaviour such as SIB and aggressive behaviour. Music interventions are widely used in many clinical settings but this chapter has looked into its effects on the emotional and psychological health of a particular group of clients. As discussed previously, musical activities are recognised as an effective means for modifying behaviour and are found to be very effective in decreasing aggression and SIB. In some cases, the effects of music therapy can go beyond to the prevention and management of mental health problems of clients. Both the White Paper 'Valuing People' (DOH 2001) and the National Service Framework (NSF) are favourable towards the integration of clients with mental health problems and learning disabilities into the society. This integration can be possible if there is an effort made towards creating and further developing new health promotion strategies. Consequently, the role of nurses will nevertheless be to promote the health and well-being of clients wherever they go, if SRV and NSF are implemented. The introduction of new interventions within nursing practice can only serve to help the practitioner to fulfil their role as health facilitator

RECOMMENDATIONS

The author suggests that health professionals should concentrate on the aspects of health promotion when attempting to enhance the quality of life of clients. This can be done by developing the right attitude and approach to complementary therapies such as the introduction of music therapy in nursing practice. Nowadays, health care professionals are more aware of the benefits that music can have on their clients but sadly little use is made of this knowledge. To implement musical interventions no expertise is required but music therapist is the appropriate person to implement music therapy. The ability to play a musical instrument can be beneficial in music interventions since the facilitator can better relate to the clients. Since musical interventions can take place in different forms, those who cannot play any musical instrument can still be fully involved in the activities. Music therapy is a failure free intervention, which has no side effects. Patients can engage in music in different ways and it is therefore essential to understand and explore the importance music plays in the life of the patients. By doing so the facilitator can start developing a professional bond with the patients. Language is a powerful tool in the treatment of patients. In the contemporary society where people with different cultures and background blend together, there can be a problem of communication. Music is a universal language, which can help break any barrier and solve problems. In psychiatric settings, patients are sometimes secluded as part of their care plans. It is suggested that when patients are unsettled in the seclusion room, there is the optimum use of music intervention especially music which are the patients' favourite.

SUMMARY

- Musical intervention reduces SIB and aggressive behaviour and is found to be useful in many other clinical areas such as Forensic psychiatry.
- Clients should be encouraged to participate in musical activities irrespective of the level of their impairment or disabilities.
- Nurses should not underestimate their capabilities as facilitator in the delivery of music sessions.

- Choice of music, culture and age of patients and clients are essential issues when implementing musical interventions.
- Heavy metal music can have a negative effect on clients whereas classical music is found to induce relaxation.
- Music therapy can be implemented with patients who have history of sexual inappropriateness.

REFERENCES

Alvin J and Warmick A (1994). *Music therapy for the autistic child* (2nd ed). Oxford University Press, Oxford.

Ann A (1995). Using music to calm nerves, ease pain *The consumer's Medical Journal* 73, 8.

Barber C (1999). The use of music and colour theory as a behaviour modifier. *British Journal of nursing* 8, 443-448.

Biley F (1992). Use of music in therapeutic care. *British Journal of Nursing* 4, 178-180.

_____ . (2000). The effects on patient well-being of music listening as a nursing intervention: a review of the literature. *Journal of Clinical Nursing* 9,668-677.

Biley F (2001). Music as therapy *In:* Rankin-Box (ed) *The nurse's handbook of complementary therapies* (2nd ed). Bailliere Tindall, London.

Bracefield H, Kirk-Smith M, Slevin E, Thompson K (2000). Music therapy in N. Ireland. *Journal of Learning disabilities* 4, 63-76.

Brewer J (1998). Healing Sounds. *Complementary Therapies in Nursing & Midwifery* 4, 7-12.

Bruscia K (1987). *Improvisational models of music therapy.* Charles C. Thomas, Springfield, IL.

Buckwater K, Hartsock J, Gaffney J (1985). *In:* Bulechek G, McCloskey J (eds) *Nursing Intervention: treatment for nursing diagnosis.* W B Saunders, Philadelphia.

Bunnell T (1997). *Music makes a difference: a practical guide developing music sessions with people with learning disabilities.* ISBN: 0953825802, www.webserve.co.uk/bunnell.

Carson G, Clare I (1998). Assessment and treatment of self-injurious behaviour with a man with profound learning disability. *British Journal of Learning disabilities* 26, 51-57.

Casey PR (1993). *A guide to psychiatry in primary care.* Wrighton Biomedical Publishing Ltd, Petersfield.

Corrigan P W (1991). Social skills training in adults with psychiatric populations: a meta analysis. *Journal of Behaviour Therapy and Experimental Psychiatry* 22, 203-210.

Covington H (2001). Therapeutic music for people with psychiatric disorders. *Holistic nursing Practice* 15, 59-69.

Dimond B (1998). *The legal aspects of complementary therapy practice: a guide for health care professionals.* Churchill Livingstone, London.

DOH (2001). *Valuing People: a new strategy for learning disability for the 21st century.* HMSO, London.

Doyle M and Dolan M (2002). Violence risk prediction *The British Journal of psychiatry* 8(3), 214-222.

Durand M, Mapstone E (1998). Influence of 'mood-inducing' music on challenging behaviour. *American Journal on Mental Retardation* 4,367-378.

Emberson J (1990). Self-injurious behaviour in people with a mental handicap. *Nursing Times* 23, 43-46.

Ferry R (1992). Self-injurious behaviour. *Senior Nurse* 12, 21-24.

Gagner-Tjellesen D, Yurkovich E, Gragert M (2001). Use of music therapy and other ITNIs in acute care. Journal of Psychological Nursing 39, 27-36.

Gillam T (1996). Sounds good. *Nursing Times* 92, 28-30.

Gilroy A, Lee C (1995). *Art and music therapy and research.* Routledge, London.

Glater S (1999). Music as therapy, *Journal* Online Internet Sanctuary Psychiatric Centre's information Network.

Glausiusz J (2001). The generic mystery of music. *Discover* 22(8), 70-76.

Goddaer J, Abraham L (1994). Effects of relaxing music on agitation during meals among nursing homes residents with severe cognitive impairment. *Arch. Psychiatric Nurse* 8, 150-158.

Hamer B (1991). Music therapy: harmony for change. *Journal of Psychological Nursing* 29, 5-7.

Holford A (1999). Keeping in tune with the times. *Healthlines* 62, 12-13.

Hooper J (1991). Music hath charms. *Nursing Times* 87, 40-41.

Hughes M (2000). A comparison of mother-infant interactions and the client-therapist relationships in music therapy session *In:* Wigram B, Saperston B, West R (eds) *The art and science of music therapy: A handbook.* Routledge, London.

Hughes R (2003). Music therapy. *Student BMJ* Vol.11, 76.

Lai, Y (1999). Effects of music listening on depressed women in Taiwan. *Mental Health Nursing* Vol 20 (3), 229-247.

Lawes C, Woodcock J (2000). Music therapy and people with severe learning disabilities who exhibit self-injurious behaviour *In:* Wigram B, Saperston B, West R (eds) *The art and science of music therapy: A handbook.* Harwood Academic Publishers, Netherlands.

Lawrenson H, Lindsay WR (1998). The treatment of anger in individuals with learning disabilities. *In:* Fraser W, Sines D, Kerr M (eds) *Hallas' the care of people with Intellectual Disabilities* (9th ed). Butterworth Heinemann, Oxford.

Layman K (1999). *Music therapy.* Gale encyclopaedia of medicine. Find articles.com.

Lund K (2003). Music through time. *Student BMJ* Vol. 11, 77.

MacDonald R, O'Donnell P, Davies J (1999). An empirical investigation into the effects of structured music workshops for individuals with intellectuals disabilities. *Journal of Applied Research in Intellectual Disabilities* 12, 225-240.

McCarty R, Barrios-Chopin B, Atkinson M, Tamasino D (1998). The effects of different types of music on mood, tension and mental clarity. *Alternative Therapies in Health and Medecine* 4, 75-84.

McClellan R (1991). *The healing forces of music: history, theory and practice.* Element, Massachusetts.

Morgan J, Mackay D (1998). Self-injurious in people with learning disabilities. *Nursing Standard* 26, 39-42.

Moss S (1995). Methodological issues in the diagnosis of psychiatric disorders in adults with learning disabilities. *In:* Emerson E, Hatton C, Bromley J, Laine A (eds) *Clinical psychology on people with intellectual disabilities.* Wiley, London.

Nordoff P, Robins C (1992). *Therapy in music for handicapped children.* Victor Gollancz, London.

NordoffP, Robins C (1975). *Music in special education.* MacDonald Evans, London.

Oldfield A, Adams M (1995). The effects of music therapy on a group of adults with profound learning disabilities. *In:* Gilroy A, Lee C (eds) *Art and music: therapy and research.* Routledge, London.

Osburn J (1998). An overview of social role valorisation theory. The international Social Role Valorization. *Journal/La Revue Internationale de la Valorization des roles sociaux* 1, 7-12.

Pavlicevic M (1995). Music and emotion: aspects of music therapy research. *In:* Gilroy A, Lee C (eds) *Art and music: therapy and research.* Routeledge, London.

Place C (2003). Simple coping strategies for people who hear voices. *Nursing Times* 99(47), 38-40.

Podalsky E (1954). *Music therapy.* Philosophical Library, New York.

Ritchie F (1993). The effects of music therapy with people who have severe learning disabilities and display challenging behaviour. *In:* Heal M, Wigram T (eds) *Music therapy in health and education.* Jessica Kingsley Publishers, London.

Saroyan J (1990). The use of music therapy on an adolescent psychiatric unit. *Journal of Group psychology, psychodrama and sociometry* Vol. 43 (3), 139-141.

Schalkwijk F (1994). *Music and people with developmental disabilities.* Jessica Kingsley Publishers, London.

Smith L D (2000). The nature of health and the effects of disorder. *In:* Thompson T, Mattias P (eds) *Lyttle's Mental Health and Disorder (3rd ed)* Bailliere Tindall, London.

Stevens K (1990). Patients' perceptions of music during surgery. *Journal of Advanced Nursing* 15, 1045-1051.

Streeter E (1993). *Making music with young child with special needs a guide for parents.* Jessica Kingsley Publishers, London.

Thompson T, Gray B (1994). *Destructive behaviour in developmental disabilities. Diagnosis and treatment.* Sage Publication, London.

Trevarthan C (1999). How music heals. *In:* Wigram T, De Backer J (eds) *Clinical application of music therapy in developmental disability, paediatrics and neurology.* Jessica Kingsley Publishers, London.

Vernon D (1997). Health. *In:* Gates B (ed) *Learning disabilities (3rd ed)* Churchill Livingstone, London.

Wigram T, Skills O (2000). The effects of music, vocalisation and vibrations on brain and muscle tissue: studies in vibroacoustic therapy. *In:* Wigram T, Saperston B, West R (eds) *The art and science of music therapy. A handbook.* Hardwood Academic Publishers, London.

Withers P (1995). Successful treatment of severe self-I jury incorporating the use of DRO, a snoezelen room and orientation cues. *British Journal of Learning Disabilities* 23, 164-167.

Wolfensberger W (1998). *A brief introduction to social role valorisation.* Syracuse, New York.

Wood M (1993). *Music for people with learning disabilities.* Souvenir Press, London.

INDEX

A

Abuse Risk Inventory for Women, 4, 13
Acetylcholine, 94, 102
acting-out, 33, 34
adolescence, 15, 20, 21, 30, 39, 57, 90, 154
Adult Attachment Interview (AAI), 18, 36
adult mental health, 15, 38
Adult Outcome of Abused Children Compared, 21, 22
aggregated responses, 3, 6, 10
aggression hypothesis, 120, 143, 154
aggressive acts, 4, 59, 71, 159
aggressive behavior(s), 63, 66, 67, 87, 88, 91-93, 96, 99, 100, 102, 106, 108-111, 116, 117, 119, 120, 124, 126, 134-137, 142, 144, 150, 156, 157, 160, 162-164, 167-171
aggressive drivers, 115, 118, 144, 155, 156
aggressive driving, 116, 117, 148, 155-159, 163, 171-173
aggressive escalation, 117
aggressive syndromes, 91, 103, 105
aggressor, 31, 33, 34, 59-62, 65-67, 70, 71, 73, 160
agitation, 91-93, 95-106, 110, 112, 175, 177, 182, 185
Alcohol abuse, 25
alexithymia, 79, 80, 83, 89, 90
Amantadine, 102, 107, 109
American Automobile Association (AAA), 158
American Automobile Association, 116, 154, 158
Anger Expression Inventory, 123, 125, 126, 146, 156
anger expression, 121, 123-126, 132, 140, 143, 144, 146, 148-150, 152-154

anger, 23, 28, 29, 33, 36, 37, 51, 72, 73, 75, 81, 84-88, 103, 111, 116-137, 139-157, 159, 162, 167, 170, 172, 177, 179, 182, 186
angry drivers, 116, 119, 123, 149, 154
angry emotion, 116
angry emotionality, 116
antipsychotic medications, 98
anxiety, 17, 20, 23, 27, 29, 31, 34, 53, 55, 56, 57, 89, 96, 101, 148, 151, 152, 157, 172, 176, 179
apathetic withdrawal, 33
appearance teasing, 54
atypical agents, 98
autism, 177
automobile, 158, 163, 174
axonal projections, 94

B

behavior of strangers, 157
behavior, 2, 5, 7, 10-12, 24, 25, 34, 43, 49, 61, 62, 67, 68, 70, 73, 74, 87, 89, 92, 95, 96, 104, 108, 109, 112, 113, 115-119, 123, 124, 126, 128, 130, 134-136, 140, 142-146, 149-152, 155-159, 161, 163, 164, 167-172
behavioral problems, 96, 102
Benzodiazepines, 101
beta blockers, 100
bipolar disorder, 98, 106, 111
birth, 15, 16, 18, 29, 38, 177
black sheep effect, 61, 67, 69, 71, 73
black sheep perspectives, 67
brain injuries, 91
brain-injured patients, 95, 99-102, 108, 111-113
British Automobile Association, 116
Brody longitudinal study, 15
bullying, 53, 54, 57
buspirone, 101, 109, 112